Ralph Bulger lives quietly in Merseyside where he helps to bring up his children and relaxes by fishing. Along with his brother Jimmy, he continues to campaign to find justice for James. **Rosie Dunn** is a freelance journalist and author. A former crime reporter for the *Sun*, she has also written for the *Daily Mail* and *Mail on Sunday*, *Daily Mirror* and the *People*. Her first book, *Playing in the Dark*, was published in 2011.

RALPH BULGER
WITH ROSIE DUNN

My James

The Heart-rending Story of
JAMES BULGER
By His Father

PAN BOOKS

First published 2013 by Sidgwick & Jackson

This edition published 2013 by Pan Books
an imprint of Pan Macmillan, a division of Macmillan Publishers Limited
Pan Macmillan, 20 New Wharf Road, London N1 9RR
Basingstoke and Oxford
Associated companies throughout the world
www.panmacmillan.com

ISBN 978-1-4472-1874-6

1 3 5 7 9 8 6 4 2

A CIP catalogue record for this book is available from the British Library.

Typeset by Ellipsis Digital Limited, Glasgow
Printed and bound by CPI Group (UK) Ltd, Croydon, CR0 4YY

Dedicated to my beautiful son James

Contents

Prologue

I've always loved to watch the damselflies skimming the water, like low-flying helicopters just above the ocean. Today was no exception as I sat on the banks of the river, watching the warm summer sun glint off their sparkling turquoise bodies. There was barely any noise apart from the chirping of the grasshoppers in the reeds and the occasional cyclist who would draw my attention for a few seconds before I returned to watch my fishing rod, waiting for that all-important bite. It couldn't have been a more peaceful or tranquil setting, but it was a stark contrast to the turbulence in my head.

I couldn't help but think how my young son would have loved this day out with his dad, trying to spot the grasshoppers and sharing ham sandwiches and crisps with me. I had always planned to teach James to fish when he was a bit older, to buy him his own little rod and tackle box, but I never got the chance. Now, my fishing trips were the times when I would try to make sense of everything, a small slice of peace in an otherwise messed-up world. As I perched on my camp stool, alone at the side of the river, watching the odd bubble float to the surface from a fish chancing its luck to feed on the flies that danced there, I began one of my many conversations with my dead child.

'My darling James, I hope you are keeping well and that you are safe and warm and happy. I hope you have made lots of new friends and that you are all playing games and having fun. I wish you were with me now, son, by my side so that I could put my arm around you and tell you how deeply sorry I am. Your dad is fishing today and I wish with all my heart I could magic you up beside me. You would love it and I looked forward so much to teaching you how to fish.

'You were such a loving and kind little boy, and I wanted to say thank you for being the most fantastic little lad ever. Not a day goes by that I don't think about you. From the moment I wake up in the morning to the time I shut my eyes at night, you are with me, and I hope you can still feel me with you. I try not to think about all the horrible things that happened to you that day and try to concentrate on your lovely smile and the glorious sound of your laughter. That was the best music I ever heard and I want to be able to hear it for the rest of my life. You were a joy to be with, James, and I miss you every single day. Whatever happens now, I want you to know that I have tried with all my heart to fight for you. I will keep on with the battle just so that you know how much you meant to me.

'Your dad is so sad without you, lad. And that's because you were so very special to everyone who was lucky enough to meet you. You made me the happiest man alive and the proudest father on earth. I sometimes thought my heart would burst with joy when I watched you play or held your hand as you were sleeping. I hope you knew how much we all loved you and that you were happy for the few short years you spent with us. You will always travel with me in my heart.

Love, your Ralph.'

1

My Beautiful Baby Boy

From the moment I laid eyes on my son, he stole my heart completely. He was the most lovely baby I had ever seen, and as I held him close for the very first time, moments after he was born, I felt like the luckiest man in the world. This tiny little child in my arms meant everything to me and, as I wrapped myself around him, I couldn't stop staring at him. His big blue eyes peeped up at me as he wriggled around and tried to adjust to his new world. He began blinking rapidly under the bright lights of the hospital delivery room and I held him even tighter to comfort him. I rocked him gently, back and forth, and tried to take in everything about him – his wet blond locks of hair, his wrinkled pink baby skin and his little button nose. He felt so light and delicate, and I knew instinctively that I would always want to cherish and protect him. It was an incredible feeling and words could barely describe the happiness I felt inside. To me he was just perfect.

'Hello, my beautiful baby boy,' I whispered to James as I kissed him gently on the forehead. 'I'm your daddy.'

My wife Denise gave birth to our son James Patrick Bulger on Friday, 16 March 1990, at the maternity unit at Liverpool's

Fazakerley Hospital. I was by her side throughout. Despite our obvious joy, the moment was tinged with sadness because we had lost our first baby. In June 1988, Denise gave birth to our daughter Kirsty, but tragically she was stillborn. We had no idea that this was going to happen and so the shock and pain were huge. I was there with Denise when she delivered Kirsty, and we were both distraught at the loss and overwhelmed with grief. Instinctively, I asked Denise to marry me that day, and she accepted. I just wanted to look after her and help her through our shared suffering. I am not a sophisticated or intelligent man, but I loved her, and that was my way of showing how much she meant to me.

We buried our daughter in a small wooden coffin on a day I will never forget. It was a simple but heartbreaking funeral service that gave us both a chance to say goodbye to the little girl we would never get to know, never see grow up. We didn't want a big funeral, and so it was just our immediate families who attended the service. It was unbelievably sad. Both Denise and I were in a bad way over the loss of Kirsty. In some respects, I think it hit Denise harder because she had carried our baby for so long inside her. We had no choice other than to get on with life, but the sadness never left us. We talked a lot together about Kirsty and we tried to imagine what sort of daughter she would have grown up to be. It was important to us never to forget her, but we were both determined that we would have another baby. We really wanted a family together even though we knew we would never be able to replace Kirsty. Denise was full of grief, but she was also very strong. Despite the sadness, she showed fantastic courage by refusing to fall apart. We dealt with our loss together and, in some ways, it made us closer as a team.

Denise and I married at Knowsley Register Office in Prescot on 16 September 1989, the day Denise turned twenty-two. I was twenty-three at the time. It was a quiet, small wedding, just the way we wanted it, and we held a family party at home to celebrate. Denise was by now already pregnant again, with James, and I did my very best to look after and care for her, as we were both terrified of losing another baby and having to go through the same grief again. Thankfully, we were spared another loss at that time, and James was born a healthy and happy baby who cemented our marriage and created our own loving family unit.

We lived in a small, pokey bedsit in the Southdene area of Kirkby, an industrial town on the outskirts of Liverpool that was an overspill to the main city. Money was tight, but where hard cash was lacking, love most certainly was not. Twenty years earlier, things had been very different because there was more work around, which made people's lives easier. Kirkby was a historic area of Merseyside that had been developed as a new town in the late 1950s, to house people who were being forced to move out from homes that were falling down and being bulldozed to make way for new developments in the city centre.

My mum and dad, Helen and James senior, had moved there from the Scotland Road area of Liverpool. 'Scottie Road', as it is known, was near to the busy docks and was once home to thousands of people. But the area had been badly damaged by bombs during the Second World War and many of the houses still standing were in poor condition and considered to be slums. At the time, people were delighted to move out of the city. The old houses they lived in were often damp and, in many cases, still had outside loos and small backyards. By contrast, Kirkby was brand new. The houses were purpose built by the council and had neat front and back gardens with all mod cons inside. And the town had local parks and open green spaces where children could play out safely. Mum and Dad saw it as a new start, a great place to bring up a family.

Opportunities for work were good in Kirkby's heyday, as the town had plenty of factories. At its height in the early 1970s, Kirkby Industrial Estate provided jobs for 26,000 people and was known to be one of the biggest of its kind in Europe. One of the main employers in the town was the giant Bird's Eye frozen-food company, which provided thousands of jobs over the years, as well as the Kraft food company and plenty of small car firms. But when the economic recession hit in the early 1980s, a lot of companies shut down or moved out because it was cheaper to manufacture abroad or elsewhere in the UK. This hit Kirkby hard and unemployment began to rise. As in many other urban areas of England, this brought social problems, in particular when heroin became widely available and many saw it as a way of escaping life's difficulties. That's not to say that everyone took to drugs and crime – they didn't. The majority of people were good, hard-working folk who were doing the best they could to get through, but the town was affected by the same inner-city problems that surfaced in a lot of places during the recession. Once it had been a sought-after area; now it had become rougher, and you needed to be pretty tough to survive there. Kirkby attracted a lot of unwanted press attention, even earning itself the dubious nickname 'Baby Beirut'.

It remains a tough town today, though there has been some recent regeneration with the building of new sports facilities, and there are major plans to overhaul the town centre. The industrial park still provides some work, even if it doesn't compare to how Kirkby thrived in its early days. But its harsh history didn't just bring problems; Kirkby became an area where the sense of community was strong and people were always willing to help each other out where they could. It is still like that today – it is a tight-knit place, and the town always protects its own. Even though life was difficult, most of the families there were good, honest people who did their best in life to survive, and everyone pulled together.

I have lived in Kirkby all my life and it has always been home to me, despite its reputation and lack of work opportunities. It is in Kirkby that I have a sense of belonging in my own community. It's not pretty or gentle, but it is very real. It is where I feel most comfortable and I remain proud of the great people of this community. When you really need support, I can't imagine where you would find a warmer, more generous and loving group.

I was the baby of our family, born on 24 June 1966, and had three older brothers, Jimmy, Philip and John, and two sisters, Lorraine and Carol. I was pretty spoilt as the youngest child but, even so, life wasn't always a bowl of cherries. Money was scarce, but at a very early age my parents instilled in me an understanding of right and wrong.

There were three bedrooms in our house, one for my

mum and dad, one for my sisters and one for us lads, and as a kid I shared a double bed with all three of my brothers. It was crowded but it was great fun too. My brothers and I were lively, and even though we were always scrapping, we were also very close. We would hang out together when we were not in school and I was always looked after because I was the youngest. And it was at the heart of this environment that I learned to have a sharp sense of humour. Everyone was in the same boat, and so I didn't really know any different. People were always telling jokes, often at their own expense – it was a very Scouse way of dealing with the hard things in life.

I was taught to have a good work ethic by my parents, but the problem was that there was no work to be had. By the time I was a young man in the 1980s, unemployment in Kirkby was terrible. The town had never really recovered after the recession. I didn't have any qualifications from school, but I could use my hands. I was constantly looking for work, with no luck, and as a result I was sent on countless Government schemes and courses to learn skills. I learned bricklaying, plastering, reupholstering, truck driving, joinery and how to be an electrician. You name it, where manual labouring skills were concerned, I had a certificate with my name on it. And at the end of it all, as hard as I tried, all I was left with was a bag of tools and no job. It was pretty soul-destroying, but I was certainly not alone. Many men from the area were forced to move away from their homes and families and travel to London or the south of England to get work to provide for their loved ones, because the north-west was on its knees at the time.

Like the rest of my family, I chose to stay at home and

continue the search for work. I didn't sit around moping about the fact that there were no jobs, I just got on with things. It makes you fairly hardy to the knocks that life throws at you, but I got through it by taking up running and training in the gym.

It was in 1987 that I met my future wife, Denise. I was on a night out at Kirkby Town Football Club when I spotted this young, pretty girl dancing away and I liked her immediately. Denise was only small but she had a big personality. She laughed a lot and I liked that. She looked carefree and happy, and with the Dutch courage of a few glasses of ale inside me, I went and asked her to dance. I was made up when she said yes. She was even prettier close up, with lovely blue eyes and wavy brown hair to her shoulders, but it was her big smile that I liked the best. I have always been a quiet, shy person and it takes quite a lot for me to open up to people, but I felt very comfortable and relaxed with Denise. In particular, she had a wicked sense of humour and a great laugh. We began going out together and in a way it was very old-fashioned. At first we just enjoyed having a few drinks until we got to know each other better, and then we really clicked and became a permanent item. Like me, Denise also had very strong family ties and we both wanted the same simple things in life.

When we moved into our own little bedsit we were over the moon; you would think we had been handed the keys to a palace. Denise was ultra house-proud and turned the flat into a warm and comfortable home for us. Even though that first year had brought us the tragedy of losing Kirsty, we were thrilled when Denise fell pregnant again in 1990. Of course, we were also scared that we might lose another baby in the same way we had lost our daughter. All we could do was hope everything would be fine, and I supported Denise and looked after her as best I could. Everyone was anxious, including our extended families, but they were there for us both throughout. When James was born healthy we felt as if we had been given a second chance in life and, naturally, we were so protective of him from the moment he was born.

We took James home and he became the centre of our world. It was one of the happiest periods of my life. James was a small baby with a smattering of blond hair and bright blue eyes. He was named after my dad, who had died of cancer not long before his arrival. At first he cried a lot, as many newborns do, but after a while we began to get him into a routine and he settled down, becoming a lively and happy young baby. We both noticed that he was as bright as a button from a very early age. He was so nosy, and even when he was just a few months old he started mumbling his words, trying his hardest to speak to us. It was wonderful to watch, especially when he started to walk even before his first birthday. They were fantastic days for us as a family. I loved my wife and my son and, despite the lack of money, James never went without. He was showered with love and affection not just from us, but from all his relatives on both sides. That was the way it was. The children were always put first and life revolved around them. If the kids were happy, then so were the grown-ups.

We led a very simple, traditional life. The grim un-employment in the region meant that nearly everyone we knew was skint, but we all chipped in and helped each other out. When we moved into our flat, family members rallied round to get us furniture, and if you needed to borrow a few quid to get by then help was always there. Likewise, if we could help others in any way, we would. I would always do odd jobs for people, fixing things or making shelves in relatives' homes. It was the least I could do. The women in the family all took it in turn to mind the kids, giving each other a break from time to time and, of course, we were never short on babysitters. Not that we were out a lot, as we couldn't afford it, but on Saturday nights it was a chance for Denise and me to go out locally and share a few drinks, have some laughs with each other and meet up with others from the family. As hard as it sometimes was, life was good in the most important ways. I had a fantastic family of my own with Denise and James; we had fun together and I was really happy. I loved being a dad and Denise was a great mum.

As James began to grow up, we were able to move to a bigger one-bedroom flat in the Northwood area of Kirkby. The town is divided up into different districts, but most areas of Kirkby are similar to each other, with fairly large housing estates and local shops for basics, all within walking distance of the main town centre. With James already toddling, we needed eyes in the back of our heads to keep up with him! He was the most boisterous, outgoing baby you could meet and he was into just about everything he could get his hands on. He loved to climb onto furniture and roar with laughter all the time. His giggle was totally infectious and everyone just adored him. He would play with anyone and didn't have an ounce of shyness in him.

Our days were spent looking after James, watching him grow into the most amazing little boy. He loved to play rough and tumble. Mischief was never far away from James, but he didn't have a bad bone in his body. After his breakfast, I would often take him to the park. One of his favourite toys was a red go-kart but, as James was short for his age, he couldn't even reach the pedals. It was so comical and cute. He had got into the habit of calling me Ralph instead of Dad because he had heard other people calling me by my name. I can still hear his little voice shouting out to me in the park as he played in his red car.

'Ralph, Ralph, come and push me, come and push me!' he cried.

'No, James, I'm your dad, not Ralph. You have to call me Daddy.'

'OK, Ralph, now come and push me,' he replied.

I couldn't help laughing. James was a little imp and got away with so much, but he was also kind and loving. I couldn't have wished for a better son. He really was the light in my life and I cherished every moment I spent with him.

Other days we would have a gentle knockabout with a football, his little legs running as fast as he could to get the ball. It was a sight to warm your heart. When he managed to push the ball into the net he would cry out, 'Ralph, Ralph, I scored a goal! Look at me!'

Each time he scored I would run over and fetch him up in my arms, throw him in the air and catch him before running around the park in celebration as James giggled at the top of his voice. Money can never buy moments like these and I will always remember them.

Those early days with James remain my most precious memories. You never imagine they will be all you have left of your child, but while they are my sacred, private memories, in many ways it helps to share them publicly, because so few people got to know James as a little boy. To the rest of the world he became a photo in the newspaper or on the news at the centre of a tragedy, a grainy image on a CCTV camera as he was being led away by his killers. But he was so much more than that. He was a living, breathing bundle of energy who was idolized by his family. He had his own giant, cheeky personality wrapped up in his short, stocky body. I want people to know more about this special little boy who was denied the chance to grow up.

It was as natural as breathing for James to smile and giggle, and as a result he would have everyone around him laughing too. His joy was completely infectious. Even though he was little, he was very strong and lively. He was often described as being like a human tornado or a Tasmanian devil, tearing around at full pelt until he just dropped with exhaustion at the end of each day. He would literally launch himself onto chairs or unsuspecting laps for loads of cuddles. It would wear us all out just watching him, especially when he started dancing to his beloved Michael Jackson tunes. He had followed in the footsteps of his mum, who was a huge fan of the singer. As soon as any of his records came on the radio or television, he would be up doing the funniest dances as he tried to impersonate the superstar's moves, flinging his little arms in and out, giggling all the way.

James loved life; he lived it to the full, and wanted to learn everything. Denise was great at teaching him and encouraging his sharp young brain. He kept us all entertained and busy for hours on end, day after day. Like most kids, he had his favourites among his toys, and Thomas the Tank Engine was definitely at the top of his list. He would ring the bell inside the tiny train and at night he couldn't wait to climb into bed under his Thomas the Tank Engine duvet.

Another firm favourite was *The Smurfs*. He was mesmerized by the sight of the little blue people and played his Smurfs video so much he almost wore it out. He had a Smurfs ball and a Smurfs cereal bowl. And then he developed a thing for chairs! Mainly, I think, because he was so short he wanted to stand taller. There was one particular white chair that he would drag around the place and climb on.

'I'm the king of the castle,' he would sing at the top of his voice as he stood up on it.

Other times he would climb on a chair and belt out his favourite nursery rhymes, 'Baa, Baa, Black Sheep' or 'Twinkle, Twinkle, Little Star'. Some chairs were just too big for him to clamber onto, and so in the end I decided I would make him his very own little throne, using the skills I had learned on my joinery and upholstery courses. I was never academic but I was good with my hands and at making things. I spent three days crafting this piece of furniture for my son.

'What you doing today, Ralph?' James asked me as he cocked his head to one side.

'Daddy's making you your own special chair,' I told him.

'Wow! I'm gonna have my own chair,' he gushed as he threw himself on me for a big cuddle.

I measured the dimensions of the chair precisely so that it would be exactly the right size for James, and I carefully and lovingly constructed it in Denise's dad's large garden shed, which doubled as his workshop. Huey was happy for me to work away in there until the chair was done, and I have to say it was pretty good at the end. I used old bits of wood and leather, finally upholstering it in bright red. When I eventually took it home and showed it to James, all I heard was a huge roar of excitement before he was off like a rocket, climbing all over it and jumping up and down on his very own seat. From that day on you couldn't part my little boy from his chair. Every day he would pull it up to watch his favourite television shows and be the happiest kid ever. I loved to do things that made him happy, as did everyone else in the family.

A lot of time was spent with our extended family, and so James had plenty of other kids to mix with, as there were loads of cousins as well as aunts and uncles. They all showered him with affection and love, and in return he adored making people laugh. He was a huge part of our family and rarely was he without that sparkling smile on his face. The only time he was quiet was when he was sleeping! Sometimes he was so exhausted he would fall asleep in my arms at night on the couch and I would gently carry him to his bed and tuck him in. Other times I would put him to bed and hold his hand while he dropped off. He always took a little torch with him, and if he woke in the middle of the night, I would hear him sneaking across the room to get into bed with us.

We would often spend time at my brother Jimmy's house, which was also in Kirkby and a short walk from our flat. He and his wife Karen already had two daughters, aged five and three, and James loved to play with them. Jimmy kept pigeons in a loft in his back garden and it was a huge treat for James to go and visit. He was completely mesmerized by them and the noises they made.

'Cor, look at the birds, Ralph,' he would gasp aloud, as I lifted him up to see them. 'When I grow up I want to have birds like that too.'

'You can do whatever you want when you get older, son,' I promised him.

He loved his Uncle Jimmy and his Aunt Karen, who were always happy to see us at their house. Karen kept her home immaculate, like a lot of Liverpudlian women. They lived in an end-of-terrace red-brick house with three bedrooms. Everything was beautifully decorated and yet you didn't feel like it was somewhere you couldn't relax; it was so inviting and friendly, you felt totally at ease and able to enjoy yourself.

Their house had the added bonus of a small but child-friendly garden, which was Jimmy's pride and joy. At the far end were his pigeon sheds, but elsewhere there was a well-kept lawn and plenty of plants and flowers. This meant that when the weather was good enough, the kids could run out the back patio doors and play outside, which they loved. We didn't have the sort of lives where you had to book appointments to tell people you were coming to see them. It was the 'norm' just to turn up and stick the kettle on, day or night. It was an open-house policy.

Both Jimmy and Karen were tall and slender, but while Karen had dark brown, almost black hair, Jimmy was the blond one in the family. Neither of them was quiet! Jimmy loved to be around people, cracking jokes and having a laugh. Karen was the same and they were rarely without smiles on their faces. They were both larger than life, and it was me who was the quieter one, but I always loved being in their company. When everyone got together, their house was filled with laughter and the kids were as content as anything to tear around and enjoy themselves. It was here that many of the kids' birthday parties would be held – there was never a dull moment in that house. Jimmy was working on the taxis at the time, and life seemed very good for him and his wife. They were happily married, enjoyed a great social life and had a brilliant family. That happiness rubbed off on anyone who walked through the front door.

James was no exception, and I will always remember the day he climbed onto Jimmy's lap and declared, 'You've got the same name as me.'

'No, son, you've got the same name as me and your granddad, because we were here before you,' Jimmy replied.

With that James let out peals of laughter before rushing off to entertain someone else. Everyone remembers his antics during a kids' Halloween party Jimmy and Karen held in October 1992, when he was two and a half. He was the centre of attention among all the other kids because he was the youngest, and totally lovable! Karen and Jimmy's girls doted on him and wanted to play with him like he was a little cute doll and, of course, James lapped it all up. There must have been about eight kids at the party that day, some family as well as others from the street, and just as many adults. That was quite a lot of people, and noise, in an ordinary-sized house, especially as the children were all screaming at the top of their lungs and having the time of their lives. Karen always threw great parties and sometimes

I think the adults enjoyed them just as much as the kids!

As ever, James was the life and soul, loving every minute of showing off in the bin-liner costume that the kids had dressed him in for the occasion. But that wasn't enough for our James. He wanted to go the whole hog, and so Jimmy's eldest daughter led him upstairs with about four other kids and they set to work on his look, raiding whatever make-up and costumes they could lay their hands on! About half an hour later, they all pounded down the stairs and there was James with the biggest grin across his face. He was plastered in *Rocky Horror Show*-style make-up. Gone were his bright chubby cheeks and the angel face. Instead he was covered in white face cream with red devil streaks painted down from his eyes and he now had green hair under a witch's hat!

'Look at me, everyone,' he shrieked. 'I'm coming to get you on my broomstick!'

The more everyone laughed at his antics, the more excited James became. He was completely in his element, running under tables and chairs and jumping out on the grown-ups, trying to scare us in his Halloween costume.

But the favourite part of everyone's day was playing duck apple in a large bowl of water. Even the adults had a go, pushing their faces into the bowl to fetch an apple with their teeth. This proved a lot harder for the mums and dads after downing a few beers during the afternoon, but it was very funny, and the children especially liked to see the adults making complete fools of themselves. When it came to James's turn to try and grab an apple, he did it with as much energy as he did everything else in his life, and launched his head into the bowl as the kids around him squealed away. There was water and mess everywhere but no one was in trouble. This was a fun day and the kids could let off some steam and play together.

By the time James had finished with the apples, his make-up had run all down his face, and so off he went upstairs with the rest of his gang to have it reapplied all over again. There were loads of goodies that day for the kids – bags of sweets and plenty of cakes, mainly made by Karen, who was a great cook. All the adults kept an eye on the children to make sure they were all safe. If things got out of hand, any one of the mums or dads would step in and have a quiet word. There was no time limit on this party or any other. The kids were taken home when they were tired or had had enough, and I can remember carrying our son home that night as he slept in my arms, totally exhausted by all the fun.

James was always up to something. He had a habit of hiding food and sweets in anything that had a lid on it. We would have to go and hunt down biscuits and cakes in pots all over the house to make sure they didn't rot and smell, but you could never be cross with James. At one family party he tried to put a whole piece of gateau in his mouth at once and ended up smearing it right across his face. It was a sight to be seen.

Despite his boisterous nature, James was also very kind and caring. He loved all types of animals and, even though he was naturally curious, he never wanted to harm them. I would take him over the nearby hills and he would run around with excitement.

'Let's go and find some grasshoppers, Ralph,' he'd shout.

'OK, son, I'll race you to see who finds one first.'

I always let him win, and when he found the grasshoppers

he would sit for ages listening to the noises they made. Then he would carefully put them on his hands and look on in fascination as they jumped away. He would collect all the caterpillars from the fuchsia plants and carnations growing in Jimmy and Karen's garden before gently letting them go again. Similarly with frogs: he would put them on his palm and stroke them before they hopped away, never hurting them. But his favourite animals were the fish in the tank at our house. He was so short that someone would always have to pick him up so he could see. He loved to gaze at the angelfish, guppies, mollies and tetras, but most of all he liked the neons that shone so brightly in the water as they swished about. You could see James's eyes darting as he tried to keep up with the pace of the fish. He was fascinated by them.

'Can I feed the fish, Ralph?' he would ask without fail.

'Of course you can, son. Let's get the food for you.'

Then he would gently drop the fish flakes into the tank and watch with wide-eyed astonishment as the food glided through the water and the fish swam to gobble it all up. Every time he left the house he would have to kiss the glass bowl and wave goodbye to the fish.

'Bye-bye, fishes, see you soon,' he chirped, waving all the way to the front door in my arms.

No one will ever know just how much James meant to me. He brought so much to all who knew him in such a short space of time. Never in a million years could anyone have imagined what was going to happen to this most special and treasured little boy.

I sometimes sat him on my shoulders and he used to try to pull my ears off in fun. I would be covered in bruises because he was so boisterous, and on one occasion he accidentally snapped the gristle at the top of one of my ears. It's an injury that has never healed. But it's odd to think that when I now touch that damaged ear it can evoke such tender memories of my little boy.

I used to tell him all the time how much I loved him, and he would reply, 'I love you too, Daddy.' Or 'Ralph', depending on how the mood took him!

The night before he vanished from our lives for ever, I put him to bed as normal after another exhausting day. It was one of the jobs I loved as a parent because even when James closed his eyes, he looked content and happy. Denise and I would always take it in turns to put him to bed. That evening when he was finally sleepy, I tucked him under his duvet and kissed him on the forehead before watching him fall asleep. He was holding my hand as he often did, and I waited until his fingers relaxed, slipping away from mine, before I dared to move away.

'Goodnight, my beautiful son,' I gently whispered in his ear.

2

The Day Everything Changed

Friday, 12 February 1993 was a bitterly cold day and, as ever, James was sitting on his special chair in his 'jim-jams' eating his breakfast in front of the fire. He was as lively as could be, even though he had just got out of bed. He was like that every day, full of beans, until it was time for him to go to sleep at night. To be honest, I can't say that the details of that morning stood out to me more than any other. But I do know that as soon as James was up and about, it meant that everyone else had to be full of energy too, because he was such a live wire. James always had cereal for his breakfast and I started my day with a cup of coffee and some toast. When I think back, it is almost unreal just how ordinary the day was and how happy and un-troubled we all were as a family. And yet in a few short hours nothing would ever be the same again. No, we didn't have a lot of money, but we had a warm and clean home, Denise and I had each other, and together we had the most amazing little boy. It is easy to take your blessings for granted until they are stolen from you.

I had agreed to go out that morning to help Denise's brother Paul fit some wardrobes at his new home, which was only a short distance from where we lived. Denise asked if I would take James with me because she was heading up to her mum's to see family, and it would give her a break and the chance to catch up on her own chores. Denise usually went and did some shopping on a Friday, but as far as I can remember she hadn't planned to go out of Kirkby when we parted that morning. I was normally happy to have James around me, but on this occasion I was concerned that he might get hurt if we weren't keeping an eye on him at all times. The doors to the wardrobes were heavy and there would be lots of electric tools and nails lying around that might pose a danger to an incredibly nosy child like James. I couldn't bear the thought of him being injured because I wasn't able to keep an eye on him properly. Both Denise and I were very protective of James, and we were both constantly checking on him because he had the potential to get into mischief in the blink of an eye.

Not taking James with me that morning is the biggest single regret of my life. It was the worst decision I have ever made, and to think that I made it trying to protect James is the most bitter irony of all.

Denise and I agreed that she would take James with her. He was dressed warmly, bundled into his long blue hooded anorak. We all left the flat together and walked to Denise's mum Eileen's house. I said goodbye to them both from there. The last I saw of James was as he waved to me from the front door. My last words to him were a simple, 'Ta-ra.'

When I arrived at Paul's house, I didn't have a care in the world. We set to work for the day fitting the wardrobes and it wasn't until late in the afternoon that I finished and called in to see my mum. I didn't stop long, and after having a chat with her I walked back to Eileen's house to meet Denise and James. I can't remember exactly what time it was, but it was already dark and approaching teatime. I had no idea until that point that my son had gone missing. We were not yet in an age where everyone had a mobile phone and people were ringing or texting each other every few minutes.

I remember that when I walked through the door I immediately sensed a strange atmosphere. I couldn't see Denise or James and I wondered if they had already gone back to our flat.

'What's up, Eileen?' I asked. I knew from her face that something was wrong.

'Ralph, the police have been on and your James is missing. I don't know much more than that, but there's a message on the answerphone for you to get to the station. I've been out shopping myself, so I don't know what time this all happened, but I've been ringing round as many people as I can and no one seems to know anything. You need to get to Marsh Lane Police Station.'

'What do you mean? How can he be missing, for God's sake?'

I felt sick to my stomach. It hit me so hard, as if someone had just punched the living daylights out of me. It was just coming up to six o'clock, and I looked out of the window only to see how dark and cold it was.

'Where's my baby boy, Eileen? I need to find him,' I choked.

I ran out of the house as fast as I could to rally relatives to start a search for James. The first person I went to was

Denise's brother, Ray Matthews, who was at home with his wife Delia eating their tea when I arrived.

'James has gone missing. They can't find him anywhere. We need to get to the police station and find out what's happened to him. I need to get out there and find him but I don't know what's gone on. I haven't even spoken to Denise. Have you heard from her?'

'How has he gone missing? What do you mean?'

Ray automatically assumed I meant that something had happened to my brother Jimmy, and then it dawned on him that I meant my son. I still knew so little. The police had told Eileen that James had gone missing during a shopping trip earlier in the afternoon, but not where they had been.

'I don't even know where he went missing, Ray. I just know they can't find him and I need to speak to the police and Denise as soon as possible. Denise is at the police station. Can you take me there?'

Without hesitation, Ray grabbed his car keys and we both raced to the front door together. Marsh Lane Police Station is in Bootle, which is a dockside Liverpool town nearly eight miles from Kirkby. Ray was driving as fast as he could and my head was racing.

The next few minutes were a bit of a blur. I was beside myself with worry and all I wanted to do was open the car door and throw up because I felt so sick at the thought of my lovely son being out there all alone. Ray kept trying to reassure me that all would be well and that James had probably wandered off to make mischief as he always did. I hoped with all my heart he was right, and that by the time

I arrived at the police station I would be greeted by my son's gorgeous face, grinning from ear to ear.

It's not until something like this happens that you realize how physical your emotions can be. Every parent in the land must surely know what it feels like to lose sight of your precious child, even for a few seconds. I felt violently ill from head to toe and was in a blind panic over the thought of James being in danger. It seemed like an eternity before we arrived at Marsh Lane, but when we did I jumped from the passenger seat of the car and legged it into the police station.

'My name's Ralph Bulger and my son has gone missing,' I blurted out to the first officer I saw. 'Please tell me you have found him . . . please,' I begged.

'I'm sorry, sir, we have no news about your son yet,' the duty officer replied. 'Come through and I'll find someone who can speak to you and bring you up to speed.'

It was obvious that everyone in the police station was on high alert and was aware that a child was missing. I was desperate to speak to Denise, because I needed to know what had happened. I also knew that I had to get out into the cold night and search for my son. Every minute I stayed at the police station was another minute *not* spent looking for the most precious little boy in my life.

I was led into an interview room where two policemen said they would need me to give a statement and as much information as possible to help them in their search for James. My fear and frustration spilled over.

'For fuck's sake, what am I doing in here answering questions when I should be out there finding my James?'

'I'm sorry, Ralph,' one of the officers replied calmly. 'It's vital we get as much information as we can to assist us in our search. I understand how you must be feeling but we are going to do everything we can to get James back to you. We just need you to tell us as much as you can.'

I realized that the police were doing their jobs, but there was no doubt about it, they were taking statements from me and Denise to establish if we may have been behind James's disappearance. They couldn't rule us out until they had spoken to us in detail. It took a long time as they tried to piece together where I had been and if I could have been with James at any time that afternoon. They asked me about Denise and where she had been that day, but I couldn't answer many of their questions because I hadn't spoken to her. I know this would be standard practice in a police investigation of this nature, to rule out immediate family and friends, but I found the line of questioning very harsh and unsettling. Perhaps I was just sensitive to their questions because I was desperate to get out and look for my son. In any case, I didn't have a choice. I wasn't going to be let out of the police station until I had completed my statement. I hadn't even seen Denise at this point, as she was being held elsewhere, answering more questions.

I felt bad about my initial outburst, but I was lashing out because I was so terrified about the safety of my son, and it was never meant as a criticism of the police. Even after I had made my statement, I still couldn't get out and join the search. Instead, the police drove me back to our flat in Kirkby because they desperately needed some up-to-date photos of James. I understood why this was important, but as a parent, as James's father, the delay was agony.

Finally, after what must have been about three hours, the

police took me to see Denise in another interview room. She looked up at me and her face just crumpled. She was in bits as she got up to hug me.

'What the hell happened?' I asked as I put my arms around her.

Denise filled me in on the details as best she could, but she kept breaking down in tears and it was hard for her to get the words out. She was in the interview room with her brother Paul's fiancée, Nicola Bailey, and it turned out that the pair of them had gone shopping earlier that day in the Strand in Bootle, a large, popular indoor mall. Denise had taken James with her and Nicola was also minding a little girl for the afternoon, the three-year-old daughter of Denise's brother John. It was the first I knew that Denise had gone to Bootle, as her shopping trip had been arranged on the spur of the moment when Nicola had also turned up at Eileen's earlier that day. Nicola was heading to the Strand and had asked Denise if she wanted to go along with her.

Nicola drove the four of them to the retail centre where they arrived just before 2 p.m. As ever, James was thrilled to be riding in a car, which was always one of his favourite pastimes. Since he had been very young he had loved cars, bikes, planes, trains – he'd always been mad about anything that moved.

It was a typical Friday afternoon in the shopping mall, ram packed with people spending their wages on food for the weekend or clothes for a night out on the town. It was also bitterly cold outside, and so that brought even more people into the mall because it was warm and sheltered from the wintry weather. Usually Denise would never take James out without his pushchair, but as the girls didn't plan to stay long at the Strand, she decided to leave it behind. She told me that James was overexcited, being his normal bubbly self, but because he was not in his pushchair, he kept trying to break free from her hand to go off exploring the shops. I had always worried when we took him to the Strand because I knew how busy it was in there and how easy it would have been for James to get lost if he went off on his own.

He was naturally nosy and friendly, and he would have been in seventh heaven looking around at all the shops and all the people there that day. Denise said they bought the kids sausage rolls and some sweets and then set off to get their grocery shopping for the weekend, calling in at Tesco and Marks & Spencer. She said the kids were getting restless and playing up a bit, running up and down the aisles and making a nuisance of themselves, as young children do. She was having trouble keeping hold of James as he kept trying to get loose from her grip and tear around the shops like a maniac. Both she and Nicola agreed it was time to get the kids back home, but they wanted to stop at a butcher's on the way out.

They called into A. R. Tyms, where Denise usually bought her meat. She was buying chops for our tea that night.

'I can't believe it,' Denise sobbed. 'I swear I only let go of him for a second and he just vanished. I went into the butcher's and got my purse out to pay, and when I looked down our James was gone. One minute he was there, the next he disappeared. I saw him by my side and then by the door and that was it. I ran out to find him, but I never saw him again. I'm so sorry, Ralph.'

She told me she just panicked and ran out of the shop.

'Where's James, where's James?' she yelled. 'James, James, where are you?'

She said the rest was a bit of a blur and that she was running about everywhere, bumping into people and shouting his name out as loud as she could. She ran in and out of shops and checked the corridors and aisles of every place she could think he may have gone to. Her shouts for James became screams of panic, begging passers-by to let her know if they had seen her lost son. Nicola was searching different shops as the two girls tried their hardest to find him, but they both said it was as if he had disappeared into thin air.

A few minutes later Denise found the security office for the mall and reported James missing. They made several announcements over the public address system, appealing to anyone who had seen a lost little boy. After that Denise went back and forth to the security office, getting more and more desperate with every visit. She said it was mayhem and that she was just running around everywhere, crying and screaming for her son. She wanted them to shut the precinct doors to prevent James from leaving the mall, but the security officers kept reassuring her that he'd turn up.

'I'm so sorry, Ralph,' she sobbed, as I held her close to me. 'I tried everything to find him but he just went. I want my little boy back, Ralph. Where has he gone? Please find him for us.'

'Don't worry, love, we will find him. I promise.'

It was all I could do to reassure her, but inside I had this huge knot in my stomach. The sick feeling of dread and frantic worry wouldn't leave me. But I had to try to look after Denise as well as find James. It was now several hours since he had gone missing and all I could think was how my son was alone and cold and scared in the dark somewhere.

Denise told me that she and Nicola had carried on searching in the mall, and it was at 4.22 p.m. that the security office called the police, forty minutes after James had disappeared. Police Constable Mandy Waller arrived at the mall to meet Denise and Nicola.

Some time later, Mandy described to me how she had been the first police officer on the scene – she was on a routine patrol in her car when that initial call was made to say that a little boy had been lost.

According to Mandy, this was a regular thing and not in the slightest bit unusual. Routine police work often involves missing children who wander off, and in most cases parents and kids are happily reunited within about fifteen minutes. What had alarmed her, though, was that by the time she arrived at the mall, James had already been missing for a lot longer than that. She could see Denise was frantic with worry and together they started scouring the mall, retracing Denise's every step earlier in the day and looking again at the places she had already searched for James.

The Strand contains more than one hundred shops, set over two floors. Together, the upper and lower malls have five entrances and exits as well as access through the main multi-storey car park. There was a lot of ground to cover, not just on the public forecourts, but in the stores themselves, which were due to close shortly after Mandy arrived. She tried to reassure Denise that it was most likely James had hidden himself under a counter or in a store cupboard as part of a mischievous game and then found himself lost.

The pair of them stopped as many people as they could, asking if anyone had seen a little boy, and then went outside to alert taxi drivers in the cab rank outside. Eventually the precinct closed as the last remaining shops shut at the end of business, but Denise still continued to scour the mall with Mandy. She said that she kept praying James had just been accidentally locked into one of the shops and that he would be found safe and warm. Maybe he had gone to sleep somewhere and was going to wake up oblivious to all the fuss? But both Denise and I knew it was highly unlikely given his reputation for being a ball of energy. What was so concerning was the speed with which he just vanished. How can a lively and loud child like James be there one moment and gone the next? It's not as if he was a quiet lad who would go unnoticed, and yet everyone who was asked that day said they had not seen a small child lost.

Eventually Mandy took Denise and Nicola back to the station, where she gently told them the police would need to ask the pair some questions to learn as much about James and his disappearance as possible. Denise had not been in a fit state to say much, but she tried to pull herself together to help detectives in any way she could. She would have done anything to have her baby back by her side again.

By the time I met up with Denise in the interview room, she was falling apart again. While I wanted to take her home, as she was so upset, I was also desperate to get out and start looking for James.

'Go home, Denise, and I'll get out and find our baby. I'll let you know the moment we hear anything,' I promised her.

'I'm not going anywhere until I find James. I'll stay out here all night if I have to. We've got to find him, Ralph.'

'I don't think you're in a fit state to go wandering around. I promise I won't give up till we find him, but just go back to your ma's and I'll ring to let you know what's happening.'

'I'm coming with you, and nothing you say is gonna change my mind.'

Denise was a strong woman and a terrific mother, but I have never seen her so devastated. We had already lost Kirsty, our first daughter, and now our only other child was missing. It was hard for me to look at the pain etched all over her face, and although I hugged her, I knew it wouldn't make her feel any better until James was back with us. I made many different pacts with God that night.

'Please, God, please bring James back to us and I swear I will do anything in return,' I prayed in my head.

The truth was, I would have laid down my life for my child at that moment if only he could be returned home safely. I think at that stage, my greatest fear was that he had suffered some kind of accident and that he had been injured somehow and couldn't get any help. That seemed to make the most sense during those early hours of the search, because no one was coming forward to say they had seen him. He was so little and vulnerable, I was certain that if anyone had come across him wandering the streets alone on a dark night, they would have gone to his rescue and brought him to the nearest police station, but there was nothing. And so I had to hold on to the hope that he would be found safely at some point. It was just that the waiting was agony.

The feeling of helplessness is possibly the very worst thing of all. It's as if you have been thrown out of a plane without a parachute and are free-falling to earth. You have absolutely no control over what is happening. To any parent, I can only say this: imagine that it was your two-year-old child who was missing. You know your son or daughter is out there somewhere, but you have no way of finding them. There is no greater torture for a mum or dad. All I wanted to do was put my arms around my baby and cuddle him for dear life. It was my job to protect my family and I had failed. There is nothing more precious than your own child and the love you have for him. I felt desperate inside.

'Let's go and find James,' I urged Denise.

'What if we can't find him, Ralph,' she replied.

'We will find him. We have to find him. He can't stay missing for ever. We will have him home tonight, tucked up safe and sound in his bed without a care in the world.'

3

The Search

The police search was well underway by the time Denise and I left the station around 8 p.m. There were patrol cars everywhere, not just in Bootle, but in the surrounding areas as well. They were using loudspeakers to appeal to the public, asking if anyone had seen a little boy, letting everyone know he was lost and missing from home. By now it had turned into a massive hunt for James. The police helicopter was scouring the skies above, shining its torch across the area. More than one hundred officers had been called out to join the hunt and the Operational Support Division (OSD), which backs up major incident teams, was being assembled to widen the search.

Mandy Waller had been assigned to continue looking after Denise and me, as she had struck up a good rapport with Denise especially. She would be our point of contact for information as the search continued. Mandy was a lovely woman. She was strong, confident and capable, but she was also gentle, kind and compassionate. We both trusted her from the beginning and that trust was not misplaced.

Denise's brother Ray took Denise back to the now-closed

mall to have another look, and when they arrived a security guard spotted them and let them in. Together with a plain-clothes detective and guards, the pair retraced Denise's steps from earlier that afternoon in the hope they might get lucky. The guards told Denise it was unlikely that James was trapped inside a closed shop because any movement from him would almost certainly have triggered highly sensitive alarms, but they were taking no chances and they continued their search anyway. Keyholders to the stores were being scrambled to make sure that nothing was left to chance.

Close relatives from both sides, as well as extended family and friends, had rushed out in force to help the search once they were alerted that James was missing. It would be impossible to name everyone who was there that night; as the evening wore on, there must have been hundreds of people from Kirkby who made their way to Bootle to offer their help in trying to find our little boy. It was quite overwhelming, the show of solidarity we received from our community, but it didn't surprise me one bit. That was the way it was where we came from. Friends and family spread out as far and as wide as possible. It was like a needle in a haystack, of course, but there were many carloads of people driving around just in the hope that someone would see something that would lead us to James. Others set out on foot to start combing every square inch of the area. I know Jimmy was there because he immediately tried to take some of the burden off my shoulders and suggested to everyone which places they should cover. His work as a taxi driver had given him a brilliant knowledge of the area. I can also remember him giving me a hug and comforting me.

'Don't worry, kid, we'll find him,' he said. 'We won't stop searching till we do.'

It was Jimmy's turn to try to reassure me, just as I had with Denise, but we needed to cling to that hope and carry on believing that we would find James safe and well. As far as Jimmy was concerned, I was the baby of the family and, as my older brother, he was now trying to look after me.

Jimmy recalls:

It was the coldest of nights and yet that seemed to be the farthest thing from anyone's mind as we started trawling the area. There were so many members of the public from Kirkby and from Bootle just turning up in droves and asking if they could help. I remember thinking that with this number of people, and the police operation in full swing, we were sure to have a lucky break somewhere.

When I saw Ralph, he just looked awful. Drained of colour and petrified. He is my baby brother and I knew I had to step up to the mark and do what I could to help him through this. We agreed that teams of people would spread out from the Strand and that we would keep returning to the police station every so often to see if there was any news.

There cannot have been a single place we didn't check that night. There were police and members of the public in playing fields, schools, housing estates, industrial sites and car parks. We checked in bins, telephone boxes, skips – anywhere a small child may have tried to take refuge from the cold or some-where that James might have found himself trapped. Some of the places were so eerie in the black of night, and there were some really rough and seedy areas we had to search.

We checked back alleys used by the homeless and drug addicts, picking our way through empty beer cans and discarded and bloodied heroin needles. I'd seen them all as a taxi driver but they were not the sort of places you would want to find a two-year-old baby.

The search continued with no joy. As every hour ticked by our nerves grew more frazzled, but we had to keep going. Tiredness didn't come into it. It was like everyone was on autopilot, focusing on one thing only – the need to find baby James.

The next time I saw Ralph, I just tried to keep his spirits up. 'Don't worry, Ralph. We won't stop until we find him.'

But the panic was well and truly set in his eyes by this stage. I could see it in everyone's faces, and I hoped it didn't show on mine as he looked at me with complete despair.

The local and national media had now been told that there was a manhunt for a missing boy and news bulletins were being carried by regional television and radio stations by 10 p.m. The police told us that a woman had reported seeing a young child crying earlier in the day on the banks of the Leeds–Liverpool Canal, which runs alongside the shopping precinct. That night the search team got down there with their torches to see if they could find anything in the dirty water. Reeds were pushed aside and rubbish bags were ripped apart on the route, but still there was nothing. The liaison officers at the station told Ralph that an underwater search team would begin dredging the canal at first light. They wouldn't have stood a chance of seeing anything in the dead of night. It was not a good moment. The focus of the search was drifting towards the canal as, at that point, it was the only known sighting of a young child, but it was just unthink-

able that his body might be found there the following day. I tried to push the notion from my mind and carry on with the search.

Jimmy was a big help to me that evening. He was my backbone – the person who was there for me, while I was trying to be there for Denise. During the evening, Denise and I returned to the precinct several times with the police, shuttling between the mall and the station. Every time we spoke with the detectives, I said a silent prayer to God that they would have something positive to tell us. I would let myself feel a moment of hope, then see from their faces there was no good news. I searched so many places that night. Sometimes Denise was with me and other times she would remain with Mandy at the station or go off with her brothers to continue looking.

At one point the police took Denise and me back to the precinct to see some of the images being extracted from the security cameras. They asked us to look at a very fuzzy frame of a little boy running from the door of a butcher's shop. My heart sank when I saw it.

'That's him,' I said without hesitation. There was no mistaking my son's little body, however grainy the images were.

Denise was exactly the same. She recognized our James immediately and screamed out, 'That's James, that's our baby.'

I wasn't sure if the sighting was a good thing or a bad thing. In one way I thought it was a positive breakthrough because we were now seeing our son leaving the butcher's shop, and I was praying that further images and information would show us where he went. If that was the case, surely it would lead us to our son? Our early hopes of finding James had quickly faded as the evening became more intense. Was this the tiny chink of light that would bring James back to us?

But in the next breath, it was so painful to see this tiny little figure all alone, and I was terrified of what we might see next. I was almost too afraid of what was around the corner. Then we were shown another frame taken seconds later, which showed Denise leaving the butcher's in a panic and beginning her search for James on the downstairs floor of the mall.

This must have been quite late in the evening, at a guess I would say about 10 or 11 p.m., because we had been in and out of the mall many times and I had been off searching elsewhere as well. By now we had still only identified this one image of James outside the butcher's shop just moments after he had slipped away from Denise's side. A police team was continuing to go through more of the images from the CCTV camera shots taken from the mall earlier that afternoon. Detectives told us there were sixteen cameras recording, which they hoped would provide a much clearer idea of where James had gone after he ran from the butcher's counter. The frame-by-frame account of that afternoon was crucial in building up a picture of what had occurred.

Late in the evening, the police persuaded us that we should go home to get some rest. They reassured us that the search would continue through the night and that we should come back at first light. We were driven home to Eileen's house, and when we got there Denise and I just sat in silence, both lost in our own thoughts. I began pacing up and down, unable to sit still for more than a few minutes. It was no good. I was not going to be able to rest and Denise felt the same. There was no way we were staying at home while James was still out there somewhere. At around 1 a.m. two of Denise's brothers, Ray and Gary, returned home to check on us and to update us. They stayed a few minutes and Denise and I returned to Bootle with them to continue looking.

At one point I remember trudging across a wet, dark field, feeling so desperate and alone. I thought about my baby James, scared and crying in the dark, and I just sank to my knees and cried. I raised my eyes towards the horrible black sky and prayed with my hands clenched close together. 'Please, God, let us have him back. Please don't let any harm come to him.'

'What have we done to deserve this?' I shouted out loud. 'Are you punishing us for something? Just take me instead of James if you have to.'

As tears streamed down my face, I didn't even feel the cold or the drizzling rain that had soaked through to my bones. There was only one thing that mattered.

Jimmy was still out searching with the rest of the family. We all refused to give up until we found James. We didn't get any sleep at all that night, but as dawn broke on Saturday morning the search was to take on a startling new twist. We were unaware at that point that highly trained technicians and police officers from the OSD had been working through the night on a series of images taken from the CCTV. The next day, 13 February, Denise and I automatically set off for the station to continue our search and to see if the police had any further news. We were told the police had found images showing that James had left the shopping mall with two young boys, probably in their early teens. There was every chance they had taken him as a prank or as a bit of mischief, as if he was their younger brother. The police were now going to concentrate on finding the boys to establish if James was still with them or, if not, where they would be able to find him.

I looked at Denise and smiled with relief.

'He's gonna be all right, Denise,' I said. 'He's with two young kids – he's gonna be all right.'

For the first time, I felt that God had answered my prayers. As soon as I heard that, I thought everything was going to be OK. It all made sense as to why we couldn't find James, because he had gone off to play with other kids. The previous night some very dark and nasty thoughts had crossed my mind. My biggest fear was that James had been stolen by a nonce, a pervert paedophile, and that he had been abused and killed. It was not something I could say out loud to anyone, and I kept telling myself I had to keep on hoping, but in the dead of night when you can't sleep and your son is missing, you can't stop such terrible fears preying on your imagination. I also worried that James had got lost and hurt himself, and was now unable to get help. There are so many things that you think, but this really was the last thing I would have imagined.

'Thank you, thank you, thank you, God,' I said over and over in my head.

We were asked if we would take part in a press conference that was being held at 11 a.m. and we agreed. Even though we still didn't know where he was, at least there was a chance that he would turn up and come home with us again. Denise was hopeful, but she was still so strung out by the events of the last thirty-six hours that she hardly had the strength to register a lot of what was going on. Neither of us was comfortable doing the press conference, but we knew it was important to get as much information out to the public as possible, as it may bring in further details that would lead to James. Both of us would have done anything at that point, but Denise's nerves and stress got the better of her when she eventually faced the cameras.

The police station was a hive of activity that morning and loads of our family had arrived at the station too, to offer moral support. The press conference was packed and I could feel myself tensing as we sat down in the full media spotlight. There were TV cameras and flashbulbs going off everywhere and I was getting hot and sweaty. Denise was in a bad state. She was exhausted and wrecked from lack of sleep and worry. She managed to describe how she was buying meat with James and then the next minute he had gone, but she was close to breaking down.

'If anyone has got my baby, please just bring him back,' she sobbed.

Denise was now crying her heart out and it was horrendous. She had to leave the room and I tried my best to pick up where she had left off. It had been a mistake to ask her to deal with the press so soon after James went missing. Her emotions were there for everyone to see, as any mother's would be in the same circumstances. I was little better, and felt like a rabbit caught in the headlights. Neither Denise nor I would have imagined this in our worst nightmares, but it was very clear to me that we needed the press to keep putting the message out there because I was convinced someone would know where James was.

'It could happen to anyone,' I said. 'She just turned away and the next thing he was gone. James is a bubbly kid who gets on with anyone. He will chat away to anyone, but we have taught him his name and address so if anyone asks him he will tell them.'

I answered a few questions as best I could, but I couldn't wait to get out of that room. The police continued on with their briefing to the media as they broke the news about the images of the two boys seen leading James away from the mall. Copies of the video images were given out, and by Saturday lunchtime the headline television news on BBC and ITV reported that detectives searching for a missing toddler on Merseyside now believed he had been abducted. It was horrible to hear those words because they felt so threatening and dangerous. But it was far better to think he was with kids than the more sinister alternative of him being led away by a strange man – that his disappearance was just a result of high jinks, and that mischief, not murder, was the motive. I remained convinced that if James was with other children then he was going to turn up safe and well.

The TV reports were accompanied by the grainy images of James holding the hand of a boy as he was led away from the shopping mall. Ironically, they were passing a Mothercare shop at the time the images were taken.

Those blurred and sketchy pictures, which were screened around the world, have become some of the most eerie and terrifying film footage ever seen, a silent witness to a savage and unthinkable crime. Now, knowing what was to later become of my little boy, I desperately want to reach into the TV screen and pluck him back from danger. But at the time, as we watched my happy-go-lucky son trotting from the mall that afternoon, holding the hand of a ten-year-old boy, no one had any idea he was being led to his brutal murder.

The picture we had already seen of James running from the shop was captured at 3.42 p.m. and was followed within moments by scenes of Denise frantically searching for him. They were all taken outside the butcher's shop on the ground floor of the mall. But just a minute later the images of James hand-in-hand with a young boy as they followed another youngster were taken on the top floor. Just four minutes after James had strayed from Denise's side, he was led away from the precinct by two strangers.

Despite the glimmer of optimism and the major breakthrough with the discovery of the images, the police search was as intense as ever. As the press conference continued at Marsh Lane, elsewhere police divers began trawling through the canal following even more reports from members of the public of a young boy seen on the banks of the water. There would be many more sightings from that point on, although not all of them were confirmed to have been James. The divers carried out a painful, inch-by-inch search, and it was an agonizing wait for them to finish, but when they did it gave us even more hope because they failed to find his body. I was more certain than ever that James was tucked away with these lads somewhere and that it was only a matter of time before he turned up. One police theory was that the two boys who had taken James could be living rough and that all three of them might be hiding in some derelict building somewhere.

By now more and more information was starting to pour into the incident room that had been set up at Marsh Lane. It was being led by Detective Superintendent Albert Kirby, head of the Merseyside Police Serious Crime Squad. He was a very experienced detective, tall and slim and with a reputation for fairness while accepting no nonsense. He was supported by Detective Chief Inspector Geoff MacDonald, a solid and decent man who was straight-talking, and Detective Inspector Jim Fitzsimmons, who was thorough and compassionate throughout the inquiry. There had been many more possible sightings of James and every last lead was being followed. But James had still not turned up and we were facing our second night without him.

We had all gone past tiredness now and carried on regard-less. I felt dizzy and disorientated at times through stress and lack of sleep, but I had to keep shaking myself to try to get rid of the spinning sensation in my head. Everyone was running on adrenaline, and it is incredible how far the body can be pushed at times like these. It is like a survival instinct that kicks in, only in our case we were fighting for the survival of James.

It was still very cold, and everyone carried on searching in the same manner as the night before until the early hours of Sunday morning. The earlier hope Denise and I had felt was beginning to diminish again as we failed to find our son. When we all returned home, Denise and I and members of the family talked for hours through the night about what could have happened to James. There was very little we didn't consider, but each time we tried to come up with a positive outcome. None of us could bring ourselves to speak out loud our darkest fears that James could be dead. Of course it crossed all of our minds, but I think instinctively we all knew it would not be helpful to start talking that way. No body had been found and so there had to remain some hope that he was still alive. Privately, I was terrified that the boys may have been used by a paedophile ring to entice James away without attracting suspicion. But I wouldn't allow myself to share these thoughts with anyone.

'What if James has fallen into a rubbish skip and can't get out? What if he is locked in a store room somewhere and no one knows he is there?' Denise questioned.

'Then he is going to be found eventually,' I reasoned. 'We both know James is a little fighter. If he's locked away somewhere, someone will realize. They have to. A little boy can't just vanish into thin air. He could still be with these young boys and they could be hiding out somewhere, anywhere. They probably think they are in a heap of shit now and are too scared to bring James back, but they can't hide for ever.'

'My guess is that he has got lost somewhere, and because it's been so cold, he's found somewhere warm to shelter. He has to turn up sometime or other,' Jimmy chipped in.

We had to keep each other going with possibilities that carried a happy ending. Some of the theories may have been lame but they were better than believing that James was dead when we really had no idea what had happened to him.

The story continued to dominate the headlines, which in turn meant that information kept pouring into the incident room, where detectives worked around the clock to collect and assess new sightings and possible leads. I didn't even bother to try and go to bed that night. We had arrived home late, and after we had all chatted for about an hour, I sat up in a chair and closed my eyes. Even if I had wanted to sleep, my mind was so scrambled it wouldn't let me. I just wanted the morning to come so we could get back out there once again, and I prayed with all my might that this would be the day that James was coming home.

On Sunday, 14 February, Valentine's Day, I returned to Marsh Lane as soon as possible. The senior detectives had called another press conference for the media, although Denise was in no fit state to take part in it. We agreed that I would read out a statement instead. It was a horrible ordeal and the mood was pretty grim. Publicly the police kept stressing that while they knew James had been taken by these two boys, they were keeping an open mind as to what had happened to him. But it was now day three and there was no sign of our baby. With all the will in the world, it was hard not to lose faith, and I think everyone carried a sense of dread that day.

You could feel an atmosphere around the police and the press, who must have known by now that it was only a matter of time before the inevitable tragic outcome was delivered. Here was a child who had been snatched from a shopping centre and three days later he was still nowhere to be seen. I felt desperate inside but, until I knew otherwise, I had to keep hoping. I am sure I must have been lying to myself, because I probably knew deep down this was not going to end well, but I was never going to give up until I knew otherwise.

With a heavy heart, I went into the media briefing, which began with a statement from DCI MacDonald.

He said, 'It is now forty-four hours since James went missing on Friday. We have continued searching buildings, open land and the canal area in the Strand. I would like to make an appeal for anyone living in the area of Bootle, and perhaps towards Walton, to search their gardens, their back sheds and anything of that nature as the child may have wandered off and found somewhere to sleep.

'We have a sighting of James at around 4.30 p.m. on Friday in the Breeze Hill area of Walton near a reservoir. This is a fully enclosed reservoir and no access can be made into the water area. A lady saw a small boy answering his description with two other boys. She viewed the video pictures of the two boys and is quite confident that they are the two boys she saw, and also, having seen the photographs of James, she is quite satisfied that that is James also. We are anxious to trace any more persons who may have knowledge of who these two boys are or who may have seen them in this particular area. I do have enlarged photographs of the boys.

'We have been getting help from the public and we are anxious that anyone who has information come forward. We request vigilance from everyone to search the area for James.'

It was then my turn to address the press. I could barely hold my head up and face them, I was so fatigued and desolate. It was also one of the most alien situations I have ever confronted – standing in front of the country's media – but I would have walked over hot coals and stuck needles in my eyes if it meant finding James.

'Me and my wife just want to say to the lads who were seen with James, whoever they are, if they could come forward and get themselves eliminated or bring my son back, so long as he gets back . . . If they could bring him to the nearest police station or somewhere safe, or phone, or something . . . or anyone who can give information, no matter how small it is, just get in contact.'

DCI MacDonald continued: 'The witness who saw James with the boys asked about the little boy. They said they were in the area having just found the child. Then they took him away and went off into Breeze Hill. She thought they were round about twelve years of age and it was about a mile away from the Strand. They left the reservoir area and went towards Breeze Hill, the main dual carriageway. It is a distinct possibility that they are frightened. We are also looking at the possibility of boys who have run away from home, either absconders or missing from their homes, possibly squatting. Initially the woman thought it was unusual but then said she was confident they all seemed to be together because the little boy seemed happy to go along with them.'

After the press conference I went to meet up with Jimmy and some of my other relatives to start a new search around the reservoir area. Jimmy remembers very clearly what happened next.

We met at the car park of The Mons pub nearby and decided to split up and go our separate ways so we could cover as wide an area as possible. Ralph looked absolutely dreadful. He was gaunt, sunken in the face and totally done in. None of us had had any sleep but we just kept plodding on in the hope that something would turn up. It was the same routine: searching housing estates, streets, bins, park-land – absolutely anywhere there was a possibility we would find the baby.

By now I had a terrible sense of foreboding, a sinking feeling in the pit of my stomach that James was never going to be found alive. I think deep down Ralph knew that too, but he had to hang on to the hope of seeing his son again. Too long had passed without any more sightings of James and the situation really was dreadful.

We carried on searching, hour after hour, and every now and again we would all meet up in the pub car park to regroup and swap any relevant information. At one stage I volunteered to go back to the police station to see if there was any news.

As soon as I got there I spoke to Geoff MacDonald and I knew it was bad news. Even before he opened his mouth the look in his eyes gave it away. Then he told me they had found a body. It is hard to describe what I felt, but the only thing I remember was this awful pain in the pit of my stomach. My legs seemed as if they were going to give way and I just felt weak from head to toe. I shook my head from side to side and swore out loud, but other than that I said very little. In my mind, all I could think about was Ralph and Denise. I knew they were going to face the most terrible moment of their lives.

Whether it was shock, sadness or anger that I felt, or all of them rolled into one, I can't say, but my body learned a coping mechanism that day which has stayed with me until now – the ability to lock my own feelings away as if they don't exist. The most important job I had to do was protect and look after my kid brother whose son had just been found dead. It didn't matter how I felt. Baby James was dead and I had to be there for Ralph.

He asked me where Ralph was and I told him he was still out searching. He said I needed to get hold of him as soon as possible and get him back to the station. The strain and distress was obvious on the faces of all the police around me.

Geoff told me the news we had all been dreading. He said they had found the body of a small boy and there was no doubt it was James. Denise had been told and we needed to get to Ralph as soon as possible. He asked me to break the news to him. It was the right decision as it was better coming from me than anyone else. I drove back to the car park to find Ralph, dreading the moment that I finally arrived there. How was I going to tell him? How do you tell someone that his son is dead?

When I got there he was already in the car with Denise's brother Ray Matthews, because a police officer involved in the search for James had told them to return to the station. It was the most awful thing to have to tell your baby brother. His life was about to change for ever. I took a deep breath and walked over to the passenger seat of the car where Ralph was sitting. Denise's brother Gary was with me, and he asked Ray to jump out of the car for a word and took him to one side.

'I've got some news, Ralph,' I said. 'It's not good, I'm afraid.'

Ralph leapt from the car and we walked a few yards across the tarmac before I just threw my arms around him and held him for dear life. My heart was beating so fast as I clung to him, not wanting to say the words.

'Ralph, they have found baby James. They have found him. I am so, so sorry, but he is dead. He's dead, Ralph.'

I moved away from hugging Ralph and held his face in my hands. He just nodded at me, unable to speak or move. His face was ashen, as if the blood had drained from him, and then I looked into his eyes. They looked like stone, as if the life had left him in that split second. His body was as limp as a rag doll with the shock. The haunted look on Ralph's face that day will never leave me.

'Where is he, Jim?' he finally said.

'I don't know, Ralph. I don't know.'

His hands were gripping my jacket by now, but still he couldn't move. He was totally stunned into silence.

'We need to get back to the station, Ralph. Denise is there and she needs you. She knows that your son is dead. Let's go back now and sort things out. Come on, let's go there now. We will find out everything when we get there, and you will need to look after Denise, but I am here for you, Ralph, whenever you need me. I am just so sorry.'

He nodded again and slowly let go of my jacket. We both just stood there for a few moments before I held his freezing cold hands in mine and squeezed them hard. I had no words of comfort to bring him in his darkest hour. I put my arm around his shoulder and guided him back to the car before the remaining convoy of vehicles at the car park headed back to the station.

The drive back to the police station was in silence. We were all lost in sorrow and disbelief. I don't even know if it had really sunk in with Ralph yet, but I knew him very well and sensed an explosion of grief was on its way. I felt physically sick. My heart was still pounding as I tried to put myself in Ralph's shoes. It was like we had been dropped into a horror movie and it was almost impossible to believe this was happening. Everyone's lives had been turned upside down and I had no idea how Ralph and Denise were ever going to get through this. How could two parents survive something so huge and devastating? None of us knew then that there was far worse to come.

4

Who Did This to My Son?

I can remember Jimmy holding me in the car park as he told me that James was dead. It was as if I was frozen to the spot. I was numb from head to foot; in a strange way it felt like I wasn't even in my own body. I just didn't have any words to say. I don't think I was in disbelief, but maybe my mind and heart weren't able to process the information that had been delivered to me. It was only as we started to drive towards the police station in silence that my whole body began to tense. The sickening knot that had gnawed away at my stomach since James had disappeared began to magnify into what felt like a huge ball of fire that was engulfing me, body and soul. I thought my body was going to explode like an erupting volcano as my rage took over me. I clenched my fists in silence, my chest tightened and I just wanted to get out of the car and scream.

When we got to Marsh Lane, I ran towards the door of the police station and got taken through to the back of the nick. The first person I saw was Geoff MacDonald and I just let rip, all my emotions pouring out of my body.

'Where's my son?' I screamed. 'I wanna see my James

now. What the fuck have they done to him? I'm gonna kill the bastards.'

'I'm sorry, Ralph, but you can't see him now,' he replied with great compassion.

'Are you sure it's him? How do you know it's my baby? What did those bastards do to him?'

'We're very sure, Ralph, and I'm so very sorry.'

The next thing I remember I was punching the walls and I was just kicking and screaming the place down before I collapsed on the floor and began wailing like a baby. My brother Phil was trying to calm me down, and when I had pulled myself together I went up to Geoff MacDonald's office. My rage was still out of control as I smashed my fists onto his desk, demanding some answers.

'Who did this to my son?' I screamed. 'Have you got the bastards? If you have, just let me at them and I will kill them. What did they do to him?' I repeated.

'We don't have the people responsible yet, Ralph, but we will get them. I promise you that.'

Geoff MacDonald couldn't have been more kind and gentle if he'd tried. I could see in his face that he really did care and that he was totally distressed by what had happened. He was one of the senior investigating officers who had been to the site where my son's body had been discovered, but at this stage he didn't tell me any details about what had happened to James, only that the police were sure it was my son and that he had definitely been murdered. I sensed that he understood how angry I was and, even though I knew I was out of control, I didn't feel as if he was judging me. I also believed him when he promised me that he would find whoever killed my son.

I was eaten up with fear that James had been abducted, sexually attacked by perverts and then murdered when they had finished with him. I realized for the first time that the horrors that had filled my head could now be a reality. I knew I had to calm down to go and see Denise, but my basic instinct as a man, and as a dad, was dictating everything. Geoff MacDonald's manner seemed to calm me for a short while – long enough for my brother Philip to take me off to the toilets and talk me down. He told me that I had to be strong for Denise, and he was right. She needed me and I had to go to her. I would have to deal with everything else later.

I walked into a toilet cubicle and felt a rush of nausea. My stomach was in agonizing spasms and my limbs turned to jelly. I began retching violently over the toilet but nothing came up. Eventually, when I could stand again, I came out and splashed some water on my face. When I looked at my reflection in the mirror I saw a stranger, a man I no longer recognized. My eyes looked like they were going to pop out of my head, blazing with anger and bloodshot from tears and rage. I looked pale and thin, but most of all I could see shame and disgust. I couldn't bear to look at the bleary-eyed face before me. I hated myself so much because my son was dead and I felt that it was my fault. I had failed to protect my own flesh and blood, that beautiful little boy who would never have harmed anyone. How could someone have hurt him?

It was then that I realized I was shaking. I was freezing cold and yet the rage I felt building inside was like a furnace. I had to see Denise, but I was dreading facing her – my lovely wife and the fantastic mother of our amazing son.

What on earth could I say? I knew that no words would ever be able to console her. And I somehow had to keep my anger from her. She needed comfort and protection; I just didn't know if I was capable of giving that to her.

As I walked into the police TV room where Denise was waiting, I saw she was sitting in a chair, rocking gently and crying. I walked over and just held her with all my might and kissed her on the head. I held her for so long, but no words came out of my mouth. We were both crying together, trapped in a world of pain that no one else could ever understand. She felt so tiny and so vulnerable. I tried to push the anger back, and just held on to her for all I was worth.

We stayed like that for a long while, our arms around each other, crying. From time to time her sobs became uncontrollable and all I could do was hold on tighter. Eventually we began to talk.

'We will get whoever did this to our son,' I promised her.

'I just want my baby back, Ralph,' she sobbed.

'I know, so do I. Let's try and be brave for our James.'

'I want him back, Ralph. I need to have him with me.'

'I want him too. I want him too.'

Denise was inconsolable. To hear your wife crying in such way is unbearable. I knew there was nothing I could do to take her pain away. It was like listening to a wounded animal. The grief was overwhelming; it takes over your body in a way that you would never imagine possible.

We must have stayed in that room for over an hour, comforting each other and trying to pull ourselves together.

We didn't have the words to express our feelings but we both felt them. Above all else we were confused and we didn't know what to do. I don't think there was any obvious reason for us to stay in that room, we just didn't know where else to go. Eventually we knew we couldn't hide there any longer; it was time to go home. It was the moment I had dreaded: returning to our little flat where just a few days before we had been a happy family, only this time it was without James and we knew for sure that he was never coming back to us. All our hopes had gone for ever, and all we were left with was an emptiness and feelings that I could never describe to another living soul. I remember seeing Jimmy when I came out of the police room and that's about all I know. My memory from that moment is hazy. I don't even remember getting home, but Denise and I went to her mum's house where she took herself off to the bedroom and locked herself away in silence.

I sat with the men of the family downstairs and they tried their best to console me, but I can't say that I remember much of what they said. I was in total despair, sometimes crying, other times in complete silence. The rage would still rise up from time to time, but my body was exhausted and all I really wanted to do was go and see James. To be with him and hold him close to me for the very last time. There was so much I wanted to say to him. A little later the police arrived to say they would need someone to formally iden- tify James's body.

'I'll do it,' I volunteered without hesitation.

He was my son and I wanted to see him. I needed the chance to tell him how sorry I was for failing to save him.

'I don't think that's a good idea,' Jimmy said straight away. He recalls:

We knew that James had been badly injured but didn't know the full extent of how he had been mutilated. I just knew that I didn't want that to be Ralph's last image of his son. Ralph and Denise had looked distraught at the police station when they'd been told the news. It was one of the most terrible things I have ever seen. I have never felt so sad or so angry. I knew there was nothing I could do to make them feel any better, but at the very least I could spare Ralph the gruesome sight of James's body.

The police agreed with me and advised Ralph not to see his son because of the extent of the injuries he had suffered. I quietly spoke to the police and said that I would do it as soon as possible because otherwise Ralph would change his mind and insist on seeing James himself. That was the last thing I wanted him to do. As it turned out, the police were also keen for the identification to take place as quickly as possible, even if it was to be a legal formality.

It wasn't a job I wanted to do, but I knew I had no choice. I just wanted Ralph to remember his son as he had last seen him – a happy, bubbly, giggling child. I knew that if James was my son I would want my last image of him to be a good one, and not the mashed-up body of a small baby.

It was agreed that I would do the identification and I went home to my wife Karen, not far away in Kirkby.

'Are you sure you want to do this? Will you be able to cope?' she asked.

'I have no choice, Karen. I can't bring back baby James, but I have to do all I can to protect Ralph. He's my brother

and I owe him that much. I wouldn't want to see my child lying on a mortuary slab,' I replied.

I asked Karen if she would come with me and she agreed straight away. I was going to need all the support and back-up possible after what I was about to do.

Karen has always been my strength, my backbone, and she is a strong and decent woman. She was totally devastated at the death of James, as we all were, but she was still trying to look after me too.

At about 9 p.m. that night, a police traffic control car arrived to take us both to the morgue at Broad Green Hospital, about a fifteen-minute drive away. As I sat in the back of the car with Karen, I tried to prepare myself for what I was going to see. I felt strangely detached, as if my body was trying to protect me from the horror I was about to witness.

Every single minute of that night has stayed with me to this very day. It is like it has been scorched into my memory and it plays in my head over and over again. Nothing I do can ever get rid of the images I saw that evening.

When we got to the mortuary, Geoff MacDonald and Albert Kirby were both there to meet us. They wanted us to go into a briefing with them and the pathologist before I saw the body. They outlined what I could expect and warned me that James was horrifically injured. They told me that James's little body had been severed in two by a train where it had been left on a railway track. The two senior detectives kept stressing how important it was that I didn't touch James's body because it could interfere with forensic examinations that still needed to be carried out.

I didn't ask many questions. I just listened in silence as I felt the palms of my hands start to sweat. Albert spoke to me *quietly and gently before he asked, 'Are you sure you're capable of doing this, Jimmy?'*

'Yes, I'm sure,' I replied.

He then said it was important that I take my time to iden-tify the body and not to rush, despite how difficult the job was going to be. No one was in any doubt that this was James, but it was vital that no errors were made and that all proced-ures were followed correctly. I understood what they were saying.

'Have a good look, Jimmy, and then let us know if this is James. If you are not sure, then just say so,' Albert Kirby re-iterated.

As I stood up to get the job done, they both stressed again how crucial it was that I didn't touch the body. When I entered the room it was cold, clinical and eerie. I could feel my breath shorten as I began to gasp for air.

The first thing I saw was the adult-size mortuary table. It was about eight feet long and covered in a white sheet. And then it hit me like a car crash – the minuscule outline of a little body under the cover. I will never forget how incredibly tiny the trace of that childish figure looked against the back-drop of that huge table.

The pathologist gestured to me to go towards the table and nodded at me with raised eyebrows, silently asking if I was still OK to go through with it. I nodded in return and slowly edged towards the body. Geoff MacDonald and Albert Kirby were both in the room with me also.

'Are you happy to go ahead with this, Jimmy?' Albert asked again.

'Yes,' I replied.

'Take your time,' he repeated.

With that, the pathologist slowly and deliberately drew back the cover from James to just below his chest. I gasped aloud and drew a long, hard breath as if I was terrified my heart was going to stop beating. I have seen many things in my lifetime – fights, injuries, horrific car crashes on the roads – but absolutely nothing could have prepared me for what I saw before me.

There was no mistaking that it was James, despite the obvious and brutal injuries all over his body. Lying before me was the corpse of a precious little boy. Just a few days earlier he had been the light of his parents' life, giggling and charging around with the innocence of a small child. Now there was nothing there. Nothing but a shell, a mutilated body replacing the vibrant and much-loved child who hadn't even reached his third birthday.

Even though the rest of his torso was covered up, I could still tell that his body was in two bits lying on that table. There was a separate mortuary table in the room that was empty, and I assumed that was where the post mortem for one half of his body was carried out while the top half was examined on another. The two had been placed together for the identification.

His bright blue eyes were still open, just staring outwards, and his little mouth was slightly apart too. His thick, soft, strawberry-blond hair was still splattered red, matted with his own blood. There were hideous marks all over his face and body and the skin on his forehead had been pushed back, exposing his brain.

I remember feeling sick – not just physically sick, but violently traumatized to think that any living human being could possibly have done this to such a warm and loving boy.

I felt a rage well up inside. It was a pure venom and at that moment I just wanted to take revenge on whoever had done such a wicked thing to James. I kept thinking about his parents, Ralph and Denise, and how important it was that they never see what had been done to their baby boy, so they could keep their memories of James intact. It was truly horrific.

Despite all the reminders, I instinctively reached out to cradle him and to stroke his head to bring him comfort, but Geoff swiftly stepped in to stop me.

'I'm sorry, I couldn't help it,' I whispered.

James's skull was badly mutilated and there were savage marks on his face where he had been kicked and battered and tortured to death. I can remember clearly the blue paint on his face – it looked so odd and out of place.

I stood staring in disbelief for a long time as tears rolled down my face and splashed onto my hands. I could hear James's voice crying out for his mummy and daddy. I could hear him begging his attackers to stop, pleading for mercy through the terrible pain he must have suffered. Never could anyone have been confronted with something so unimaginably violent and evil.

Eventually, Albert Kirby interrupted the silence. 'Is this baby James, Jimmy?' he gently prodded.

'Yes, that's our James,' I replied.

'Are you certain?' he coaxed.

'Yes, I'm sure.'

My head hung low as I stood frozen in grief and anger while the white sheet was pulled back over James's broken body.

We all left the room together and I heard Geoff MacDonald ask me, 'Are you OK, Jimmy?'

I nodded and asked him, 'Will they be able to do anything to put his face back together so that Ralph and Denise can see him one last time?'

'It is highly unlikely,' he said.

'In that case, I don't think they should ever see James like that. He might be their son, but I would never want them to see him like that. I will never be able to rid my mind of those images now, and I think it will finish them both off to see what has been done to him.'

Geoff nodded in agreement.

I went out and sat down beside Karen, who was waiting for me. She held my hand as I sunk into the chair beside her and she asked if I was all right. I just nodded and said it was time to go. The police said they would need me to sign a statement confirming the positive identification I had just made, and I agreed.

The traffic car drove us home again and both Karen and I stayed silent. It was a chance to gather my thoughts in the quiet as I tried to pull up the emotional drawbridge and lock the experience away. But, as hard as I tried, what I had seen that evening would stay with me for ever. I've learned you can't put your feelings on standby. Certain smells can trigger instant flashbacks to that day, in high-definition technicolour. Certain colours and weird shapes still take me back to the sight of this little boy's battered brain. But the strangest thing is, you cannot see what it does to you. You don't witness the change in yourself that your loved ones around you see.

5

The Boys Were Just
Ten Years Old

They discovered James's body on that cold Sunday afternoon on Valentine's Day. A group of teenage boys were playing alongside a railway track near their homes in Walton when they spotted what they thought at first was a toy doll or a dead cat on the freight track between Edge Hill and Bootle.

As they moved closer the full horror struck them. The 'doll' on the track was, in fact, my son. James's lifeless body lay on the railway line in two pieces, severed in half after a train careered over him. The four boys screamed and ran as fast as they could down the railway embankment to Walton Lane Police Station, which was just 100 yards away. They crashed through the doors and blurted out to the desk sergeant what they had seen. Police officers scrambled to the scene. The long search for James was finally over.

His killers had brutalized him, battered, kicked and tortured him before carrying his blood-soaked body to the railway track and laying him over it. He was still wearing his coat on his upper body, but his lower body, which was further down the tracks, was completely naked. There was blood everywhere at the scene and we later learned that

James suffered forty-two injuries, mainly to his head and face as well as his body. He didn't die during his torture but some time before the train hit him. He was still alive when his attackers left him on the track to die alone.

Albert Kirby, Geoff MacDonald and Jim Fitzsimmons all went to the crime scene that day and were deeply horrified at what they saw. They said there was no question that James had been deliberately and brutally attacked and murdered. Because James's body was cut in two and the two halves found some distance apart, the police effectively had to deal with this as two crime scenes, preserving as much evidence as possible. James had been laid on the rail at the waist and his upper body was on the inside of the tracks. It was thought his head may have been weighted down with bricks, and when the train hit him his lower body was carried further down the track.

The clothes that had been removed from James's lower body were found close by, his underwear soaked in blood. Detectives also discovered blood-stained bricks, stones and iron bars at the scene, as well as some AA batteries and a tin of blue modelling paint.

It was very clear to the detectives that James had been savagely beaten around the head and body. He showed multiple cuts and fractures to the head and there had been severe bleeding. On one cheek there was bruising thought to have been caused by the imprint of a shoe. There was some damage to my son's genitals and his body was spattered with blue paint.

The police spared us nearly all of the gruesome details about James's injuries in those initial hours, and a decision was taken by Albert Kirby to withhold much of this information, not just from the press and the public, but from the investigation officers also. The senior officers who had been at the crime scene knew the full extent of what had happened to James because they had seen it for themselves, but many others on the investigation were not told until a long time afterwards. Albert Kirby took the view that it would be unnecessarily distressing for his team, and he was trying to keep them focused on the job ahead of them. It was only over a period of time that the full horror would inevitably unfold.

I can remember getting a visit from Detective Sergeant Jim Green, a smart and polite young officer in his thirties. He had now been appointed as our family liaison officer along with Mandy Waller. The night after Jimmy had identified James's body, Jim Green came to see Denise and me at Eileen's house. It was well known in the media that James's body had been cut in two by a train, and this information would not stay secret for long. Jim had the awful job of breaking the dreadful news to us so we didn't find out from the newspapers or television.

Denise and I sat in the kitchen together as we listened to the officer and neither of us said a word. Denise held her head down and I am not sure she was able to take in anything that was being said. I was just like a block of stone. I listened but I was beyond responding. After he left, Denise went back up to the bedroom and I sat alone, trying to get the images out of my head of James being injured and cut in half by a train. I veered between rage and grief. Sometimes I would sob, other times I wanted to explode with anger.

There was much going on in Liverpool, but for the first few days Denise and I were unaware of almost everything.

We didn't leave the house and stayed locked in private, silent grief for most of the time. I can remember wandering out of the house on occasion to go and see my mum. She was utterly devastated by James's murder and, like everyone else, was trying to find ways to cope with it and understand it. As well as dealing with her own grief for her grandson, Mum was trying to protect not just me, but Denise too. Several hours after the news was released that James's body had been found, it was obviously all over the media. That evening people began ringing in to the Pete Price talk show on the city's independent Radio City channel. One caller cruelly started blaming Denise for James's murder, and my mum just snapped and picked up the phone to publicly defend her. She went on air to say that Denise was a great mum who loved her son and that she was not to blame for James's death. It was quite an extreme thing to do, but that's how protective Mum was of both of us. She couldn't sit back and listen to strangers making judgements about her family without coming out and having her say.

I often sat with Mum and cried like a baby myself as she held me in her arms and hugged me. I told her that I wanted to hold James and make everything OK again. I can remember grabbing his pillow, his toys or his clothes and holding them tight to my face because I could still smell James on them. It was an intense period of grieving that no words can properly describe. I couldn't reach Denise and she couldn't reach me. I didn't know a human being could hurt so much and, when I look back, I have no idea how we survived it.

We had regular updates from Mandy and Jim and they

did their very best for us in the most terrible of circumstances. All I kept repeating to them like a broken record
was the same question.

'Have you got them yet? Have you got the bastards that
killed my baby?'

We didn't watch the news or read the papers. It was all
too much for us to bear. And so the days ticked by. I wish
I could say I remembered more about those early few days,
but the truth is one hour just rolled into another with the
same miserable suffering. It is a blur to a large extent, but
I will never forget the pain.

The police, of course, were busy as ever with their investigation. They did an outstanding job and worked around
the clock to find the culprits for James's murder. They were
still frantically hunting for the two boys seen in the CCTV
video images and about sixty young kids were interviewed
as they worked through class registers of all the kids who
had failed to turn up at school that day. But still they had
no positive lead. On the Tuesday evening after James had
been killed, a boy of twelve was arrested in the area of
Kirkdale, which is very close to Liverpool city centre. Police
wanted to question him about James's murder and it sparked
a near-riot in the area. Television crews and reporters got
wind of the arrest of a boy named as Jonathan Green and
began arriving at his home, where he lived with his mum,
dad and grandmother. Their presence alerted local people
and soon a huge crowd began gathering in the street outside
his house. They started stoning the property, smashing
windows and shouting abuse, and police were forced to call
for back-up to disperse the mob that had formed. Gossip
was rife, and as rumours spread that the police had nicked

a kid for James's murder, another angry crowd started gathering at Marsh Lane Police Station.

It was mayhem because the mood across the city was so angry at what had happened to James. Denise and I were also receiving calls that night from people telling us about the arrest of a kid who was thought to have been behind the murder. We didn't know what to think and so we called the police station and spoke to Geoff MacDonald, who reassured us that this was just one of a number of arrests and that no charges had been made. Later that same night, Jim Green came out in person to see us because he didn't want us to get our hopes up that the killer had been caught. As it turned out, Jonathan Green had nothing to do with the murder whatsoever and he was released without being charged, but the damage had already been done.

Gangs continued to harass Jonathan Green and his family and eventually they had to be moved away to a secret location. It was a classic example of mob rule getting out of hand, and some people were baying for blood. I could not forget that complete strangers had turned out in their hundreds to look for James when he was missing, and I will always be grateful for that help. As a family we had received so much support from the people of my city and I understood that Merseyside now felt shocked and angry – I was angry too – but I didn't want vigilantism in my son's name. I didn't want innocent people to be hurt. On top of that, I didn't want this sort of stuff to be getting in the way of the police investigation to find James's real killers. I wanted the police to be able to do their jobs properly without local feelings boiling over into chaos.

In homes across Liverpool, anxious parents questioned

their young sons about the murder of baby James. Some asked outright if their child had anything to do with the crime, including the mother of a young boy called Robert Thompson.

'Is that you on that video, son?' Ann Thompson demanded.

'Nah, it's got nothing to do with me,' he replied.

As if to prove his point, Robert went to a makeshift memorial that had been growing near the railway in Walton, close to where he lived, where local mourners had been leaving flowers, teddies, cards and messages of sympathy. He later took some flowers to lay at the site, where news crews were filming everything that was going on, including those who turned up to pay their respects to James.

When he got home he said to his mother, 'Why would I take flowers to the baby if I had killed him?'

At another home nearby, after the security camera footage hit the news, Jon Venables told his mum, Susan, 'If I'd seen them kids hurting the baby, I'd have kicked their heads in.'

When his mum later told him that James had been found dead, he said, 'That must be awful for his mum.'

Jon's father, meanwhile, asked his son about the blue paint that was splattered on his mustard-coloured coat. He said that his friend Robert Thompson had thrown it at him.

I later learned that on the Wednesday evening an anonymous woman walked through the doors of Marsh Lane Police Station and said she had some information about James Bulger. She was a friend of the Venables family and knew that the son, a boy called Jon Venables, had skipped school with a friend called Robert Thompson on the Friday that

James went missing. He had returned home with blue paint on his jacket. She also said she thought she recognized his outline from the CCTV video. The woman's identity has never been revealed, but her visit to the police station set off a vital chain of events.

Detective Sergeant Phil Roberts was in charge of a group of officers who were assigned to talk to Robert Thompson and arrest him for questioning. Another group of detectives would arrest Jon Venables. The police set out early on the morning of Thursday, 18 February, and DS Roberts has recalled his experience for several television documentaries. He described how, when the information came in, no one on the team could believe Robert or Jon could be guilty. How could two ten-year-old boys do such terrible things? Nevertheless, the information had to be followed up.

The Thompson family lived a few hundred yards away from the railway at Walton. When Ann Thompson opened the door to the police and DS Roberts explained why they were there, she looked 'petrified'. Inside the house, DS Roberts saw Robert's younger brother Simon and told him that he wanted to speak about James Bulger. Simon told him Robert knew about the murder and had taken some flowers to leave at the scene.

Then Robert came downstairs, neatly dressed in his school uniform. DS Roberts was struck by how small and young the boy looked and thought again that he couldn't be responsible for killing a baby. He sat Robert on the sofa and crouched down in front of him so he could make eye contact, then he explained that the police had been told Robert might be involved in James's murder. At that point,

Robert panicked and started to cry, although he didn't shed any tears. He shuffled his feet and DS Roberts could tell that the boy was frightened.

As Robert was led away with his mother, police search units began scouring the house, collecting his clothes for examination. Officers immediately noticed there was blood on his shoes.

Jon Venables was also visited at his home in Norris Green in Liverpool, which is about three miles from where Robert lived in Walton. He too was taken away for questioning. His mother, Susan, was unsurprised when the police turned up, but put their visit down to his bunking off school. They asked for his mustard-coloured coat, which showed the outline of a small handprint in paint on the sleeve where James had tried to grab hold of it.

Jon Venables also burst into tears and officers said he looked genuinely petrified.

'I don't want to go to prison, Mum. I didn't kill the baby,' he cried. 'It's that Robert Thompson, he always gets me into trouble.'

Both boys were taken to separate police stations to be questioned, but as Jon was driven away, he kept asking about Robert and told police that he thought they should speak to him.

As Phil Roberts was about to start interviewing Robert he knew what was at stake. He prepared himself well.

'The age and the size of Robert was shocking,' he said. 'I just couldn't believe he was old enough to have done something so terrible. It was so unusual to have suspects this young, which made the importance of what I was about to do all the more significant. I couldn't afford to make a mistake and I also knew that I couldn't be aggressive, despite the horrific nature of the murder of baby James.

'I planned to take it nice and easy, and I knew that I had to sit off my own feelings and do a professional job.'

'It was crucial that I established whether he knew the difference between right and wrong and the difference between telling lies and the truth.'

Denise and I were informed throughout that police were formally interviewing two ten-year-olds about James's murder and, like everyone else, we just couldn't believe what we were hearing.

'How can ten-year-old boys do something so evil towards a little baby like James?' I asked. 'There has to be some mistake. They must have the wrong people, which means James's killers are still out there.'

I would find myself talking to James all the time. I kept asking if he was all right and I kept repeating to him how sorry I was not to have saved him. I told him how much I loved him and that I missed him.

And I got drunk. Very, very drunk. There is no rule book for grief, and I was just trying to get through each minute of every hour the best I could. I have no doubt that grief alters the brain and feels like a temporary insanity. And I started to fall apart.

I can remember sitting with Jimmy one day as he tried to support me through it.

'I don't know how to do this on my own,' I said. 'Please help me.'

'I'm here for whatever you need,' he replied gently.

My emotions would run away with me sometimes and

I would sit and imagine all sorts of things. In particular, I kept thinking about all the times I had spent with James, and I could constantly hear his voice and his happy, infectious giggle. Other times my emotions would just vanish and I would feel cold and distant as I tried to switch off from the horror story that had become my life. I wanted to help Denise more, but it felt as if she had withdrawn completely, numb and paralysed by the shock of what had happened.

I obviously wasn't present during the long hours of police interviews, but in his book, *Every Mother's Nightmare*, Liverpool journalist Mark Thomas, who covered the case from start to finish, gives a full account of what happened when Robert Thompson and Jon Venables were quizzed about killing my son. He has kindly allowed me to reproduce his account of what took place, for which I am very grateful. The rest of this chapter is an abridged version of what he wrote:

The little boy looked frightened. He looked tiny next to the burly figure of DS Phil Roberts sitting alongside him at the table in the interview room at Walton Lane Police Station. Robert's mother Ann sat at his left-hand side, a portly, unkempt woman who was almost as scared as her son. A solicitor, Jason Lee, sat at the end of the table next to her, while DC Bob Jacobs sat at the other end, to Phil's right.

It was three minutes before six o'clock on the evening of Thursday, 18 February, when Phil began his questioning, recording the precise time on the tape machine and stating who was present for the legal record.

Phil knew that his first job was to try to put Robert at

his ease. It would not be easy, but if anyone could bring it off, it was Phil Roberts. He had been on a special course to learn the techniques of interviewing distressed children, but he was also a born detective, a Serious Crime Squad man with the kinds of instincts and experience that you can't teach on a course.

The first thing was to establish eye contact. Phil sat hunched forward, crouching in his chair to keep his head on a level with Robert's. It was an uncomfortable posture for such a big man, but one he would maintain throughout the interviews to help Robert feel more secure. Phil spoke softly and slowly, making his sentences short, his questions simple.

Phil began with establishing if Robert knew the difference between telling the truth and telling lies. He kept the tone light, trying to gain the boy's confidence. At one point Phil actually had him laughing as he broke the ice.

'What football team do you support?' Phil asked him.

'Everton.'

'Everton. Right, if I said Everton won 10–nil last Saturday, what would you say that was?'

'A lie.'

'OK, and if I said there was five of us in this room, what would say that was?'

'True.'

After ten minutes, the detective sensed that Robert was relaxed and the time had come to move on to the facts of the case.

Now Robert's legs began to move, swinging listlessly back and forth under his chair. It was a small body language clue that Phil learned to spot whenever he believed Robert was not telling the truth. Robert readily admitted to 'sagging' school that Friday and going to the Strand with Jon Venables, and he claimed he had seen 'little James' holding his mother's hand in the precinct. He confirmed he had heard about the James Bulger case, revealing that he had taken flowers to the scene on Wednesday.

The detective then asked, 'Now, is it right or is it wrong that James should have been killed?'

'Wrong.'

'It's wrong, isn't it?'

'Yeah.'

Exactly five minutes after the start of Robert Thompson's first interview, detectives at Lower Lane Police Station began questioning Jon Venables. DC Mark Dale, the arresting officer, led the questioning, backed up by DC George Scott.

Mark Dale sat at the opposite end of the table from Jon. The others in the room sat nearby and included Jon's mother, their lawyer Laurence Lee and George Scott. The detectives began just like Phil, trying to put Jon at ease. He confirmed that Robert Thompson was his 'mate'.

'I don't go near him at school sometimes 'cos he causes trouble at school. He just wants me to stay out late and say we can do good things and I say to him what is there to do in the dark?'

Mark asked, 'And what does he say?'

'He just says come on the railway with me and that . . . you know, by the police station.' Jon claimed that Robert slept on the railway sometimes and lit fires, but he insisted he had never been on the railway with Robert. He said Robert was not a good friend because he got him into trouble and added, 'He's much of a girl. He sucks dummies – and sucks his thumb.'

He then described some of the mischief they got up to when they 'sagged' school, climbing into back gardens and getting people to chase them. 'We rob bouncy balls and throw them at windows and one day this fat man came running out getting his mop and throwing it at us.'

'You have a riot, don't you?' asked Mark.

'Yeah.'

He said that on the Friday of James's death Robert had tried to get him to go 'pinching'. 'He just steals. He just goes, "I'll have that and that," and just stuffs it in his coat.' Robert would then give him things outside.

The detectives got Jon a can of Coke and a Mars bar from a vending machine before they started their second interview that night.

George recalled, 'We questioned Jon about where he had been on the Friday James Bulger was abducted. He led us on a wild goose chase. He told us he went everywhere, all over Walton and even as far as Scotland Road, but denied he ever went to the Strand.'

Asked about the paint on his coat, he claimed Robert had thrown it over him.

Back at Walton Lane, Phil Roberts and Bob Jacobs were deliberately keeping their questioning sessions short. It was a break the adults valued as much as the child.

Phil said, 'I was totally focused while I was interviewing Robert. The thought of what happened to James Bulger never entered my mind at all. I was there to do the job – to find out what the hell went on.'

Robert told detectives that his hobby was skipping

school. They put it to him that boys wearing clothes similar to his and Jon's had been seen with James on the security video, and Robert said, 'I never touched him.'

Asked again about the video, Robert said, 'Yeah, but that may not have been me and Jon that killed him. But I know it wasn't me that killed him, or Jon.'

He admitted stealing from shops in the precinct but insisted again, 'I never took the baby.'

Asked what did happen, Robert repeated, 'No, but I never touched him.'

Phil said, 'Well, we're going to find out what happened to him.'

Robert started to cry then and insisted, 'I never touched him.'

Then Robert admitted that James had been walking round the Strand on his own and added, 'He [Jon] grabbed the baby's hand and just walked round the Strand and then he let him go loose. When we were by the church he let him go.'

Phil's heart jumped. 'You don't lose concentration but you lose the focus for a moment,' he recalled. 'The fact he had escorted him out of the Strand was a big step. He blamed everything on Jon.'

Robert said James had been asking for his mother, actually mimicking the toddler's voice as he called for his mum. Later, Robert insisted, 'I told him to take him back.' He started to cry again and added, 'I'm going to get all the blame.'

Robert's crying was not winning the detectives over to his side.

'When he admitted things he would cry at the same time, but there were no actual tears,' recalled Phil. 'It was part of his act. I really thought he was evil, looking at him. He was astute and very streetwise. He wasn't educationally intelligent but he was shrewd.'

At the end of another interview, Robert asked, 'Will I be able to go home tonight?'

'We don't know yet, we don't know,' was the gentle response.

At Lower Lane Police Station, Jon Venables tucked into his special fried rice with enthusiasm before his third and final interview for the night.

Eventually Jon admitted to being at the Strand but he denied taking any children. He also admitted to petty stealing and general mischief. The interview ended just after 10 p.m. and Jon was bedded down for the night in the unlocked juvenile detention room. Susan stayed with him on a specially arranged mattress in the room.

At Walton Lane, Robert Thompson also went through one last interview. Robert admitted that they all left the Strand together but insisted it was Jon who had actually taken James. 'You'll get his face up on the video,' he added.

Earlier, Robert had denied it was him and Jon who were seen by a witness on the enclosed reservoir site at Breeze Hill, but by the time this interview had finished he admitted that it was them. He said they had taken James to Breeze Hill and left him there on top of the hill after playing with him. Robert was then settled down for the night.

On the Friday morning, detectives began their questioning of the two boys again. Jon talked about going to various shops with Robert, including Tandy, from where police knew the batteries found at the murder scene had been stolen.

Phil Roberts and Bob Jacobs began their fourth interview with Robert at 11.35 that morning. Phil had the feeling
that Robert was ready to tell him more. He steered the
questioning in the direction of the paint that was found on
James. Robert admitted for the first time being in posses-
sion of a small tin of enamel paint. He said it was Jon who
had taken James, and that they had taken him up on the
railway. He was asked about blood on his clothing and said
it was his own blood where Jon's mother had hit him. After
killing James, the boys were found later that evening
hanging out at a video shop, by Susan Venables. Robert
claimed she hit him, which she denies. Robert claimed that
Jon threw the paint in James's face and also threw the hood
of his anorak on the line.

'He threw it in his eye,' said Robert.

'Why was that?'

'I don't know and I ran away from him then, from Jon.'

'What did baby James do?'

'He sat on the floor.'

'Was he crying?'

'Yeah, I was crying myself.'

'Why?'

''Cos he threw it in his face. He could have blinded him.'

He said that after the paint was thrown in James's face,
they ran off, but Jon might have hit him slyly. Crying again,
Robert insisted, 'We never killed him.' He said James had
been crying because he wanted his mum.

Meanwhile, Jon Venables was still denying almost everything. When he was told that Robert had said Jon had taken
James by the hand, he threw a tantrum, looking really upset
and insisting that Robert was lying.

'I never killed him. We took him and left him by the canal, that's all,' he said, sobbing.

Detectives got the distinct impression that Jon wanted to talk and had some horrific things to tell that were causing him a lot of concern. As Jon was having his lunch in the detention room, Susan shouted to Detective Constable Dave Tanner and asked if he could come in to the room. Jon was sitting on the bench when both his parents and the detective walked in.

Susan held her son in a tight embrace and said, 'I love you, Jon. I want you to tell the truth, whatever it might be.'

Jon Venables started to cry, and just blurted out, 'I did kill him.'

The boy looked across the room at the detective and said, 'What about his mum? Will you tell her I'm sorry.'

Robert Thompson still continued to deny murdering James until he volunteered, 'Jon threw a brick in his face.'

He then said that Jon threw another brick at him, which hit him in the stomach, and hit him with a fishplate, a metal bar with holes used to join tracks together on the railway. This blow, claimed Robert, knocked James out. Robert said he put his ear to James's stomach and he was not breathing as he lay on the railway track. They had left the scene and not discussed it together since, he said.

Jon continued to blame everything on Robert, but confirmed on the police tape, 'I killed James'.

He went on to speak of their attempt to abduct another child from the Strand before they found James, the two-year-old toddler son of a local woman called Diane Power. He said it was Robert Thompson's idea and the plan was that the toddler would go into the road and get knocked over, making his death look like an accident. He said they found James outside the butcher's shop. He said it was his own idea to take him but it was Robert's idea to kill him. They took him to the canal, where Robert planned to throw him in. James would not kneel down to look at his reflection in the water as they wanted, so Robert picked him up and threw him on the ground. This was how James had first injured his head. He said that James kept crying, 'I want my mummy.'

Jon admitted going up to the reservoir and to the railway.

'I can't tell you anything else.' When pressed why, he replied, "Cos that's the worst bit.'

Under gentle coaxing, he continued: 'We took him on the railway track and started throwing bricks at him.'

He claimed Robert threw bricks at James and hit him with an iron bar. Jon said he had thrown small stones, but that Robert had thrown house bricks.

When asked what he thought about what they had done to James, he cried and said, 'It was terrible. I was thinking about it all the time.'

The next day, Robert still maintained his stance that he had nothing to do with the attack on James. He denied taking any of James's clothes. He said Jon had thrown paint in the child's face 'because he felt like it'. He said Jon had thrown bricks in his face and stomach and hit him with a metal bar and claimed that Jon had a smirk on his face afterwards.

Jon, meanwhile, went on to deliver the most graphic and terrible account of the attack they carried out. He described James screaming and falling down under ruthless assault but getting back up again. He claimed Robert told the help-less child, 'Stay down, you stupid divvie.'

Mark asked Jon why Robert had said this. 'He wanted him dead, probably,' he responded.

'Why?'

'I don't know. I didn't want to, really. Robert was prob-ably doing it for fun because he was laughing his head off.'

'That was as full an admission as we were ever going to get of what happened on that railway line,' George recalled. 'It was utterly horrific to think that this child of ten could carry out the acts that he did to another human being.'

Robert Thompson was interviewed again and he was formally arrested for the attempted abduction of Diane Power's son. Phil pressed on, but Robert was still not about to admit to any involvement in the attack on James.

'He never actually told me the truth in the end – far from it,' said Phil. 'He lied from the minute we started to inter-view him.'

In Jon Venables' final interview he said that he knelt down by James, who grabbed his coat and said, 'Don't hurt me.'

He said it had been Robert's idea to put bricks over James so nobody would see him. Robert had kicked him, Jon stamped on him. Robert had kicked him in the face lots of times.

After going for a ride in a police car to retrace James's last journey, Jon returned to the police station and started drawing some pictures. George said to him that he thought Diane Power's son was the luckiest boy alive the day James was killed.

Jon looked up at George and said, 'Yes'. There was a big,

beaming smile on his face. It was a moment that will haunt the police team for ever.

At 6.15 p.m. Jon Venables was formally charged with the abduction and murder of James Bulger. He began to weep. Then at 6.40 p.m., detectives at Walton Lane Police Station put the same charges to Robert Thompson. He seemed completely unconcerned when the charges were read out to him. He replied simply, 'It was Jon that done that.'

Phil recalled, 'When he was charged he had no problem at all with it. I suppose he knew that if he was found guilty he would have a better life than he would outside. I thought to myself, "This boy has caused so much misery and evil." I didn't look for the three sixes on the back of his head, but at that moment I thought he was the Devil.'

6

Prisoners of Our Grief

It was an agonizing wait as the detectives continued questioning the two boys. It was completely mind-blowing that ten-year-olds could be responsible for the abduction, torture and murder of my son.

'This can't be right,' I kept muttering. 'There has to be some mistake.'

It felt like we were in limbo, waiting for news, waiting for something, but in the end, none of it really made any difference because James was never coming back to us.

Denise and I remained prisoners of our grief, so immersed in our sorrow that the days rolled into one another. I just ran out of things to say because the pain was so intense. One minute I found myself sobbing, the next I was struck numb, before that terrible anger and hatred began to rise up in me again.

The one thing I can clearly remember is Albert Kirby coming to see Denise and me on Saturday afternoon, little more than a week after our beautiful boy was taken. Jim Green was also with him. The two men came into our home and sat down opposite us.

'I just wanted to come in person to see you both to let

you know that we have charged Robert Thompson and Jon Venables with the abduction and murder of James,' Albert Kirby said. 'It's hard to believe because they are both ten years old, but we are not in any doubt that they are responsible. I wanted to tell you before it is made public knowledge to the media, and if you have any questions about anything, then you get in contact with us any time.'

'Thanks for letting us know,' I replied.

I didn't say any more than that. I just stared ahead of me and Denise sat with her head bowed down. What was there to say?

His face was pained and he looked exhausted. I knew the police had done a good job. I also knew that they cared a great deal. I appreciated the fact that Albert Kirby had come to see us himself and I was relieved that James's killers had been caught, but we were left with the new horror that my son had been tortured and killed by a pair of children. And for what?

After the police left, I went out and just started walking. I felt as if I could hardly breathe and I needed to get some air. I was caught in a waking nightmare and no matter where I went it always came with me.

For nearly twenty years, experts and ordinary people have analysed and probed this case to find out how two children could have acted in such a way, and much was made of their upbringings. But I have never been persuaded that their difficult childhoods had any bearing on what they did to my son. I grew up in a tough community and knew many children who had awful lives through no fault of their own. But they did not go out and murder an innocent child.

I didn't know much about this pair of kids when they

were first charged, but a lot came out in the media after the trial. In the early days, it was always thought that Robert Thompson was the more aggressive of the two boys, harder, tougher and the natural ring leader, but history has shown that Jon Venables was just as nasty and devious as his partner in crime. Some experts have concluded that Venables was possibly even more inclined to violence and cruelty than Robert, a view shared by some of the detectives involved in the case.

Robert certainly had the more brutal upbringing, and from a young age had developed a thick skin to deal with the troubles he faced at home. According to NSPCC Case notes, which the author Blake Morrison obtained and wrote about in his book *As If*, Robert was used to seeing his father beat his wife, and it seemed the beatings were not just reserved for his mother. Robert's eldest brother had been put on the child protection register when he was four after he was spotted with a black eye, bruises and a cigarette burn to the face.

When Robert was about six, his father left the family for good to take up with another woman. Robert was the fifth of six brothers and life got a lot worse when their father left. His mother, Ann, admitted she turned to the bottle when her husband left. She became well known in the area for her drinking and neighbours talked to the press about how she would get into fights with other women or even, on occasions, men. It was normal for her children to see her 'rotten drunk' according to one local. However, in the last few years she had stopped drinking, after getting pregnant again by another man and giving birth to a seventh son, and was trying to cope.

The Thompson household was in freefall, with each of the brothers beating their younger siblings as if in a domino effect. The eldest boy picked on a younger brother, that brother battered the next in line, right down to the youngest child. Instead of protecting each other without their parents to look after them, the siblings needed protection from one another. Robert was very small for his age and was frightened of his older brothers. But it didn't stop him from beating those younger than him.

Robert was often seen wandering the streets past midnight and on one occasion terrified his younger brother Ryan by taking him to a local canal and abandoning him there alone. It was the same place to which he would later take James on his final journey. Another brother, Philip, even volunteered to be taken into care to get away from the family home, and on the rare occasions his mother tried to punish him, Robert would taunt her and say she couldn't touch him or else he would go to the police. He was reported as being a very bright youngster, but life at home meant that he took to regular truanting and rarely spent much time on his education. Robert was moody and quiet at school but well skilled in the art of manipulation. He had few friends to speak of, but the limited number he did have included Jon Venables.

One expert put forward the theory that Robert was replicating on James the violence that he had suffered from his older brothers, but even if that was the case, it doesn't take away from the fact that Thompson was capable of dealing out extreme violence and cruelty, without showing any remorse. I believe Thompson and Venables are wired wrong and were from the start. And that makes them dangerous.

Jon Venables was also a troubled child but had a different background to his friend. His mum and dad, Neil and Susan Venables, had three children. Jon was the middle child.

His parents divorced when he was just three and life was unsettled for the children. Susan, like Ann, was also reported to be a regular visitor to the local pubs. On one occasion, police were called to their house in the Norris Green area of Liverpool after the three siblings, aged seven, five and three at the time, had been left unsupervised for more than three hours.

His brother and sister were known to have learning problems, but Jon was said to be bright and educationally normal. However, he was hyperactive, prone to wild outbursts and tantrums, and was constantly seeking attention. He was just as aggressive as Thompson and his school teachers recalled how he would fling himself at the walls, knocking off posters, pictures and artwork done by other children. He would curl up under desks and stick paper all over his face, cut himself with scissors and tear his clothes apart. He would stand on his desk and throw things at other pupils and his teachers were exasperated with his behaviour, describing it as unlike anything they had ever seen before. His antics grew more and more violent as he sought ever more attention.

He spent time with his mum and dad, but both of them found his outbursts and tantrum fits hard to deal with and eventually he was referred to his school's psychologist. He became marginalized, for not only was he aggressive and antisocial to other kids, but he was also bullied for his strange behaviour. His teachers believed that he knew his behaviour was wrong but carried on because it brought him lots of attention. One day he tried to choke another boy at school. He stood behind the pupil and tightened a 12-inch ruler across his neck to stop him breathing. After this, he was suspended and his mother made arrangements for him to start afresh at Walton St Marys Church of England Primary School.

Jon started his new school eighteen months before James was killed and it was there that he met Robert Thompson. Neither of them had many friends, and as a result of their poor school records, they were both put into a class a year below their age. In September 1991 they struck up a friendship, and as two loners they seemed naturally to be drawn to each other.

It was then that Jon started to play truant from school with Robert, something he had never done before. When he was in school, he was the more disruptive of the two in the classroom, Robert remaining quiet and moody. Both would get into trouble in the playground, scrapping with other younger children, and when Jon was made to stand against the wall as a punishment, he would bash his head against the brickwork continually, trying to get the attention of his teachers and dinner ladies. He only stopped when he failed to get the attention he was seeking.

Jon's home life was nowhere near as chaotic as Robert's and so his behaviour is harder to explain. It may not have been a perfect environment, but he didn't suffer violence from his family, and despite the fact that his parents split up, they both carried on looking after him. Regardless, his aggressive, disruptive and spiteful manner was obvious to those around him

Teachers later recalled how Jon and Robert seemed to bring out the worst in each other, often egging one another on, as each felt bolder and more aggressive in the other's company. In the classroom, they were always kept apart, but there was little anyone could do outside of school, and the pair began to bunk off more and more regularly. Together they bullied weaker, younger and more vulnerable kids, picking on them in the playground and starting fights they were confident they would win. Jon and Robert's behaviour began to spiral out of control as they grew more daring. They would often go to the Strand shopping centre and make mischief, steal sweets and toys, and roam the streets until late at night. It seemed that Jon was the one who led the way when it came to luring James away, as well as in their plans to snatch the other little boy earlier in the day.

Robert was always seen by teachers as sly, devious and quiet, and was an accomplished liar. Jon, on the other hand, was more volatile and prone to violent outbursts. Jon's father, Neil, tried to warn his son to stay away from Robert, insisting he was bad news. But the young Robert Thompson may not have been the only bad influence on Jon.

It was suggested at his later trial that when he stayed with his father, he had begun to watch some of the movies that Neil had rented. Many of the films were ultra-violent or contained pornography, including a notorious video nasty called *I Spit on Your Grave* in which a young woman is gang raped in a cabin. She takes her revenge on the gang, picking them off one by one in a series of gruesome killings. Another of the films was the horror movie *Child's Play 3*, which stars a demonic doll called Chucky that springs to life in a military academy. The doll then abducts a young cadet and tries to kill him under the wheels of a fairground ghost train. In the end it is Chucky, wearing toddler's dungarees, with his face splashed with blue war-games paint, that meets a gruesome end. The violent plot has terrible echoes of the attack on James and it was reported in the trial that this video was the last film rented by Jon's dad before James was abducted. Jon was known to have an active imagination and fantasized about being a hero. He was resentful of the attention his brother and sister received for their learning difficulties and often lost himself in a world of fantasy films and violence. The result was a hostile, angry and violent young boy who would do anything for attention.

It has long been debated whether these films had any influence on him. I accept that the movies may have fuelled the violence already within him, or even just been something he enjoyed, but I have never believed that a horror film can put evil inside a child in the first place or turn him into a killer. *Child's Play 3* did not make Jon Venables kill my James.

One of the many articles written about Thompson and Venables suggests that they saw my son as a doll, something for them to play with and discard afterwards. In particular, reference was made to police suspicions that the batteries found at the murder scene had been forced into James's bottom. The author of this article suggested that Robert placed the batteries inside James's backside as if he was a walking, talking doll that Robert tried to bring back to life again. I understand society's need to try to make sense of something so horrific, but I have never believed this was a plausible reason for what he did, and still believe it was a sexual assault and that the motive for James's murder was sexual. The fact that my son's lower clothes had been removed and there was evidence of some damage to his genitals, as well as what they did with the batteries, shows that sexual abuse was a prime part of the attack.

Thompson was quizzed about sexually assaulting James and it has been reported that he became very upset and jittery. He was terrified he would be labelled as a pervert and was scared that Venables would tell police that he had sexually assaulted James.

'I'm not a pervert, you know,' he would tell police.

The biggest shock of all was the scale of violence inflicted on James by boys so young themselves. And because children who are capable of such terrible deeds are the exception, thankfully, society doesn't want to believe they can exist – that they are born with this violence in them. But in all the debate it is often overlooked that these two boys were not mentally subnormal. They were canny, manipulative and violent, and so it has always been hard to stomach some of the arguments put forward to explain their behaviour, blaming it on their upbringing. They knew right from wrong, they knew truth from lies, and they chose deliberately to mutilate and kill a child who was begging for mercy.

They knew what they were doing was wicked. Some may criticize my attitude, but I would have liked to have seen more attention paid to the real punishment of these boys instead of finding excuses for their crime. On that long walk to James's death, Thompson and Venables had plenty of opportunities to walk away from him, to let him live, but they never once showed an ounce of compassion or feeling for a tiny little boy whose life had barely started. They were happy to abuse, hurt and kill James, leaving him alone to be dismembered by a train. Their only concern was to cover up their crime and their only regret was that they got caught.

It may oversimplify the arguments, but that to my mind makes them evil beyond belief. And evil does exist among humans. Just look at people like the Moors murderers Ian Brady and Myra Hindley, or the serial killer Peter Sutcliffe. Society has far less difficulty condemning their crimes because they were adults when they hurt others. Thompson and Venables just showed their true colours before they reached their eighteenth birthdays.

I am never going to be in a position to analyse this objectively because it was my baby boy who was murdered, and I am sure most parents would feel the same as me if their child had been the victim of one of the most shocking crimes of all time. I wish I didn't have to talk about these little bastards in this book because I get so angry that it always seems to be about them and not my baby. I know I have to talk about them because they are the ones who caused so much misery and suffering but, for me, it will always be about James and what he endured. Whatever lives these boys had before they committed this crime, nothing can ever be as bad as what they did that day to my son. It is also why I never believed they could be rehabilitated. It is my job, as James's father, to tell how much he suffered and how it feels to lose the most precious thing in your life. It is something that the world should never forget because James was the only victim of this crime, not Robert Thompson or Jon Venables.

Two days after the boys were charged with murdering James, Robert Thompson and Jon Venables were to make their first appearance before the magistrates in Liverpool. Denise and I decided not to attend after being advised by the police that it would be a formality to remand them in custody and that a full trial could only be carried out before a Crown Court. But it would prove to be an eventful day regardless.

Tight security surrounded their arrival at South Sefton Magistrates' Court, which was only a few hundred yards from where James had been abducted at the Strand. Emotions were still running very high in Liverpool, much of which Denise and I had been shielded from because we were still isolated and in deep mourning. I knew about the mobs that had threatened Jonathan Green but I didn't know until then the extent of how the rest of the community and the world at large had reacted to James's murder. The police had spoken to us about the possibility of disturbances at the court appearance and asked for our help to appeal to the public to stay calm. I agreed instantly and, through the police, Denise and I urged people to act with restraint because the last thing we wanted was an ugly backlash to tarnish our son's name.

I have a terrible dilemma over this issue, which I struggle to address. I will readily admit that I wanted James's killers dead and I would be lying if I said I felt any other way. But I am not a sadistic or nasty man. I am not a killer. As a father, I would never in reality harm or be cruel to children. I felt terrible that, as an adult man, I had these feelings inside me towards two ten-year-old boys, and I found these emotions so hard to deal with. But my responses were primal. Having these thoughts in my head does not mean that I will ever spill over into being a killer myself.

Over the years, I have met other parents whose children

have been murdered and they feel the very same way. A lot of them have said they have wanted to avenge their child's death by killing the person responsible. It is a natural response for a bereaved parent, but it is very different to actually going out and committing that same crime. Unless you have experienced it, it is almost impossible to understand. It is something many parents will feel and say, but not carry through.

During that initial short hearing at court, Thompson and Venables confirmed their names and ages, and within just a few minutes it was over. They had appeared before magistrates at a juvenile court that was not open to the public, although the room was packed with journalists, who did have the right to attend. However, at this time reporting restrictions meant the boys could not be publicly named, and were to be referred to in the media as Child A and Child B.

The killers' earlier entrance into court passed without incident because the police had taken the precaution of delivering them into the court building before 7 a.m. to avoid any ugly confrontations with members of the public. It was a very different story as they left. Despite our pleas for calm, there were some terrible scenes that morning outside the court. Thompson and Venables had been formally remanded in custody and were to be taken back to local authority detention. Crowds had gathered outside the court, aware that the two boys were appearing there, and two windowless police vans with a heavy police escort pulled through the gates of the court building as a screaming mob surged towards the vehicles. Mayhem broke out as mums and dads, teenagers and kids all hurled abuse, stones, eggs and bricks at the vans, believing the boys to be inside them.

'Bastards,' they jeered. 'Let them hang.'

The scenes were captured by television cameras and shown across the news later that day. It was shaming. I understood the fury more than anyone, and instinctively knew that the protestors had acted out of grief and fear for their own loved ones, and it was just a lot of emotions boiling over. But I also knew that I didn't want my son's memory to be marred by such behaviour.

As it turned out, the boys weren't even in those two vans that were attacked. Police had predicted a backlash from the crowd and had organized a decoy convoy to throw the mob off the scent. Thompson and Venables were still sitting inside the courthouse, and when the crowds had finally dispersed, they were escorted into secure local authority care in separate waiting vans.

7

My Son's Last Journey

Once Thompson and Venables were charged and put before magistrates, it meant that Denise and I were finally able to start making plans for James's funeral. There could have been lengthy delays had the legal teams for Thompson and Venables insisted on independent autopsies, but that was not the case, and the coroner was now free to consent to release the body of our baby for burial.

We had already buried our first-born child, Kirsty, and now we were forced to bury our only other child. But the circumstances couldn't have been more different. It was hard even to begin to think about funeral arrangements, but we had no choice. We were going to need all the help we could find to get through it. As anyone who has lost a loved one knows, a funeral gives you a sense of purpose in the darkness. It is not something you want to do, but somehow your body carries you through your grief to get the arrangements made.

Neither Denise nor I was sleeping or eating properly. I would lie down at night and close my eyes and all I would do was see images of my son, screaming and crying in agony as he was tortured. If I dozed off through exhaustion,

I would wake shortly after, covered in sweat and with my heart thumping against my chest. I could hardly hold any food down and so I just snatched the odd snack to keep me going.

Although Denise and I were aware that this was a murder that was being reported across the world, we hardly watched the television or saw reports in the newspapers. If the news came on and James was mentioned, I had to get up and turn it off.

Our police liaison officers, Mandy and Jim, sat down and spoke with us about the intense interest from the media and how much attention there was likely to be on the day of James's funeral. I would have given anything to be allowed a quiet, dignified funeral for our little boy but there was also a part of me that wanted the whole world never to forget what had happened to him. One of the issues we had to consider was how to give the media the access they would need to cover the service without taking over this very sacred day. The police suggested allowing live television coverage of the funeral mass inside the church, which would provide the worldwide press with what they needed in the least intrusive way. Denise and I agreed because it was better than having hundreds of journalists and cameras trying to get inside.

The first job was to call the funeral directors, Graham Clegg, to ask if they would take on the task of burying James. They are a firm that we had used many times in our family and they agreed without hesitation. They also kindly refused to let us pay, insisting that they wanted to help us in any way they could.

Denise and I went to Kirkdale Cemetery to meet with

the funeral directors, as I had to choose a plot where James was to be buried. Later on my brothers Jimmy and Philip came with me to see the plot and we decided on a peaceful, pretty opening under a tree. It just seemed a very gentle space for my son.

I remember sitting down under the tree and I began to well up. I was so distraught at the realization that this was where my son's tiny body was going to rest, and I cried as I thought of how he would be lying there night after night in the dark and all alone, when he should have been climbing into our bed for warmth and comfort.

Denise and I then had the unbearable agony of choosing a casket for James. He was so small that it would have to be handmade for his little body, but once again the company refused to let us pay for their services. The public support was quite overwhelming for us as a family, but we had seen nothing yet.

For any parent, to lose a child is the most horrific thing. But not only did we have James snatched from us so savagely, we were also denied the chance to say goodbye to him. It's bad enough that I couldn't stop imagining what he must have looked like and what he had been through, but I would have lost it completely if I had seen the state of his body. This also meant that the casket would have to be sealed for the funeral service. I would dearly have loved to hold James one last time, to kiss him gently on the forehead and say my final goodbye, but I was cheated of that chance. I often torture myself in the dead of night, wondering whether I should have seen him anyway, regardless of his injuries. Was I weak to stay away and not see my own son? Not only did I fail to save him from such a terrible fate, I couldn't even cradle him and say goodbye properly.

The funeral director asked us what we would like to place in James's coffin and Denise and I talked it through carefully. We decided on his favourite trousers and a waistcoat, a teddy bear to bring him comfort, his favourite motorbike toy and a torch, because he never went to bed without his torch. We also decided it would be appropriate to put James's special chair that I had made for him on the altar during the service, placing some more of his toys on the seat.

It fell to Graham Clegg to drive to the mortuary at Broad Green Hospital to collect the remains of James's body. It must have been a truly dreadful task for him, but he placed James's possessions in the coffin with him and sealed the casket up.

James's funeral was to take place at the Sacred Heart Church in Northwood, Kirkby. We went to see our local parish priest, Father Michael O'Connell, who had been a great source of comfort to us since the murder. He told us it was important that we had the kind of funeral that we wanted for our baby, and he was very gentle and kind. Denise and I spent a lot of time choosing the right songs, hymns and prayers for our boy, and it was a deeply emotional process. We had to put our own feelings to one side and think only about what was right for James. It had always been about James when he was alive and we had to do right by him in his death.

Organizing the funeral meant that we were leaving the flat far more than we had since James was murdered. It was a very scary and daunting process. If I could have, I think I would have locked myself away for a very long time, but we had no choice but to get on and do things for our son. For the first time I could sense people looking at us, recognizing us from the television and newspapers. I was completely thrown by this and I felt panicked and uneasy. I didn't want people to see me or look at me; I just wanted to get back home as quickly as possible, to retreat into my private world of grief.

A couple of days before the funeral service, Denise and I went to the chapel of rest in Maghull where we would see James's casket for the first time. It was a devastating moment, knowing that inside lay what was left of our son's battered and broken body. As I laid my hands on the little white coffin, I just wanted to rip open the lid and hold my baby close to me. I put both my hands on the casket to steady myself.

'I'm so sorry, son,' I spoke out loud. 'I love you so much and just want to take you back home with me. I will always love you.'

There were many tears that day. Denise cried and so did I as we held on to each other hopelessly.

We had already worked out who would be pall-bearers for James – myself, my brother Philip and two of Denise's brothers, Ray and Gary Matthews. They all said it would be an honour to carry James, even though I knew it would be an extremely daunting task for them.

News crews, journalists, photographers and radio stations had flown in from around the world to cover James's funeral. The police had to make sure the route was carefully planned to deal with not just the press but also the possibility of thousands of people turning out in Kirkby. We had accepted that we would have to allow the service to be broadcast and seen across the globe, but through the police, we asked that we be left in private at James's burial at the cemetery. That would be our final goodbye and we wanted it to remain sacred.

With the preparations for the funeral complete, Denise and I retreated to the privacy of our home to steel ourselves for the next day. There was a horrible silence in the flat as we moved around, trying to get everything ready. My suit was hung up and my shirt was pressed. Denise laid out her clothes too, and finally it was time to go to bed, knowing that we would wake the next day to bury our beloved son.

I hardly slept that night as so many emotions swept over me. I kept thinking of James in his coffin, all alone and cold. Then I thought about the two little bastards who had brutally ended his life and I have never felt so much hatred. I wanted those feelings to leave me but they wouldn't. And as I lay in the dark, trapped inside my own mind, I just wanted the light to come.

It was Monday, 1 March 1993, when we laid James to rest. The weather was freezing cold, grey and gloomy. We got ourselves ready and made our way to Denise's mother's house, from where the funeral procession was leaving. As I walked along the pavement in silence, I felt sick and my legs were like jelly. I didn't know how I was going to get through this day. I just had to keep thinking of James and make sure that I did right by him.

The house was packed that day as the funeral cars began to arrive. In total, there were fourteen matching limousines for close family as well as a small bus for those who couldn't fit into the vehicles. Additional cars had been laid on by several more funeral directors around the area, to cope with the number of people attending. Again, they were provided free of charge. Three of the hearses that led the procession were brimming with flowers that had been sent from around the world. Behind them was the hearse carrying James to the church; inside was a clean, white oak coffin with gold handles and a gold cross. His gold name plate was on the top along with a tiny bunch of flowers. It was simple but beautiful. Alongside James's coffin were a large floral wreath spelling out his name and a teddy bear made from carnations.

Denise and I were in the car behind James's casket and it was only a few short minutes from Eileen's house to the church, but even so, the drive felt like it was taking an eternity. Many of the neighbours along the route had closed their curtains as a mark of respect while literally thousands of people came out onto the pavements to line the route. Nearly all had their heads bowed down in grief.

When we arrived at the church gates, I took a deep breath as I climbed from the car, knowing I was about to carry my son on his final journey to heaven. I went to the front of the casket with Ray while Philip and Gary took the back of the coffin. I remember thinking how light this little white box felt on my shoulders; it was the pain and heartbreak that weighed so heavily on all of us who shared that burden that day. My biggest fear was that I would collapse under the huge weight of the grief that was engulfing me. I just thought of my beautiful son as I kept my head bowed and began the slow and agonizing walk into the church.

The sight that met me was quite overwhelming and a wave of emotions rushed over me. The church was packed and there were flowers everywhere, many of which had been left at makeshift shrines to James both at the Strand and at the railway line where he was murdered. I could feel my bottom lip trembling and it took all my strength not to cry in front of everyone. I had to stay dignified for James and it was the thought of my little boy that got me through that moment. The congregation was silent at first and then they began singing the traditional hymn 'The Old Rugged Cross' with all their might, and you could almost touch the emotion in the church it was so strong. When we arrived at the front of the altar with James, we gently and carefully placed him down. Denise had followed the coffin from behind and together we took our place in the front row of the church.

The first thing I saw as I looked up from my seat was the little red chair I had so lovingly made for my wonderful son. All I could picture was the chair in our flat, with James bouncing all over it and giggling away to his heart's content. Now, instead, two of his teddies sat on the seat on the altar of a church at his funeral. How could this be happening? I could feel tears rolling down my cheeks. Denise was distraught. I put my arm around her but she was inconsolable. I could hear Father Michael talking but I couldn't concentrate on the words.

Albert Kirby was among those we had asked to make a Bible reading and he did so with huge dignity and care. And then Father Michael spoke publicly to Denise and me about James.

'Everyone's heart absolutely goes out to you,' he said. 'We wish we could turn the clock back two and a half weeks. We wish we could make things better. We wish so much we could bring James back to you both and to all of us, but we can't. All we can do is offer you our support, share with you our faith, acknowledge with you the loss you are feeling and the gift God gave us in James Patrick.

'Almost three years ago James was born. In those three years James shared so much with us.

'Even though we can't touch him, he is still influencing us, having a power over us. His death is not in vain. Something in James Patrick has touched the whole world and maybe they will respond. It has brought something out of us deep down. The death of an innocent little child is causing us to do something about it and make life better.

'For three years we had James and in those three years from what I can gather he certainly developed a personality of his own, fond of his dancing, putting on his Michael Jackson music, someone who liked to make people laugh, someone who was always in good form, someone who liked his own chair, someone we are going to miss very much.

'James Patrick didn't waste life. He lived those three years to the full and put all his energies into it, staying up at night right until the last minute. Jesus Christ didn't turn the children away from him. James Patrick has his very own little chair up in heaven now. Maybe He has James Patrick on his knee. We are going to miss him every day for the rest of our lives because we will never forget and won't ever get over him. Time does not heal. Time just helps us cope a little bit better. Let all he stood for, his innocence, love of life and music, his good humour and fun, his spontaneity, let all that continue to come to us now. Let us spread it out throughout the rest of Northwood, Kirkby and Merseyside. Life has changed. It hasn't ended. Let that change be as best we can make it, supporting one another in our tears and giving one another help and encouragement. Let us put our faith and trust in God and one another. Let this be a beginning.'

Father Michael's words were very beautiful and captured the essence of James perfectly. But life had ended for James and it was to prove to be the beginning of an unrelenting, painful journey for those of us left behind. I knew James would have his own chair in heaven and that he would make all those around him laugh and be happy. I just wished with all my heart he was still here with us to make us smile once again. Denise and I just held each other in silence as we tried to draw comfort from the words being offered to us. But the sadness was overpowering.

We had chosen Michael Jackson's song 'Heal the World' to be played amidst the more traditional hymns, and as the recording began to play, so many people broke down and cried. Denise was sobbing and all I could do was hold her. We were both distraught and we knew our hearts had been broken that day. Some days later, Michael Jackson heard about the funeral and delivered a bouquet of flowers and a message of condolence to us. It was an extraordinary gesture and I know James would have loved that.

After the Requiem Mass finished, it was time for me to carry my son for one last time. As I bore his casket on my shoulder, a recording of Eric Clapton's heartbreaking song 'Tears in Heaven' played throughout the church. With every step I was edging closer to the moment I had to let my son go. I wanted to sob there and then but I refused to break down before my job was done. The agony of bearing your child in a coffin is almost beyond words. And I kept thinking about how he had been deliberately mutilated and murdered.

If anything, it was my hatred for his killers that got me through that day. Had I allowed my pain and sorrow to flood out, I would have broken down, but I had to be strong one final time for Denise and for my son.

From the church, we began the long and harrowing journey in the cars to the cemetery where James was to be buried. There were thousands of people lining the streets along the route. The people of Kirkby were sharing our grief and pain, just as I knew they would. Everywhere people were stopping their business to bow their heads and pay their respects to the sorry procession of funeral cars that slowly made its way to its final destination. It was an outstanding tribute to James and to the people of my town, who had so little themselves but freely gave their love and compassion, and I will never forget the way they rallied to our support.

It wasn't a huge gathering at the graveside. It was just close family and friends and a handful of the police officers who had been intimately involved with the case. They had all been so deeply affected by what they had seen, especially those who were present when James's body was found, that it seemed to bring them some comfort and closure to what had undoubtedly been the worst case they had ever had to deal with. It was a peaceful time and a stark contrast to the violence and pain that James endured while he was still alive. The police showed us that they cared deeply for our son and about what had happened to him, and they were very welcome at his graveside.

As I stood looking into the ground that was to be my son's final resting place, I felt nothing but profound sorrow. Denise and I placed single stems of red roses on James's coffin and, as I bent down to my knees, I just wanted to climb down into the grave and lie still with my son. I wanted the world to go away and let me be with James one more time.

The funeral home had organized for the other relatives to be given bags of rose petals to scatter on the coffin instead of the traditional earth. It was a thoughtful and loving touch for which we were very grateful, allowing James go to rest in a bed of beautiful roses.

Our final goodbye to our son was contained in a poem that Denise and I had chosen for James. A local man named Archie, who drank in the Roughwood pub, had written the poem as a tribute to James and it touched us so much we asked him if we could use it as our final goodbye to our son. We laid it alongside a floral wreath at his graveside in the form of the gates of Heaven, to which we had no doubt that our son had now gone. Our final message to James read: 'James, our beautiful baby son. We didn't get to say goodbye and that really makes us cry. You brought so much love in our lives, that love for you will never die. The only thing that we can do, is sit and pray for you. In our hearts you will still be there, locked inside our loving care. God, look after him as we would do, for we are sure that he is with you. Goodnight and God bless, James Patrick. All our love, hugs and kisses, Mum and Dad. xxxx'

From the graveside we all left to attend a wake at the Sacred Heart Club in Kirkby. It was very much a family affair and not just confined to the adults. Several generations of relatives, including all the children, gathered together to share their loss and bring comfort where they could. For me, it was a chance to shed some of the emotions that had built up during the day. It was a pretty full-on do, and as drink began to flow, so too did the tears from almost everyone who was there that evening. That night I got drunk, very drunk, until the moment I was able to pass out under the heavy anaesthetic of the alcohol. I didn't want to feel anything any more. Not the anger or the hatred. Not the pain or torture in my soul. Every waking hour felt like my heart had been ripped apart, my soul wrenched from my body, and the alcohol brought the smallest refuge from the agony I was feeling.

A few days after James was buried, I returned to his grave with my brother Jimmy. We saw a young couple standing at his plot. Beside them were their own two young children. They were crying and very distressed and I wondered if they too had suffered the kind of loss that we were going through. They recognized me when they saw me.

'Hello, are you Ralph?' the woman asked.

'Yes,' I replied.

'I'm so sorry if you think we are intruding but we felt we had to come here to pay our respects to your son. I hope you don't mind us being here, but as parents ourselves, we felt we couldn't do nothing.'

'No, it's OK. I appreciate the fact that you care so much. You are welcome here.'

It turned out that this anonymous young couple, who never knew James or his family, had travelled nearly 150 miles with their own children from Sunderland to bring flowers to my son's grave. It wasn't the only time they would visit his final resting place. For the next couple of years, they regularly continued to visit James once a month to lay fresh flowers on his grave. They showed genuine compassion for us and for what had happened to James, and they were not the only ones. So many people responded with such overwhelming love and kindness, as well as shock and outrage, that it taught me there are more good people in the world than bad.

8

The Aftermath

Gradually, after the funeral, Denise and I started to recognize the impact James's murder had had on others. You would expect an outpouring of grief and anger in Liverpool – this is a community that fiercely protects its own, and to discover that two local boys were responsible for the heinous crime only added to the intensity of feelings. But James's murder shook the world. Parents everywhere were terrified for the safety of their children, realizing that their precious offspring may no longer even be safe with other children. In the weeks after James was killed, mothers and fathers held their children's hands tighter in public, and there was a sharp increase in the sale of baby reins, so that youngsters could not wander off into potential danger.

Denise and I began to receive thousands of messages of support from the four corners of the globe. Letters and cards of sympathy arrived in sack loads on a daily basis. Like the couple at the graveside, everyone felt they had to do something to show their solidarity and outrage at the dreadful course of events. Some of the letters were simply addressed to the parents of James Bulger, Liverpool, but they all arrived through our letterbox.

One handwritten letter had added poignancy and really showed just how this crime had touched people from all walks of life. It read:

Dear Ralph and Denise,

I know you are inundated with messages and flowers, but I could not let James's journey to a better place go by without expressing my deepest, deepest sympathy. I am so shocked and upset that this could have happened, and cannot in any way comprehend the total suffering you must be going through.

Last night I went to see my little babies in their beds. I thought of James and the pain I would feel if I walked back into these bedrooms and could not see my girls in their beds – and feeling the suffering of knowing they would never come back. It made me cry and they were there. It was a small feeling of the agonies in your heart. You must be going over and over in your mind what happened and if only . . .

But James is in a better place. This world we live in was not for James and he was such a special person that God needed his soul. I know nothing can ever ease your suffering, you both have been through so much. If there is anything I can do at all to help you, please let me know. I give you all my support and strength, for what it is worth.

With love, Sarah.

The note had arrived from Buckingham Palace and was from the Duchess of York, Sarah Ferguson. It touched us both very deeply and mirrored the kind of sentiments that so many people were sending to us in the wake of losing James. We really did appreciate the messages of support from everyone, but I don't think they sunk in until a lot later on when I was able to go back over them, and that's when they helped me to grasp how much people had cared about James. In the early days, I was just too wrapped up in my own pain to look outside of myself.

After James's funeral, my life began to unravel in spectacular fashion. Now I no longer had the planning and the day itself to give me a reason to keep going, I felt this terrible, dark void, as if life just wasn't worth living any more. That feeling intensified on 16 March, the date that should have been James's third birthday. It was just over a month since James had been murdered. As we had done in the previous two years, we would have had a party for him with all his cousins and friends. There would have been jelly sweets and ice cream, chocolate cake and party games. Instead, I sat alone in our bedroom where James used to sleep alongside us. I didn't know what to do with myself and found myself staring at the walls, or pacing up and down, all the time wishing more than anything that James was back with me once again. I could hear the echoes of him laughing. 'Look at me, Ralph, look at me.' I remembered his voice so vividly. In my imagination, I could see him trying to shove as much cake as possible into his mouth at once, making everyone around him laugh. And I could see him happily blowing out the candles on his birthday cake: three little candles he never got to see. I missed James more than ever that day and couldn't bring myself to talk to anyone. The only person I spoke to was in my head.

'Happy birthday, son,' I whispered. 'I hope you are having

a great day in heaven and that you have chocolate birthday cake with all your friends. I miss you so much, James, and I love you more than you can ever know.'

Denise was also suffering from enormous grief and we tried so hard to comfort each other, but it was impossible. We were both so angry it wasn't true. I think I found it hard to speak to Denise about it because I was not the type of person who was used to opening up about my feelings, and this was so huge, it felt as if it might finish me off if I confronted how I felt. For that reason, it almost felt easier, possibly even safer, to say nothing in the hope that it would go away. It never would, of course, but I didn't know that then.

I'm not even sure how to describe some of my feelings properly. All I knew was that I felt so badly broken that I didn't believe anything could ever put me back together again. The result was that a lot of emotions continued to fester inside of me, which was unhealthy, but I didn't know any other way. There is no handbook to tell you how to deal with the awful murder of your own son by two young boys.

I had a recurring sense that I just wanted to run away, to get away from what I was feeling, and inevitably that led to me starting to drink heavily. I would drink anything I could lay my hands on cheaply, and often that would be pints of lager washed down with large whisky chasers. I would drink in the pub or I would drink at home, I really didn't care. In so many ways I had given up on life. I would lie in bed during the day, hungover, ill and in a world of physical and mental pain.

In the beginning, I was drinking a bottle of cheap whisky

a day, but that quickly doubled to two. I would buy the drink and then take myself off in private somewhere. The truth is, I do not remember half the places I went to. My head was in a permanent fog. I know that I often used to walk through the night drinking until I arrived at James's grave, where I would sit for hours and hours just talking to him aloud. It was crazy, stupid stuff, but it was like my grief was a kind of insanity.

'Hello, my beautiful boy, your daddy's here beside you,' I would tell him. 'I miss you so much, James, with all my heart. I hope you are OK in heaven and that you have made lots of new friends. I hope you have got your own special chair too. I know everyone who meets you will love you, just as we did. We still love you so much and we wish you were back here with us. I'm gonna stay a while with you now. I don't want to leave you ever again.'

My drunken ramblings continued into the night and I would sob my heart out in such distress. Often I would pass out from drinking beside James's grave. When I didn't come home, Denise would call Jimmy and he'd come out to find me. She probably thought Jimmy would be better at dealing with me and calming me down, as she was still going through her own traumas. Jimmy would drive to a number of different haunts of mine, but he always checked the grave because I went there so often.

'Come on, Ralph, kid. Let's get you home,' Jimmy would say as he shook me awake. I'd be drowsy and weak and he would have to use all his strength to get me standing before taking me home to sleep it off.

I'm not sure what drew me to James's grave. I just felt it was a way of getting closer to him, to be with him once again. I also wanted to protect him. I know that sounds ridiculous as he was already dead, but I almost felt I was standing guard over him at night when I was at the graveside. There was another very strong reason that I went there of a night. I have already described how I had developed a hatred for going out and facing people, and I didn't want to go and visit James in the daytime because there would be too many people around. On top of that, members of the public might have recognized me if they realized which grave I was at, and I couldn't bear the thought of having to talk to people.

I realize that this must have been a terrible time for Denise too. She was trying to cope with losing our son and she also had a husband who kept going missing and was bent on self-destruction with the drink. The truth is, I couldn't cope, and my life would remain this way for a very long time.

I don't know if anyone could properly deal with something as terrible as this, but I didn't come from the kind of background where you went to the doctor to ask for counselling or antidepressants. As far as I was concerned, the booze was my medication, even though I was most certainly chronically depressed and grief-stricken. Everyone knew I was drinking way too much but, to an extent, I think people almost expected me to. That was the way it was for a lot of men in Kirkby. I don't even think it's a macho thing. I was of the generation who were just supposed to get on with it, and my way of doing that was to get blotto all the time. I don't remember anyone challenging me about my drinking, but I did get a lot of support from the people of Kirkby, in particular some of the lads in the town. Some of the toughest men I knew did all they could to get me through this period. They knew I was on the ale heavily and that nothing was going to stop me, and so they would often pick me up in a car, drive me out of town to a pub and buy me a meal and a few pints. It was their way of keeping an eye on me, and making sure that I didn't do anything daft or cause myself any harm – deliberately or by accident.

I realize now that the drinking was only making everything a hundred times worse by heaping on more depression and fuelling my fears and anxieties. There is no question that I considered killing myself. The only thing that stopped me from doing it was the thought that I would be letting James down once again. I couldn't let that happen. As with everything else, I kept those feelings to myself, but I suspect close family members knew because they were constantly keeping a watch over me. I'm not the brains of Britain but I am a very emotional person. The fact that I struggle to show those feelings makes it all the harder because there is nowhere for me to put them. The drink was my only salvation because it meant I didn't have to put up with such unbearable emotions twenty-four hours a day. I didn't even have the energy to try and put on a brave face. I just fell headlong into the daily oblivion of drink. I didn't know what else to do.

The heavy drinking pattern continued for a long time and I sank to a very dark place. To escape from my feelings I would get in my car and start driving. I never knew where I was going; I just thought that if I drove away from Kirkby I would be leaving my pain and suffering behind. But wherever I went the misery came with me. I would end up in Wales or the Lake District, hours from home. When

I arrived, I would get out and buy my bottle of whisky and just go walking through the night until I returned to my car and fell asleep. I would sometimes stay away from home for two or three days. Denise was always worried about me and she would go round to see Karen and Jimmy to ask for their help, but she also had her own intense grief to contend with, and I suppose in a way she just got used to my erratic behaviour. It wasn't good for either of us, but I felt like I was stuck in *Groundhog Day*. I would drink to ease the pain, wake up feeling terrible and so take more drink just to make it all go away again for a while.

At one point the pressure became so great that I just went off and locked myself away in the bedroom at home for almost two weeks, refusing to go out or eat properly. I couldn't get on with my life. I would lie there and think about James constantly. I would grab some of his clothes or his bed linen and hold them to my face so I could still smell him, and I would sob like a baby for hours on end. I couldn't wash or even look after myself properly. I was really falling apart. Relatives did call round to see me and try to get me to go out, but they knew it was useless until I was ready to do it for myself. No one suggested professional help because that's not the way things were done in our family. As far as we were concerned, you don't take tablets for grief. You just have to find a way to get over it.

We were delivered a tiny sliver of hope in April when we learned that Denise was pregnant again. I was stunned at the news. Of course, I was thrilled but I was also terrified at the prospect. We had already lost two babies and I don't think I would have coped if we had lost any more children.

For Denise, it was a godsend. Having that baby was the reason she was able to carry on with life. Without it, she believes she would have gone under.

I knew I had to pull myself together for Denise and the baby, but I still felt so wretched inside. I knew the drink was killing me and so I tried to cope without it, but my attempts didn't always last very long. Instead of giving up completely, I began to reduce how much I was drinking in a bid to sort my head out. Rather than sinking two bottles of Scotch a day, as I had been in the early days after James's death, I made a huge effort to cut back to drinking in the evenings and start looking after myself better, but there was no miracle cure. A pattern of binge drinking emerged. I would go through spells of being dry, and then if something happened that brought back the overwhelming emotions I felt over James's murder, I would pick up the drink to help me deal with things. This is how my life remained for almost ten years after James died. There were good periods and bad periods. All I know is that if I had carried on drinking at such a heavy rate, I wouldn't be alive today.

I didn't find life easy without the drink because it had become my mask, but things hadn't been much easier with it. With ale on board, my mind automatically drifted to thoughts of James and I would become morose and tearful. The body can only take so much punishment and my heavy drinking at times made me feel dreadful, but it was my crutch. Afterwards I had to rebuild my strength again and try to get on with my life.

On the good days, I would take myself off running as I was trying to get myself back into shape to offset the damage done by my drinking. I began going to the gym to do weight training as it was a proper alternative to drinking and it did help to clear my mind. When I ran, I felt a sense of freedom. I thought about James all the time, but my thoughts about him during my private hours of running were far more positive than in the weepy hours I spent drinking. I kept happy images of him in my head as I pounded the roads and attempted to release some of my feelings.

Denise and I tried to pull together when we found out about the pregnancy, but the cracks were already there. It was hardly surprising considering that we had been through so much, and I had been a mess for months. Our relationship wasn't helped by the fact that in the early days, I blamed Denise for what had happened to James, and I was wrong. Very, very wrong. It was just part of my raging grief, frustration and anger. I wanted to scream, 'Why did you let go of his hand? Why did you let him out of your sight? He would still be here if it wasn't for you.'

If we bickered together, I would end up blurting out that she was the last person to be with James and that she should never have let go of his hand. I am deeply ashamed of blaming Denise because nothing could be further from the truth, but once I had said it aloud, I could never take it back. I suppose it is inevitable for couples to blame one another. Denise could equally blame me for not taking James with me that day when I went to fix the wardrobes. I know I blame myself and I wish I could turn the clock back, but I can't. And the truth is that Denise was and still is an outstanding mother, and I would never have anyone say anything otherwise. She loved James with all her heart and soul, and what happened that day was not her fault. She was attentive and protective of James and he was a little live wire. No one could possibly have known that such evil was lurking just yards away – it really could have been any parent's child that day. I saw how James's murder devastated Denise and I regret feeling that blame. It wasn't that I didn't love Denise any more. I just wasn't capable of loving anyone or feeling anything other than my emotions around James's murder.

The only ones I blame are Thompson and Venables, and myself.

If only I had done as Denise asked that day and taken James with me. If only I had been with him at the time to prevent those murderous boys from carrying out their vicious perversions. If only I had been able to save my son in some way. I didn't, and I will always feel that I failed our child as a father. It was my job to love, protect and nurture that precious baby at all times, and I let him down. That is one of the hardest things I have to deal with.

In the months leading up to Thompson and Venables' trial, Denise and I tried to get on with our lives as best as possible, but we just couldn't get out from under the news spotlight. It was an added pressure on top of our mourning. We had become used to seeing cars parked up in our road with journalists and photographers inside them, and it seemed that our everyday lives were under scrutiny. Even though we tried to keep out of the media spotlight, the requests for interviews never ceased and the presence of the press in the town seemed to be permanent. Newspaper, television and radio journalists knocked on our door all the time asking if we would consider talking to them, but we were not fit to take on such demands.

The most intrusive part of the press interest came just after James's murder and then again when the trial started up in the November of that year. And they weren't just asking Denise and me for interviews. All our family members were approached, but they closed ranks. When the reporters didn't get very far with us, they turned their attention to neighbours and people in the town of Kirkby, and we know that many persistent journalists were sent on wild goose chases by people who knew us and tried to protect us. One example of this was when reporters went into one of our local pubs, The Golden Eagle, to ask questions about our family and James. The canny staff in there told them they would find me and Jimmy at a pub on the other side of town, knowing full well that we would not be there. Although the attention was fierce, we did appreciate that the press crews were only doing their jobs, and in many ways they were always on our side. It was just that we couldn't deal with them as well as our own suffering.

My emotions became even more fragile after one particular visit from the police. Detectives were frantically preparing their case for the pending trial of Thompson and Venables. Albert Kirby came to see me one day just a few weeks before the trial was due to start in November and said he wanted to talk to me about what I might hear during the court case. I still hadn't learned the full extent of James's injuries, and Albert explained, as gently as possible, that I should be warned of what would be put before the jurors. It was then that I learned exactly what these creatures had done to my little boy and I would never be able to get those images out of my head ever again.

Albert broke it to me for the very first time just how badly James had been tortured. I didn't want to know these details, but I had to sit and listen to the terrible truth of how my son was killed. It was devastating. Even in my darkest moments I had never imagined his ordeal could have been this bad. I was totally dumbstruck by what I was hearing and it cut straight to my heart. It was hard to take in because I kept going back to the reality that these injuries had been inflicted by two ten-year-old boys. There was no easy way for Albert to tell me these details that day, and it must have been an awful job for him, but he couldn't have allowed me to go to court unprepared for what I would hear in evidence against his killers. I couldn't speak to anyone about what Albert had told me and I think it threw me into even deeper shock. Denise was shielded from those awful details because we all knew she would be unable to cope with them. As far as I can gather, she still doesn't know the full extent of James's torture all these years down the line. There was no way she was going to be able to sit through court day after day and hear this gruesome list of injuries to her son.

Thompson and Venables slowly ripped my son apart like two wild and savage dogs, then went home for their tea as his little body lay flung across a railway line.

Their torture began when they made him walk several miles from the shopping centre to the place at the side of the railway line where they would eventually kill him. They dropped him on his head, they pelted him with sticks and stones and laughed at him as he cried for his mummy and daddy. They threw blue paint in his face, in his eyes, and forced him to drink the remainder while he was still conscious. I can still hear him crying out and begging them to stop, their eyes filled with hatred as they jeered him. That would have been one of the last images my son saw before he died.

I felt like I was going to explode as the details kept coming at me. My whole body was shaking. I listened in disbelief as I learned how they used iron bars and bricks to smash him apart. They stamped on his face with their boots and when his bloodied skull was smashed apart they exposed parts of his brain. They smashed him with planks of wood with metal bolts screwed through them, found at the side of the railway. As a final degrading act, they removed his lower clothes, ripped his genitals and inserted batteries inside his rectum. With their torture complete, they took his limp body and lay it across the railway track for a train to come and cut him in two. James was thought to have still been alive but unconscious and unresponsive when he was laid on the track, but he died before his body was cut in two, according to the pathologist who examined him.

That is what I face every day from the moment I open my eyes. Tell me what man, what father, can deal with knowing such evil? James was so young and innocent. He couldn't fight back and they knew that. That's why they murdered him – because they could.

The full details of James's torture almost destroyed me. I began to have horrific nightmares about Thompson and Venables standing at James's blood-soaked grave, laughing about what they'd done. I had built up a picture of the boys in my imagination and in my mind their faces were blank, almost like a mask, but their eyes blazed and squinted with hatred and their mouths snarled like wild animals. I would wake up sweating, and picture my son's headstone dripping with blood. The pain was like a raw and gaping wound that refused to heal. I could never shut off the soundtrack of James's dying screams.

9

The Trial

By the end of October, Denise was in the final stages of her pregnancy as the trial of Robert Thompson and Jon Venables was about to start. We hadn't really moved on with our grief, but we had been forced to adapt to living with our loss. Denise remained really strong as her pregnancy progressed, but we were both dreading the trial. I was determined to go along for the sake of James. As Denise was due to give birth the following month, we decided it was best for her to stay home, to save her any distress.

The two boys were now eleven years old and were to appear before a judge and jury at Preston Crown Court on 1 November. The trial had been deliberately taken away from Merseyside because feelings were still running high in Liverpool and the police wanted to avoid any repeat of the ugly scenes witnessed at their initial court appearance before the magistrates.

On the morning of the first day of the trial, I got up with that familiar knot in my stomach. I felt quite ill knowing I'd be facing James's killers in court for the first time. I had thought of nothing else for the last few weeks as the date edged closer and closer. How would I react when they stood before me? I couldn't eat a thing as I started to get ready, and then I sat down on the bed and said a silent prayer.

'Dear God, you've taken James from us, but please give me the strength to get through this day. I can't do this on my own.'

The police had organized to take me, Jimmy and Denise's brother Ray up to the court at Preston, but we were not alone. There were other members of the family and plenty of friends who were going along too, to give us moral support. I know I was angry. I was always angry. But I think I was scared witless as well because I didn't want to lose control when confronted by Thompson and Venables, especially as I now knew just what they had done to James. I kissed Denise goodbye and told her I would be back later. On the way to the court, I stayed silent. That's often the way with me. I may not have said a lot but there was plenty going on in my head.

The police told us that legal arguments would take place in the morning and the trial would open in the afternoon. When we arrived in court, it was extremely daunting. There were so many people packed into the courtroom it was unbelievable. There was press everywhere outside and inside Court Number One where the trial was taking place. It was an old and grand courthouse, which made the surroundings seem even sterner. This was to be a historic criminal trial, but that really meant nothing to me. I just wanted to see the boys who had killed my James punished. Unlike at the Magistrates' Court some months earlier, the crowds did not turn out in force to protest, most likely because the trial was taking place some 40 miles away from Liverpool. It didn't mean that the public didn't attend, but this time they were people who wanted to sit in the court and watch the trial unfold, unlike the angry crowds of before. Our family couldn't imagine why anyone would want to go to watch and hear such a hideous event. I understood that it was a unique trial, and I also got that it was of huge interest for the media to report, but I just couldn't get my head around ordinary people wanting to be there. It seemed morbid that people should take such an interest in something so awful.

Seats had been reserved for family members in the front row of the public gallery in the courtroom, and as I walked into court, I sensed all eyes were on me. It was horrible and I couldn't wait to sit down. Jimmy and Ray sat either side of me and I felt myself getting really hot with stress. My nervousness made my jaw clench tight and my palms were wet with sweat. It seemed like an eternity before the judge came into court. We all rose in silence as he took his seat, and as soon as he sat down he ordered that the two defendants be brought up from the holding room downstairs. The trial was about to begin.

I could not believe my eyes as Thompson and Venables walked up the steps into the courtroom. Standing just ten feet away from me in the dock were two short, chubby-faced kids in their school blazers and ties. I was stunned beyond belief. They were both so tiny. I felt like someone had just knocked me sideways.

'This cannot be happening,' I silently screamed inside.

I will never forget that moment when I saw them both for the first time. I had steeled myself to deal with the occasion, but the shock was overwhelming, momentarily taking my breath away as I stared intently at the boys who sat before me. Where were the demonic forces that had carried out such unparalleled acts of atrocity? Had I really expected to see horns growing from their heads and blood-drenched fangs dripping from their mouths? I was totally unable to grapple with the idea these boys could be capable of such gruesome and wicked acts.

The scene before me had run through my mind on a thousand different occasions as I imagined how I might react. I had wondered if I might scream at them or make a lunge towards them or dissolve in a fit of grief. Now the moment had arrived, instead I sat rooted to the spot, oblivious to anyone else in the room. I felt my hands clench tight and I could almost hear my heart smashing frantically against the walls of my chest amid the stunned hush of the room.

The fact they were in the dock in their school uniforms really struck home. They were so short that special provision had been made to raise the platform they would sit on to make sure they could see over the brass rails surrounding the dock. My head was completely scrambled and I felt like I was going to pass out. I desperately needed some air and I felt the knot in my tummy rising into blind fury. I couldn't lash out, but I wanted to jump from my seat and smash them to pieces. I didn't see innocent children before me. I saw two disciples of the Devil wrapped in children's bodies.

A hand gripped my arm. It was Jimmy, who was holding on to me for dear life, as if he sensed what I wanted to do. I didn't hear anything that was being said in the court and it was as if the events before me were playing out in slow motion. At that moment, when Jimmy gripped me, I think I had almost taken leave of my senses.

And then it hit me like a tidal wave. Hatred. It was a pure, undiluted hatred that coursed through my veins as if it had replaced every last drop of blood in my body. I still wanted them dead and I am ashamed to say it. How could I hate two boys who hadn't even reached their teenage years yet? Before James's death I would not have believed it was possible for me to feel this way. But from that day to this, I have never doubted that, regardless of their tender age and stature, I was staring into the faces of evil: the faces of Jon Venables and Robert Thompson who abducted, repeatedly tortured, sexually assaulted and murdered my beautiful two-year-old son.

It was hard to look at the two boys, let alone assess how I felt, but at the same time I couldn't avert my stare. My heart was beating so fast, I thought that everyone in the courtroom would be able to hear it. Boom, boom, boom. That was all I could hear.

The boys remained standing for the first few moments before the judge addressed them and asked them to confirm their names. Both just nodded in reply.

Thompson and Venables then sat and began fidgeting and shuffling in their seats. I wanted them to look at me so I could see into their eyes but they continued to mess around in the dock. Eventually, one by one, their eyes met mine. I don't suppose for one moment they knew who I was, or how much they had destroyed my life. I was just another face in the crowd to them.

I remember locking eyes with Robert Thompson first. He just seemed to stare ahead in my direction as if he didn't have a bother in the world. I felt a coldness to him that I will never forget. If he was feeling anything inside, he did not seem to show it. His expression seemed blank. He looked neither scared nor upset and I began to see what he was really like inside. Jon Venables was no different, just a more twitchy child whose eyes seemed as cold as rock when I looked at him. I peered into their eyes searching desperately for signs of sorrow, remorse, fear or regret – anything that would show me that they too were made of flesh and blood with human emotions, but to me their stares were spine-chillingly vacant.

As the two boys sat in that dock, I felt certain they were not thinking about the little baby whose life they had destroyed so unnecessarily. Had they ever thought about James? The pain and cruelty they had inflicted on him? Looking at them, I don't believe that James had ever crossed their minds. They might have been worried about what was going to happen to them as they sat in that courtroom, but they seemed monumentally oblivious to the human suffering they had caused on a catastrophic scale.

I was sick to the pit of my stomach, but I had calmed down enough to know I would not try to lunge at the boys or jump over the dock. Where would that have got me? James deserved so much more dignity than that. He died without dignity and I was determined that I would not shame my son with behaviour that belonged to his killers. Still, I was very glad that I was sandwiched between close family members. All of us felt the same way about these child killers, but they were there looking out for me, for which I will be eternally grateful. I don't think I came close to crying that day because I was so angry. I felt so ill, but I wasn't going to show an ounce of emotion to these little bastards who had taken so much pleasure in killing my son.

As the court proceedings started, my heartbeat began to slow and I managed to get a grip on my emotions. One by one, potential jurors were called into the room to swear their oaths before the court. It was quite a lengthy process and it gave me a chance to settle down a bit. The formal proceedings were important, but my mind was elsewhere. Although I tried to listen as intently as I could to what was going on around me, I still couldn't stop looking at the two boys in the dock, and images of how they had tortured James kept flashing through my mind. My brain was in chaos and I didn't know the name of the judge, or the prosecuting and defence barristers; all I knew was that my son was dead because of these two monsters. Through archive material of the proceedings, I learned a lot of these details as the months and years ticked by.

The judge in the case was the Honourable Mr Justice Morland. When all the jurors were accepted and settled in their seats, the three charges against Thompson and Venables were read out for their benefit: the attempted abduction of a child, Diane Power's son, the abduction of James and the murder of James. Thompson and Venables had already pleaded not guilty to all three at an earlier hearing. Mr Richard Henriques QC was prosecuting for the Crown, and here is how he opened the trial.

'James Bulger was two years and eleven months old when he died. He was the only child of Ralph and Denise Bulger and they live in Kirkby. They always called him James and we will refer to him as James throughout this trial. He died on Friday, 12 February this year. In short, these two defendants abducted James from his mother in a shopping precinct in Bootle. They walked him some two and a half miles across Liverpool to Walton, a very long and distressing walk for a two-year-old toddler. James was then taken up to a railway line and subjected to a prolonged and violent attack. Bricks, stones and a piece of metal appear to have been thrown at James on that railway line. He sustained many fractures of the skull. Death resulted from multiple blunt force injuries to the head. There were several lacerated wounds. At some point James's lower clothing was removed. His body was placed across a railway line and some time later his body was run over by a train, which cut his body in two. The pathologist concludes that death occurred prior to the impact of the train. The prosecution alleges that the two defendants acting together took James from the precinct and together were responsible for causing his death.

'Both defendants are now eleven years of age. On Friday, 12 February, they were both ten years and six months old, both born in August 1982. Notwithstanding their ages, it is alleged that they both intended either to kill James or at least to cause him really serious injury and they both knew that their behaviour was really seriously wrong. Not only is it alleged that they both abducted and murdered James, but that they attempted, prior to abducting James, to abduct another two-year-old boy. He was in the same shopping precinct three hours earlier. That attempt failed because the boy's mother saw one of the defendants beckoning to him to follow him. She called to him, thus preventing the abduction.

'It was between 5.30 p.m. and 6.45 p.m. that James was stoned and beaten to death before being placed across a railway line.'

It was a shocking opening to the trial and there was

silence in the courtroom as he spoke. I could feel the hairs on the back of my neck stand on end as I listened to the gruesome description of how James met his death. Hearing the words spoken aloud in public made it even worse because you could see from the looks on the faces in that room that no one could believe what they were hearing.

Mr Henriques told the court that bloodstains found on Jon's shoes were consistent with a DNA sample of James's blood, as was the blood found on Robert's shoe. He also added that there was a close match between marks on James's face and the imprint of the shoes worn by Robert that day. He didn't need to spell it out that Robert had kicked and stamped on James's face.

After hearing the prosecution outline, court ended for the day with Mr Henriques telling the jurors that the next day he would describe to them details of the police interviews with the two boys, after they had been arrested.

I couldn't wait to get out of that room. I felt like I was suffocating.

When we got back to Denise, I found it so hard to talk about all the things I had heard that day, and so her brother Ray briefed her as simply as possible, leaving out the gory details of how they had battered James to death.

I barely slept a wink that night. I couldn't erase the faces of the two little kids who had devastated so many lives. The difference now was that I had seen the vacant and cold expressions in their eyes and I realized that is what James would have seen before he died. I think I knew at that moment that I was never going to feel normal again, that my life was going to be a long and painful journey.

I felt drained and exhausted and I didn't want to go back

to court the following day. I didn't want to see their faces ever again, but I knew I had to keep going for James. It would be wrong if I didn't show up.

The police had spent a lot of time with our family trying to explain the most important aspects of the case. They said that they were not just relying on the evidence of Thompson and Venables admitting to abducting and attacking James, but on the accounts of thirty-seven witnesses who had been traced during the investigation. All of them put James with the boys. He had been forced to walk nearly three miles that day over a period of one and a quarter hours. All of those witnesses could provide a different snapshot of the events as they unfolded.

Everyone accepted there was little doubt that the boys had carried out the crime, but a successful conviction hinged on whether the defendants knew and understood that taking James away, torturing and killing him, was wrong. The prosecution needed to prove to the jury that Thompson and Venables knew the difference between right and wrong and could tell truth from lies. If that could be proved, it would show that they both knew what they were doing and deliberately intended to injure and kill James. I knew they did before I even reached the court.

The jury was made up of nine men and three women and I put my trust in them that they would come to the right verdict. When we arrived at court the following day, it was with a heavy heart that I forced myself to go back inside. Mr Henriques began to take the jury through some of the police transcripts of the interviews with Thompson and Venables. It was horrific.

The court heard how the two boys continually blamed

each other for the attacks on James. Jurors looked shocked when they heard how Thompson had said that Jon threw a brick in James's face and that he fell on the floor, his face bleeding profusely. Thompson continued with blaming Venables, insisting that he had smashed James in the face with a stick and battered him with an iron bar. Venables, they were told, said that Thompson picked James up and slammed him to the ground, leaving him with injuries to his head. And so the evidence went on, with everyone in the room listening in stunned silence.

When Mr Henriques was finished, he spoke to the jurors about the importance of establishing that the boys knew that what they were doing was wrong, just as the police had explained to us. Then they were handed a bundle of photographs depicting scenes from that day. He talked them through each picture and then warned them as they came to the most horrific ones.

'Members of the jury,' he said, 'the remaining photographs are unpleasant to look at and I invite you to steel yourselves. I should warn you now that you are going to see pictures of the scene after James's body was found.'

It was almost too much for me to bear. I put my head in my hands and closed my eyes, trying to block out what these poor jurors were being forced to witness. All I could see and hear in my mind was James screaming for help, blood pouring down his face. I wanted to throw up but sat motionless in my seat.

The graphic pictures the jurors were shown demonstrated the savage injuries to James's head and body. I don't know if those twelve men and women will ever have been able to get those visions out of their heads.

Thompson and Venables squirmed and fidgeted through-out but still I saw no shame, no sorrow or remorse. The evidence continued on, outlining minute by minute what had occurred on 12 February. I was glad when the day was over as it was really beginning to take its toll on me.

The following day I went with Denise to hospital for a check-up on the pregnancy. The doctor said that she and the baby were doing great. It was welcome news to know that our baby was safe and well, especially after the stress of the previous two days. As Kirsty had been stillborn, the fear for our unborn child was always in the back of our minds. And James had now been taken from us as well, so the life of this unborn child was unbelievably important to us. It also brought so many mixed emotions. Here I was, soon to be a father again, and yet I was hearing the most unthinkable details of what had happened to my son only a few months before. I couldn't help thinking that it was a fucked-up world that we lived in. I wanted this baby so much, but I was also petrified of bringing another child into a society that could be so cruel and heartless. I held Denise's hand as we left the hospital that day, and we both allowed ourselves to smile a little at the good news we had received. We had to hold on to something positive because everything else was so grim.

'We'll get through this,' I told Denise. 'At least we have each other and our new baby.'

'I know,' she replied softly.

The CCTV videotape of James being led away from the shopping centre was played to the jury that day when I was absent from court. I was glad I didn't have to sit and watch that again. I thought back to the first time I had seen it shortly after James went missing. I remember feeling so relieved that he was with two young boys because I believed with all my heart that he would be OK and would be brought home to us.

When I returned to court the following day, I saw many of the witnesses who had seen James that day describe in detail what had happened. Some of them looked destroyed and shaken, but to this day I have never blamed them for not stepping in to help my son. They were not bad people. They didn't know that two kids were about to brutalize and murder a little boy. They also have to live with knowing they didn't intervene and I am sure that is a heavy burden to bear. When I had first seen the CCTV footage of the boys with James, it didn't cross my mind that they were going to cause him any harm, and he was my son. So how on earth could total strangers have guessed any other way? Every one of them should have a clear conscience.

The final straw for me came that morning as the emotional and tearful witnesses took the stand, one by one. I kept looking at Thompson and Venables in the dock, watching to see if they would react in any way to what they were hearing, but they weren't even listening. And then it happened. As one woman broke down in tears giving her evidence, I saw these two boys giggling and laughing to each other, heads bowed down, oblivious to the distress of everyone around them. They were smirking and sharing a private joke between them and I felt something snap inside of me.

When the court broke for lunch, I said to Jimmy and Ray, 'I can't take this any more. I cannot sit and watch those evil monsters smirking and laughing as I listen to how they butchered my baby to death. I'll end up doing something stupid if I go back in there and I never want to see their faces again. It's too much for me. I didn't think it was possible for children to be so cruel and calculating.'

'Go home, Ralph,' said Jimmy. 'You've done your duty and we will stay in court and let you know what is happening.'

I didn't return to court after that for the duration of the trial, until near the end, when the verdict was due. Ray and Jimmy would report back to us at the close of each day, although I didn't really want to hear what they had to say. It was like the 'full up' sign had come on and I was close to breaking point. I learned that some of the weapons used on James were shown to the jury, including bloodstained stones and bricks, and a rusty fishplate metal bar. James's clothes were also shown to the court.

The Home Office pathologist, Dr Alan Williams, talked the jury through his examinations and spoke of how James had met his death.

He said, 'In my opinion the cause of death was the result of multiple head injuries. There were forty-two injuries externally, including fifteen to the front of his face. There were extensive skull fractures. There are so many injuries to the scalp and skull, one cannot single out one particular blow to the head and say that was the one that was fatal. I would estimate there were at least thirty separate blows to the body. The majority were due to heavy blunt objects and, given the amount of brick dust at the scene, I consider bricks to be a likely implement. The imprint on James's face appeared to have been caused by stamping or kicking from a shoe. I am certain that death was caused by the head injuries and not by transection by the train, but there is evidence to show he did not die immediately. There may have been a short period of survival, maybe only a few minutes, after the fractures.'

Expert witnesses were also called to explain much of the evidence and how it linked the two boys to James and his killing. Child psychiatrists, who had interviewed Thompson and Venables, testified that they were sure the boys knew that what they were doing was wrong. Consultant child psychiatrist Dr Eileen Vizard told the court how she had interviewed Robert a fortnight before the start of the trial. She insisted she was satisfied that he knew the difference between right and wrong and that he would have known so on the day of James's murder. Her evidence included her findings that she believed Robert would also have known it was wrong to take a child from a mother, wrong to cause injuries to a child and wrong to leave an injured child on a railway line. She was cross-examined by Robert's barrister, Mr David Turner, who asked her if she thought Robert was suffering from post-traumatic stress symptoms and she replied, 'Yes'.

Prosecutor Mr Henriques responded to this evidence when he re-examined Dr Vizard.

'Did you find that there was any abnormality of mind at the time of the alleged killing?' he asked.

She replied, 'There was no evidence in my opinion on the balance of probability of post-traumatic stress disorder being present before the killing. What I have indicated in my report was that on the balance of probabilities this boy seemed to be suffering from two things: academic disorder and conduct disorder.'

Academic disorder, she explained, was when a child may

have problems at school such as keeping up with lessons or playing truant. Conduct disorder, she added, was unusually disturbed behaviour resulting in lying, bullying or picking fights.

'It is possible to have both these disorders and still distinguish between right and wrong as a child,' she concluded.

It was the job of Consultant Adolescent Forensic Psychiatrist Dr Susan Bailey to assess Jon Venables. She confirmed that he too would have known it was wrong to take a child, injure him and leave him on a railway track. She added that he was of average intelligence. During her cross-examination she said that each time she asked Jon about James, he had cried inconsolably.

The police began to give their evidence and several days were spent listening to the taped interviews of the boys. It was, apparently, deeply disturbing to hear the squeaky, high-pitched voices of children talking about the murder they had committed. As the prosecution case drew to a close, it was time for the defence to make their case. But no witnesses were called and neither of the boys was called to give evidence on their own behalf.

Mr Henriques finished the week in court with his closing speech, insisting to the jury that Thompson and Venables had carried out a murderous act on a small child.

'If ever a crime was committed jointly and together, then this was that crime,' he continued.

Counsel on behalf of the boys began their closing speeches on Monday, 22 November, the fifteenth day of the trial. Mr Turner, representing Robert Thompson, took to his feet first to give his closing speech.

He said, 'The sorrow and the pain of Denise Bulger and

her husband dominate this trial. Those of us who have children must find the depth of their grief unimaginable. As I address you I can only hope to reflect the dignity that has been shown by the Bulger family in this harrowing trial.

'When the news of young James Bulger and the manner of his death became known on St Valentine's Day this year, the city of Liverpool missed a heartbeat and the nation was shrouded in grief. This case is not the tragedy of one family, but three families – a tragedy for the Bulger family, yes, but also for the families of Jon Venables and Robert Thompson.

'In this case there have been many tears shed, public tears and private tears, tears in the witness box, tears in the public gallery, tears in the dock – but those who have been dry-eyed in this case may also be feeling pain and misery. No one who has been involved with this case will ever be the same again. None of us will ever see a child separated from his or her mother in a shopping centre without remembering James Bulger.

'And what of you? Those of you with children will inevitably have identified yourselves and your children and your own experience with the facts that have occurred in this case. You will each take with you from this trial some terrible moment.'

He went on to argue that the murder was not planned, but was a case of mischief that went badly wrong. He added, 'They did get on the railway. What happened there was terrible and terrifying. You know that Robert's case is, and always has been, that the attack on little James was initiated and carried out by Jon Venables. It is no pleasant case for us to make that accusation against another eleven-year-old boy, but we say for whatever reason, petulant tiredness, a sudden mood swing, Jon Venables unhappily and tragically carried out a sudden but sustained attack on little James.'

Mr Brian Walsh QC followed with his closing speech on behalf of Jon Venables. He said, 'The prosecution say that Robert Thompson is a liar, a sophisticated liar who lied from beginning to end. I regret to say we agree. He lied to put the blame on Jon Venables and shuffle it off himself. He treated the police interview as a debate, a challenge, a sparring match. He was confident and assertive, the sort of person who would only admit something if you caught him in the act or produced a film of him doing it. Was there a word of remorse, an expression of sympathy or shame for what undoubtedly happened in his presence?'

He went on to stress to the jury that it was Jon Venables who had told the truth and deliberately missed James with bricks and only threw small stones, not wanting to hurt him. If he only wanted to hurt James, he concluded, then he was guilty of manslaughter and not murder.

The case was finished for both the prosecution and the defence, and all that remained was for the judge to carry out his summing-up of the trial before the jury retired to consider their verdict. Denise and I intended to be in court for their decision.

10

The Verdict

The judge, the Honourable Mr Justice Morland, spoke to the jury at length the following day. I wasn't in court to hear him, but the court transcripts relay some of what he said.

'All of those involved in this case will have been emotionally affected by the circumstances of James Bulger's death, but I am sure each of you will assess the evidence and reach your conclusions dispassionately and objectively and will not allow your emotions to cloud your judgement.

'You may think the evidence is overwhelming that James Bulger was abducted and that both defendants were involved physically in taking James Bulger from the Strand precinct to the railway line. You may also think that by the conclusions of their separate interviews each defendant had admitted the abduction of James Bulger.

'You may think the evidence is overwhelming that James Bulger was unlawfully killed and whichever of the defendants it was who inflicted those injuries intended either to kill James Bulger or to do him really serious injury.

'The crucial question is not what was their intention when James Bulger was taken from the Strand or during the long walk of over two miles to the railway line, but what was the intention of each defendant on the railway line when the fatal injuries were inflicted. This was not a single throwing of a stone or brick but involved a number of blows to the skull of a two-, nearly three-year-old boy. You will consider why James Bulger was stripped of his shoes, trousers and underpants when he was attacked, and why the body was moved from one part of the track near the wall to the other line. Was that to suggest that the child had been subject to some form of assault by an adult, and then run over by a train? Was that to conceal or attempt to conceal the true cause of death?'

The judge continued a lengthy examination of the prosecution case for the jury, outlining the injuries and the witness accounts of what they had seen. His summing-up continued into the last day of the trial, when I returned to the court for the final time, this time with Denise. It was Wednesday, 24 November 1993.

It was an incredibly nerve-wracking day for us both, but more so for Denise because this would be the first time she would see her son's killers. I know how it had affected me so I was really worried about her health, and the impact this might have on her, as she was only weeks from giving birth. I knew I would have to be there for her, to protect her. I didn't want to see Venables and Thompson again myself, but we both knew we had to hear the verdict passed on the animals who had taken our baby boy.

We decided that it was best for her not to go into the courtroom for longer than absolutely necessary, and so the court provided a private waiting room for our family where she stayed while the trial wrapped up. I went back and forth throughout the day, giving Denise updates. I remember walking into the waiting room and seeing her sitting there looking so small and lost.

'Don't worry, Denise, the jury will see them for what they are.' I tried in vain to convince her that the outcome of the trial would be good.

'What if they find them not guilty? What if they let them go?' her anguished voice replied.

'They won't, I'm sure of it,' I responded. 'But are you sure you want to see them?'

'I have no choice,' she whispered bravely. 'I have to look at them and see for myself who was responsible for killing our son. I hate them but I have to be here for James.'

I had the same fears running through my mind. What if the jury found them not guilty of murdering James? Would that mean these boys would be back on the streets looking for more victims? I prayed that they would come to the right decision. I felt exactly the same as Denise. This was the last place on earth I wanted to be, but we both had to be there in the hope that justice would be served for the slaughter of our innocent baby.

It was a horrible morning that seemed to last for ever. We had plenty of family in court that day to support us but the waiting was almost intolerable. When the judge had finished summing up, the jury retired with a long list of questions they had been asked to consider in order to determine the appropriate verdict. In the meantime, a legal argument was held regarding the identities of the two boys on trial. Until this point, they had only been referred to as Child A and Child B. Their identities were still not known to the wider public. The judge ruled that he would not make a decision on releasing the boys' identities until the jury had delivered their verdict.

We were warned that the jury was likely to spend at least one night away from court deliberating the case as there was so much to consider. I spent most of the afternoon pacing up and down and trying to bring comfort to Denise. The tension was almost unbearable for us both.

It was towards the end of the day, and already dark outside, when our police liaison officers came into the waiting room to tell us that the jury was about to return to court and that they had reached their verdict. I couldn't believe it.

'Oh God,' I thought. 'This must mean they have found them not guilty.'

I looked at Denise and she stared back at me. Her face had dropped and she was visibly shaken. I felt myself shaking inside too, but I had to get a grip on myself.

'Are you ready for this, Denise?' I asked her softly. 'Are you sure you want to go in there?'

'Yes, let's go,' she said, her eyes blazing with determination.

I was so proud of Denise and marvelled at how strong she was being. I held her hand and squeezed it tight as we were ushered discreetly into the courtroom without having to go through the public waiting areas. We took our reserved seats in silence and I put my arm around Denise.

'It will be OK,' I whispered to her.

Robert Thompson and Jon Venables were by now in the dock waiting for the jury to return. They sat like stone, not showing any emotion at what was about to occur. The public and press began to pour back into the room and there was some chaos as people tried to scramble for their seats. It was mayhem for a few short minutes.

I sensed Denise staring at the boys and tightened my grip around her.

'I can't believe it,' she said, as she shook her head in shock. 'They are only children themselves.'

Once the chaos settled down and everyone was in their seats, the atmosphere seemed to freeze. It was so tense and quiet, you could have heard a pin drop. My heart was beating ten to the dozen and my mouth went as dry as the desert as we watched and waited for something to happen.

The court clerk asked the jury foreman if they had reached a verdict on the first charge of attempting to abduct Diane Power's son.

'No,' he replied.

There was a huge gasp around the room and I hung my head, waiting for more terrible news.

Then the clerk asked if the jury had a reached a verdict on the second charge and the foreman responded:

'Yes.'

The gasp went round again. The suspense was intolerable.

'Do you find Robert Thompson guilty or not guilty of abducting James Bulger?' the clerk continued.

'Guilty,' he replied.

'Do you find Jon Venables guilty or not guilty of abducting James Bulger?'

'Guilty,' he repeated.

'And that is the verdict of you all?'

'Yes.'

I tightened my grip around Denise as we waited for more. Neither of us spoke a word, rooted to the spot.

The foreman said the jury had also reached a verdict on the third charge.

Once more, in a calm and unruffled manner, the clerk asked, 'Do you find Robert Thompson guilty or not guilty of the murder of James Bulger?'

'Guilty,' he replied.

'Do you find Jon Venables guilty or not guilty of the murder of James Bulger?'

'Guilty,' came his final response.

At that point, the whole room breathed out collectively and gasped as one at the verdicts.

All around me I could hear people whispering and chattering their delight. I thought I was going to combust on the spot. It was the right result; it meant that my son's killers were now going to be punished for the terrible crimes they had committed against him, but I didn't feel euphoric. I slowly leant in and kissed Denise on the cheek. Less than six hours after retiring to consider the case, the jury had returned unanimous verdicts that these two little devils had deliberately tortured and murdered James.

'We got them,' I whispered.

She didn't move, almost overwhelmed by the events of the last few minutes. Albert Kirby came over and kissed Denise on her cheek and firmly shook my hand. I squeezed his hand tight. This man and his team had been responsible for ensuring James's killers were brought to justice and, for that, we would always be in his debt.

I looked to the dock and Robert Thompson sat unmoved, as he had done throughout. Jon Venables, meanwhile, was sobbing hysterically. They were tears of self-pity and concern for himself. They were not tears of remorse or sorrow for our defenceless baby. I felt not one ounce of compassion for either of them.

The jury was dismissed after they failed to reach a unanimous decision on the attempted abduction of Diane Power's son. This was a difficult verdict for them to arrive at because the boys had not actually taken the little boy away, and proving their intent was not easy. It was a lesser charge, but it was still the one that they got away with. I'm not sure why they didn't find them guilty, because Venables had admitted to the police they had planned to snatch the child and shove him under a bus to make his death look accidental, but if any of the jurors had any doubts then they would have had to acquit them both. I was just so relieved that they had been found guilty of the worst charges against James.

There were still a few loose ends for the judge to tie up, including the issue of the boys' identification. It was a tense moment, because at this point the general public still had no idea who James's killers were. His ruling that followed was exactly what my whole family had hoped for. He took the decision to lift his original ban on naming the two boys. This would mean that the whole world would now learn the names of the boys who had killed James. All that was left was for the judge to pass sentence on the child defendants. His words have often been repeated, but on that day he spoke directly to the little schoolboys in the dock. I don't think the gravity of what he had to say had any impact on either of them, but here is what he told them.

'The killing of James Bulger was an act of unparalleled evil and barbarity. This child of two was taken from his mother on a journey of over two miles and then, on the railway line, was battered to death without mercy. Then his body was placed across a railway line so that it would be run over by a train, in an attempt to conceal the murder. In my judgement, your conduct was both cunning and very wicked.

'The sentence that I pass upon you both is that you should be detained during Her Majesty's pleasure in such a place and under such conditions as the Secretary of State may now direct and that means you will be securely detained for very, very many years until the Home Secretary is satisfied that you have matured and are fully rehabilitated and are no longer a danger.'

I continued to hold Denise close and the judge's words brought me some very real comfort, for he too had recognized that they were evil, cunning and wicked. It would be easy for me to say that as James's dad, but here was a clever, learned and experienced judge who shared the same opinion as me. Denise remained motionless, but I could feel her body shaking as she hung on tight to me for all she was worth.

As Venables continued crying and Thompson appeared to gasp for air, the judge ordered the boys to be taken down from the court, and as they stood to go, Denise's brother Ray stood up and yelled at them.

'How do you feel now, you little bastards?'

I couldn't have put it better myself.

I think the judge must have known that feelings would be running very high, and he had watched as my family acted with dignity and restraint throughout the whole trial. It says a lot that he didn't react to Ray's outburst, which in many instances would have been seriously frowned upon.

It was said in the heat of the moment and the judge allowed it to pass without comment.

After they had gone, the judge continued:

'How it came about that two mentally normal boys aged ten, of average intelligence, committed this terrible crime is very hard to comprehend. It is not for me to pass judgement on their upbringing, but I suspect that exposure to violent video films may in part be an explanation. In fairness to Mrs Thompson and Mr and Mrs Venables, it is very much to their credit that during the police interviews they used every effort to get their sons to tell the truth.

'The people of Bootle and Walton and all involved in this tragic case will never forget the tragic circumstances of James Bulger's murder. Everyone in court will especially wish Mrs Bulger well in the months ahead and hope that the new baby will bring her peace and happiness. I hope that all involved in this case, whether witness or otherwise, will find peace at Christmas time.'

The judge had spoken from the heart, but nothing was ever going to bring James back. As much as we were excited and overjoyed to be having a new baby, it could never be a replacement for the son we had lost, and nothing could ever erase the horrors in our minds about what had befallen our baby that terrible day.

The police had done a brilliant job, as had the courts, and as for the jury I will never be able to thank them enough. I put my trust in their wisdom and judgement and they did not let us down. They saw with their own eyes what these two boys did to a little child and they delivered the right verdict. The burden on any jury is heavy, but for a trial like this it must have been immense.

The long day was over and I felt drained. Both Denise and I just wanted to leave the court, and Preston, and return to the safety of Kirkby and our home. There were no celebrations that night. We were relieved at the outcome, but we could not find anything to be happy about. If anything, seeing two young boys convicted of such a heinous crime made us feel even worse. James had died so needlessly, and even though the jury had unanimously convicted both boys, we still didn't know why it had happened. No reasons had ever been put forward in the court and Thompson and Venables themselves had never tried to explain why they carried out this sickening crime. Their only response when asked by police why they killed James was to blame each other, and so neither of them ever took responsibility for their actions, burying our chance of ever finding out why they behaved as they did. That has never changed. Even the judge could not fathom how this terrible crime had come about. He recognized their evil and cunning but not their motives.

When I got home, I retreated into my shell. Denise did the same. It was a pattern that was emerging between us because we had simply run out of words. Denise also needed to rest, as to say the day had taken its toll on her would be an understatement. It had been a gruelling few weeks, and we all wanted it over. Now it was, I couldn't understand why I didn't feel more jubilant. Of course I wanted the killers to be convicted for murdering James, but it didn't bring him back to me. That's all I had ever wanted: my normal and simple life with my wife and my child. I had never asked for much. I didn't expect riches or a life of glamour and luxury. I didn't even expect life to be that easy.

I was used to struggling to make ends meet, but I certainly didn't expect it to be this hard. I had always been content to be at the heart of my family life and that was enough for me.

Now I began to question why such a terrible thing had happened to my son and to our family. I'm not saying that it should have happened to any family, far from it. But you can't help question why you are singled out to bear such tragedy. Worse still, why was James subjected to such horror, before he even had the chance to grow up? Every time I thought of my own pain, it took me back to what my son must have endured that day, and I realized that I would never know suffering on the scale that he did.

That night, I took a bottle of scotch, slumped into a corner of the bedroom and held one of James's pillows from his bed. I cradled it as tightly but as gently as I could, wishing with all my might that it was my baby boy. I would have loved to write him a letter, but I am not educated and didn't have the ability to put my thoughts into words. As ever, I began to talk out loud to him. I felt I owed it to him to let him know what had happened.

'My beautiful James. I went to court today to see the boys that hurt you. The judge has said they are going to be punished for what they did to you and I am very glad. I'm sorry they hurt you so badly and I'm sorry I wasn't there to protect you or help you, but we got some justice for you today, son. I hate the boys who did this to you. Now I can see what you had to go through and it breaks my heart, but I know you are in a better place. I know how much you suffered and I know you screamed for your mummy and daddy and we weren't there. It wasn't because we didn't love you. We didn't know where you were or how to help you.

'I tried, James, I really did. I tried to find you and I hope you can forgive me for not being there. If I could give my life for yours, I would do it in a second. You were the most precious thing I have ever had. I would give anything to hear you laugh again. I would give anything to see you running around like a maniac and making everyone laugh. Most of all I would give anything to hold you in my arms right now and hear you calling me "your Ralph". You are my James and I will always be your Ralph, darling boy. I will always be your daddy, who cared so much you will never know. I am holding your pillow close to me right now. I can still smell you. I can still feel you, close to me. I like to think you are still close to me and I hope you feel me close to you.

'Do you remember when you played on your go-kart and when we used to play football? They were the most wonderful times of my life, James. No one is ever going to hurt you again now, my precious boy. Your mummy loves you and misses you so much. I know she has told you that. When I think of you, I think of nothing but joy and happiness. I am going to hang on to those memories because I am so sad to be without you. I think all the time of you in heaven, running around and being mischievous but loving at the same time. I see your smiling face and it makes me happy, but I am devastated that I will never feel you in my arms again. I want to feel you curl up in bed with me, getting warm and feeling safe, loved and cherished.

'You would have been an amazing person if you had been given the chance to live. I know you would have grown into the most special human being with so much love and kindness to give. The boys that hurt you didn't have what you have – a soul and a heart as big as the moon. I wish you could teach the world how to be so lovely. I miss you so much, James.

'I love you with all my heart. I'm so sorry I didn't save you. Goodnight, my beautiful boy. Your Ralph.'

When I finished speaking to James, I just broke down and wept like a child myself. Those boys had ripped a baby apart like a rag doll, and in the process they had torn a family to shreds. Any hint of joy in our lives from here on in would forever be laced with sadness because James will be missing from us always. His killers may have been taken away to a secure unit, but they were still drawing breath, having their needs catered for and being looked after. They would wake up in their beds every morning and start a new day. That is a luxury they stole from my boy. I knew they would never understand what misery and suffering they had caused and I prayed they would be locked up for ever, never to see daylight again.

Stringent gagging orders had replaced the judge's original ban on the media revealing the boys' identities. Now the press could print their names, and photographs from the time of their arrest, but from that point on, strict injunctions were placed on revealing anything about their subsequent whereabouts and the release of any further photographs other than those that had already been seen. It was a very tight order and it was made clear to the media that anyone who broke the injunction would be in very serious trouble.

We knew the press attention would be on an unprecedented scale as the conviction of two children, so young, was making headlines around the world. What we didn't realize then was that the spotlight would never leave this case, and that so much more was to come.

11

The Battles Begin

Shortly after the trial, on 29 November, the judge recommended that the two boys serve a minimum sentence of eight years, which would have meant they would be eligible for release at the age of eighteen. That was the very first kick in the teeth we received from the judicial system. We learned of the sentence from our police liaison officers who came to visit me and Denise, and I suspect they were as gutted as I was, but both Jim and Mandy managed to keep their feelings in check because I don't think they wanted us to feel any worse than we already did. At least we were forewarned before the news got out, and we were able to bunker down and get out of the way of the inevitable media frenzy that was on its way.

'Eight fucking years! Is that all my son's life was worth?' I screamed in despair.

How could they judge that the life of a tiny baby, who suffered so much pain, be worth so little? It was as if someone was telling us that James's life meant nothing!

I understood that a minimum tariff didn't guarantee their release, but even the possibility of them being considered for freedom at that point was horrendous enough. If they only served eight years in juvenile detention, they would still be teenagers when they were released. What kind of a message was that sending out to society? It says that if you go and torture and murder a child you can be free again a few years later. I felt sick to the core and deeply disgusted with a country that I had always held in such high esteem.

After the trial judge set his tariff, the Lord Chief Justice at the time, Lord Taylor of Gosforth, almost immediately increased the minimum tariff to ten years without explanation, but that was still nowhere near enough in my eyes. They would still only be twenty if they were released. Both Denise and I knew we had to do something, so we launched a petition calling for the tariff to be substantially increased. Our campaign was immediately backed by the *Sun* newspaper and we were grateful that our message was being put out to the public. We threw everything we had at trying to get as many people as possible to sign the appeal, and that included a limited number of press interviews. This is where Denise and I were at our best. When our backs were against the wall, we came out fighting. It was a natural instinct for us both. We may not have been very good at talking to one another, or expressing our emotions in words, but this was one way we could show how we felt about our son in actions.

The campaign to collect signatures was not going to be an overnight job, but at least we had got it started. The *Sun* had printed a cut-out coupon in the paper for people to sign and send off if they agreed on the need to increase the minimum tariff for Thompson and Venables.

There had been some major changes in our lives in the run-up to the trial. Thousands of cards and letters, gifts and toys from across the UK and around the world had continued to pour into the police station on a daily basis, and a lot of the packages contained money. The general public were so generous and wanted to help in some way by donating cash. This made Denise and me feel very uncomfortable. We didn't want to appear ungrateful because we knew this was a way of people showing how much they cared, but we didn't feel it was right to take money because James had been murdered. The response to this crime was huge, as was the media attention, and so the police advised us that it might be a good idea to get ourselves a solicitor who could deal with all this on our behalf. We made some inquiries and decided to ask a locally based solicitor called Sean Sexton for help. He was distantly related to Denise's side of the family and thankfully he was happy to get involved. He became our legal adviser. This was important for us, because up until that point we had relied on our police family liaison officers for everything. We knew that their involvement with us would come to an end shortly after the trial, as the police's work on this case would be finished.

One of Sean's first jobs was to help us deal with all the post that was mounting up. He joined a team of four police officers who had already been tasked to start going through it all, and it took them a lot of man hours to sift through the piles of mail. Sean set up the James Bulger Memorial Appeal to be run by independent trustees, and by the time the trial started, a staggering £161,000 had been collected in donations. Denise and I just didn't know what to say when Sean broke the news to us. We were adamant that the money would be put to good use, in particular for young people. We really wanted a lasting memorial for James and so we came up with the idea to build the James Bulger Memorial Garden in the grounds of the Sacred Heart RC Primary School. It was the school I had attended, as well as several of James's cousins, and it would have been the school he would have gone to, if he had survived to start school. A special little place for the children to go and chat with friends if they wanted a bit of peace instead of playing games would be created and would be known as James's Corner. Both Denise and I loved the idea of this. Physically disabled children at a special school in Kirkby were also to benefit from the fund and a number of great schemes were put forward. It made things far more comfortable for us to know that it was the trustees who decided how the money should be spent and not us as a family. Obviously we had input, but the most important thing was that we did not hold the purse strings, because we wanted everyone who had donated even the smallest amount to know that their cash was being used properly and for the right causes.

Our first instinct had been to instruct Sean to give every last penny away to deserving causes in James's name. Sean, however, tried to persuade us that we could reach a compromise by using the money for worthy causes as well as providing some security for our own future. He knew that there would be many difficult days ahead for us emotionally, and easing the financial burden was one way of relieving some of the pressures. We also had a new baby on the way we needed to care for. It still didn't sit well with us, but we trusted in Sean's advice and we did accept some help from the trust early on to buy a small house in the Quarry Green area of Kirkby. It meant that we could move from our tiny one-bedroom flat to a modest three-bedroom house with its own back garden. With our new baby this would make a huge difference in our lives, and it was hoped that it would also provide us with a fresh start. It was so hard to remain in the flat where James had once lived with us.

The move meant we had a very busy time ahead. Denise was frantically preparing for the baby and couldn't keep still most days, while I was focusing on packing our belongings into boxes and making sure that Denise was well looked after. It was a relief to have something to occupy my mind and it also felt good to try to look forwards for a change, instead of permanently backwards. It didn't mean the damage from James's murder had healed. It just meant we had an alternative focus and an understanding that, however much it hurt, life still carried on. I knew I was never going to get over James, but I also had to be a good dad to my new baby. It was almost as if I had to break my life up into pieces and deal with one thing at a time. It was the only way I could manage it.

We moved into the new house after the trial and before Denise gave birth. One of the bonuses was that we were able to decorate and furnish a room for the new baby, a luxury we hadn't enjoyed in our small flat. It took my mind off my grief temporarily and kept me busy. We chose furniture together and I moved things around the house where Denise wanted them to go. I also painted and tinkered about the place, putting up curtains and fixing odd jobs. I smartened the house up for us and tried my best to move forward inch by inch. I enjoyed using my hands to do things and it helped to keep me off the drink, so I was at least functioning normally some of the time.

The imminent arrival of our new baby was certainly a great incentive to keep going. I have already described how Denise was putting all her energies into protecting the life growing inside of her, but as her due date drew closer, it gave me a focus too. I think it is harder for a man to be connected with his baby before it is born, but knowing my child was about to come into the world made me all the more determined to do my best. And so day-to-day life went on, but so, too, did the ache I felt for the loss of James and Kirsty. On the outside, I made every effort to stay strong for my children, even if I was falling apart inside.

On 16 December 1993, Michael James Bulger came into our lives and, for the very first time since our son was murdered, I felt real happiness. As with Kirsty and James, I was with Denise when she gave birth to Michael and it was magical when he appeared in the world for the first time. The relief was written all over Denise's face when she saw that he was a healthy little boy. She was exhausted and emotional, but her smile said it all. I could see she was fighting back the tears.

Just as I had with James, I fell in love instantly. When I held Michael close to me, I felt overwhelmed with love. It took me back to when I had held James for the first time and I could feel the tears welling up in my eyes. I didn't want my sadness for James to hijack the fantastic moment when this baby came into my life, but I couldn't make the grief disappear. It was like my happiness and sadness were all rolled into one huge emotion and it was very confusing. The birth of any child is a very moving moment, but it wasn't easy to step back from our feelings of loss over James. I think it almost made his death more noticeable.

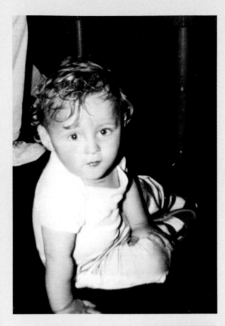

James was as bright as a button and the centre of our world.

I loved my wife and son so much and those years with James were fantastic for us as a family.

It's hard to look at how happy I was in this photograph and the one above.

We spent a lot of time at Jimmy and Karen's house. Here James is rushing after his cousins at their Halloween party (*right*), just before they dressed him up. And here he is smiling happily with his cousins (*at the back on his cousin Barry's lap*).

Jimmy and Karen in their kitchen.

The police asked us to do a press conference, to appeal for James's safe return. Denise's heartbreak was there for the world to see, and I wasn't in a much better shape.

MOTHERCARE

15:42:32 12/02/93 3HR

The image that haunted the world, of James being led away by his killers in the Strand shopping centre. When I saw the video I desperately wanted to reach inside the screen and pluck my son from danger.

This blurry image was also released, showing Robert Thompson and Jon Venables in the Strand.

ABOVE: The railway track where James was murdered and left to be cut in two by a train.

BELOW: Robert Thompson and Jon Venables, the ten-year-old killers of my beautiful son.

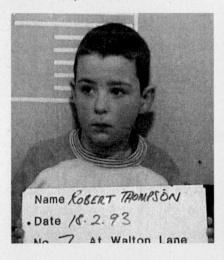

Name *ROBERT THOMPSON*

Date *18.2.93*

No. 7 At Walton Lane

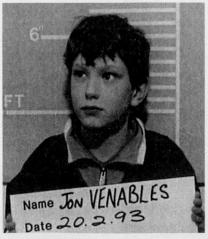

Name *JON VENABLES*

Date *20.2.93*

ABOVE: Carrying James on his last journey. My biggest fear was that I would collapse under the huge weight of grief.

RIGHT: After the funeral, I started drinking to numb the pain and would often find myself sitting by James's grave late at night. I felt I was protecting him by being there.

LEFT: Nothing can prepare you for the grief of losing a child. After James's death, it felt as if Denise and I were prisoners of our pain.

BELOW: With Denise and our baby son Michael, handing in a petition asking for the tariff on Venables and Thompson to be increased to life, in May 1994. It had been increased from eight to ten years; shortly after the petition was handed in it was increased to fifteen years.

LEFT: In October 2000 the original eight-year tariff was reinstated, which meant Thompson and Venables would soon be released. As part of our public appeal against Lord Woolf's decision, we released a video of James on the trampoline. For a brief moment my son was brought back to life.

RIGHT: Ten years after James had died and the pain was just as strong. I knew I should forgive myself for not protecting my son, but I couldn't.

LEFT: With our solicitor Robin Makin outside Liverpool Crown Court in June 2011, after our victim impact statements had been read to the Parole Board in Leeds. For once we had some success, and Venables, who was in prison for possessing child pornography, was not released.

With my brother Jimmy, who pledged to be with me all the way and has never let me down. He couldn't have been a better or more loving brother.

BELOW LEFT: My new partner Natalie has changed my world and has shown me that I can enjoy some happiness in my life.

BELOW RIGHT: My beautiful son James, with the cheeky grin that lit up the room. Sharing his love and joy in this book has given me a chance to celebrate all that he was.

Michael and James are two traditional names that have been used throughout the Bulger family history, but James was always chosen for the first-born son of each new generation. And so we opted for Michael for our new baby, with his second name chosen in memory of his elder brother.

'Hello, Michael James,' I whispered to him as I squashed my face into his warm skin. 'Your daddy is always going to protect you from danger, son. No one is ever going to hurt you, and when you are older, I'm gonna tell you all about your big brother and sister that you never got to meet. You would have loved them both and they will always be part of our family.'

I turned to Denise and said, 'Our son is beautiful. He's amazing.'

'He's gorgeous, isn't he?' she whispered, smiling back at me.

His hair seemed darker than James's, but he was so cute with the same blue eyes. He was as light as a feather and I wanted him to feel all my love and care as I held him to me before passing him back to his mum. Denise and I were overjoyed with Michael's arrival, but I felt enormous pressure too. All parents experience some nerves with a new baby, but this was different. I was petrified of anything happening to my son; I felt a real and acute fear lodged in the pit of my stomach. I never wanted to let this child be hurt or harmed in any way.

When James had come home with us I obviously wanted to nurture and take care of him, but never in my wildest dreams could I have imagined what dangers lay ahead for him. No one would have thought that such a murder was possible, but now I knew it was, and my view of the world had changed for ever. Would I ever allow Michael to go and play with his friends and have a normal childhood after what had happened to James? The whole thought of it filled me with horror. I wanted to keep this boy under lock and key, but what sort of life would he have then?

Denise and I had been overprotective of James after the loss of Kirsty, but this was a whole new ball game, and I wasn't sure how I was going to adapt. I even questioned if I was fit to be a parent, continually blaming myself for James's murder. What if I couldn't protect my new son? What if someone tried to hurt him too?

'Please, God,' I prayed. 'Don't let any harm come to this baby. Don't let us suffer any more. We have already been through too much and I couldn't bear the pain of losing another baby.'

It was a silent prayer but, with every fibre in my body, I hoped that someone out there would hear me.

When we brought Michael home, the conflicting emotions kept gnawing away at me. He was a sheer delight and, as with James, every day spent with him was a joy. He was a quiet baby, unlike his brother, and he was very easy to care for. I felt a great deal of comfort when I held him, knowing that he was safe and in my arms. It was a relief to have moved from our old flat, as the memories of having James there would have been almost too tragic to deal with. In our new place, Michael had his own room, which meant there were no comparisons to be made with where James had once slept as a baby.

Michael was born just a few days before Christmas, and we couldn't have been blessed with a more perfect gift. Even so, it was a difficult Christmas that year, as it would come to be every year. But the first one without James left the biggest void imaginable. I'm glad Michael was too young to know anything about that Christmas, because I don't think I would have been able to put on a brave face for him and pretend to enjoy such a traditionally happy time of year. The reality was, it was sheer hell. Gone was the boisterous Christmas morning noise from James I had loved so much the previous year. There was no tearing of wrapping paper or squealing with delight at his new toys. No son to fling himself in my arms and shout, 'Cor, thanks, Ralph! Look at my new toys!'

James had adored Christmas. It was a time of year that could have been made especially for him, and he had just reached the age where he could really appreciate everything about it. He had loved the presents, the food, the family gatherings and, of course, being spoiled to high heaven by everyone who saw him. I remembered the last Christmas, when he was so happy sitting around playing games and watching his new videos on the television. It was impossible trying to get him to bed in the evening because he was so overexcited, but he made Christmas such a special and happy occasion. Now there was nothing left and nothing to celebrate.

I knew I had a lot still to be thankful for. I had my wife and our new son, but that Christmas morning my grief seemed to grow out of proportion. Maybe it was because everyone expects you to be happy and full of ho-ho-ho, but I couldn't bring myself to lie and make out that I was feeling OK. I spent the day at home with Denise and Michael, and though a Christmas dinner was served up for me, I hardly touched it. The festivities meant absolutely nothing to me, and so I reached for the bottle and got drunk, hoping that when I woke up it would all be over and I could get back on with normal life. The rest of the day was just a blur. Relatives came and went – I would have another drink with them and I suppose I must have had some conversations with them and wished them Merry Christmas, but I have very little recollection of the day itself. For the best part I sat and stared into space, living my life in my head and thinking of happier times with James.

The one thing I can remember is looking out the window once it had gone dark. It was very black and cold outside with a tiny spattering of stars. There was one particular star that was brighter than all the rest and it seemed to be winking at me. I smiled and allowed myself to believe it was James looking down on me to see if I was OK. It reminded me of his favourite nursery rhyme too – 'Twinkle, Twinkle, Little Star'.

'Merry Christmas, my beautiful James,' I said. 'I miss you more than you will ever know.'

In my head, I imagined him repling, 'Merry Christmas, Ralph. I love you.'

I carried on drinking for the rest of the evening until I passed out where I was sitting, waking up on the sofa in the morning. Boxing Day was pretty much the same – more drinking and more misery. It wouldn't be until a few days later that I shook myself out of the self pity I had shrouded myself in during the Christmas period. It wasn't fair on Denise, who was shouldering all the responsibility for our new son, and I began to clear my head once again.

*

Despite having a new baby to keep us both busy, there was still tension at home. Denise and I had been through so much over the past year, we were both exhausted and wrung out. I felt as if I could no longer reach her. I couldn't talk to her about James because I had tried to protect her from knowing the worst of what had happened to him and I still wanted to do so. I was too scared to tell her how I really felt inside, because I knew it would hurt her. With hindsight, I think this is probably a common reaction for parents in our situation, and because Denise and I had shared this same tragedy, she was the wrong person for me to turn to, to pour my heart out. It was like there was this big white elephant sitting in the room, and instead of confronting it, I took huge strides to walk around it.

The chasm that had opened up between us seemed to be getting deeper and wider with every day that passed. We were both unhappy, despite the arrival of baby Michael. Our combined love for this little miracle was never in question, but I began to wonder if Denise and I would make it through together.

In times of extreme tragedy, particularly when a couple loses a child under any circumstances, it either binds you closer together or it savages you apart. Sadly, it appeared we were beginning to unravel at the seams, and we started to row and fall out. I have previously said that I blamed Denise for James's loss, but that was not why our marriage was in trouble. I no longer felt she was to blame and deeply regretted my initial feelings towards her, which were cruel and unfair. Our rows were meaningless and petty, and we weren't even arguing all the time as I was still really quiet. It was more a case of what we didn't say to each other. I can't have been easy to live with, with my silence and my drinking, but we certainly didn't set out to hurt one another.

In the New Year of 1994 I set myself some fresh targets: to quit the drinking and to get myself fit so I could look after my family properly. There was plenty for me to do around the house and I kept myself busy with DIY jobs and helping Denise to look after Michael. He was a cracking baby and he had this funny little gurgle as if he was trying to giggle. That always put a smile on my face.

The signatures on our petition against the tariff were growing all the time and so we continued to monitor those as well as get on with our ordinary day-to-day lives. We got up, fed, bathed and clothed Michael, did some jobs, went shopping, ate our dinner and eventually went to sleep at night. It was busy with a newborn but pretty humdrum. Routine helped me to stay focused, but I hadn't quit the drink completely. It came in bouts and then I would pick myself up and start all over again.

I found it hard to confide in people, but I found a true friend in Father Michael, who had conducted James's funeral. I knew him as Mick the priest, and he wasn't your average holy man. He was different to a lot of other priests I had ever met, more open and honest, and I felt that I could be myself with him. To put it bluntly, he knew I was really fucked up over James's murder, and however much I tried to act normal, I wasn't. He might have been a priest but he did things his way, and he knew that the best way to break the ice with me was to sit in the pub and talk, allowing me to get some of my sorrow and anger off my chest. He loved the people of Kirkby and he understood that drinking was the way many of them dealt with tragedies, just as I was doing. It was a little bit like have a counselling session, but over a bevvy. I wouldn't say we had arguments about things, but I would swear at him and vent my fury, and he would swear back at me. There were times we really laughed together too, although they were rare moments.

'If God exists, then why did he let this happen to my son?' I would rant at him. 'Why didn't he save James from those boys?'

Mick would respond, 'Because we know God works in mysterious ways.'

That would set me off again, but Mick never got angry with me. Instead he just allowed me to let everything out of my system. Not once did he try to drum the Catholic religion down my throat and I felt safe sharing my feelings with him. He was an amazing confidant, and if it wasn't for Mick I would have stayed locked away by myself for far longer than I did. He encouraged me to get out, even if it was to the pub. I needed answers still, and because Mick was a man of the church I believed he would be able to give them to me. I never got them and I never will, but even today, I would do anything for Father Mick. He was there for me at a terrible time and just listened and tried to help in the best way he could, and when he eventually got moved away to another parish by the church, I was devastated.

Father Mick constantly explained that I was not to blame for James's death, but it wasn't easy to accept that there was nothing I could have done. I don't think the guilt will ever leave me and so I will have to try and find some way of dealing with that in the future.

*

By February 1994, Denise and I were facing the first anniversary of James's death and it was truly awful. I didn't want to acknowledge it, but I knew I couldn't let the day pass without honouring my son's memory. Denise and I decided we would keep things simple by visiting his grave and laying some flowers for him, but it was a huge task. Neither of us could put into words how we were feeling and so we spent a quiet day, each isolated in our private thoughts and memories of James. I could scarcely believe a whole year had gone by without him, but it was to be the first of many sad and difficult anniversaries we would go through.

It also brought the case back into the media spotlight, and that was always hard for us to cope with. The pain was as fresh as it was when I was first told James was dead, and I couldn't wait for the day to end.

It was around the time of the first anniversary of James's murder that I met a woman called Eileen, who would become a huge part of my life. She lived locally in Kirkby and we were introduced by a mutual friend. Like me, she was fairly quiet, and even though she was younger than me at eighteen, she came across as mature and sensible for her age. We would bump into each other on nights out, and would end up chatting to each other. I found her easy to talk to, and chatting with her would, at least briefly, take my mind away from the horrors of the last eighteen months. She wasn't carrying any of the baggage that I was and being in her company reminded me of what life had been like before I lost James.

As we grew closer, I found her to be patient and kind. She didn't pry too much about James and that was a welcome relief. When I did open up to her about him, I didn't feel guilty in the way I would with Denise, where I was always tiptoeing around the issue because I hated to see her upset.

Eventually, the friendship spilled over into romance and I began seeing Eileen regularly. I'm not proud of this but my marriage had been ripped apart by what we had gone through and Eileen was a huge support to me when I really needed someone to turn to.

By June of that year we had managed to collect nearly 280,000 signatures supporting our petition to raise the tariff on Thompson and Venables' sentence. Six thousand of those we had collected ourselves, and the rest were made up of the coupons that had been cut out from the newspaper, as well as over a thousand supporting letters. We thought that was a great show of solidarity and it gave us renewed strength to carry on for James. Together, Denise and I travelled to Downing Street to hand the signatures to the Home Secretary of the day, Michael Howard, and our journey was covered by both print and television journalists.

We didn't know what to expect from the petition but at least this was a very public statement of protest, not just from James's family, but from ordinary people too. It didn't take long for Mr Howard to respond. The next month he publicly announced that he was raising the tariff again so that James's killers would be kept in custody for a minimum of fifteen years, by which time they would be twenty-five years old.

I would have liked them to serve life imprisonment, but at least this increase was better than an eight-year tariff. From the outset, Denise and I made our views very clear. We never wanted either of them to be released, but given that this outcome was unlikely, we wanted to ensure they would never be freed while there was even a slight possibility that either of them posed a risk to other children. As I believed they would always pose a risk, that remained my argument throughout for keeping them locked up for ever.

Michael Howard's new tariff had restored a little bit of our faith in the legal system, but even the news from Downing Street didn't relieve our suffering. We still had to live with the knowledge that James had died in such a terrible way and we would face that for the rest of our lives. The strain was with us constantly.

Then Denise found out about Eileen and we had some very difficult conversations about our future. As much as I cared for Eileen, I also had so much history with Denise and I felt terrible that I had failed her as well as failing James. She wanted to try to save the marriage and thought a trip away would give us the chance to work on our problems, as well as giving us some distance from the events of the last year.

I have some relatives who live in Australia, and so Denise organized for us to fly out to Adelaide to stay with my Uncle Jim and Aunt Moira. The problem was, she hadn't told me about the trip beforehand. She had packed my bags, organized the passports and made plans for family to look after baby Michael. She finally broke the news to me when she told me we were leaving for the airport that day and that a car would be round to collect us. I was stunned when she told me and although I was happy to try and make things work between us, I was upset at leaving Michael behind because I had all these paranoid issues about his safety. It wasn't a good start to the trip and put further strain upon us.

My state of mind wasn't great by this stage, but I had no idea what was wrong with me. I was still having vivid nightmares about James's torture and murder, eighteen months after his death. In particular the dream about James's gravestone being soaked in blood continued to haunt my sleep on a regular basis. I would wake up bathed in cold sweat during the night, terrified out of my life, my heart beating so fast I thought I was going to die, gasping for breath. It would take quite a while for my body to settle down and to realize that it had been a nightmare. Often it would wake Denise from her sleep, which was exhausting for her.

It was with all this baggage that I agreed to get on a plane and fly to the other side of the world, even though most of the time I didn't want to be around people and only felt safe in the confines of my own home. I had gone from being a young man with a sharp sense of humour to a loner who didn't laugh and found it hard to connect with others.

I can clearly remember the long flight to the other side of the world and, bizarrely, being up there in the sky was one of the few occasions when I found a little peace. It was as if I was suspended from reality, soaring through the clouds and the dark night. In a silly way, I also felt that I was closer to James up there. I wished I could put my hand outside and try to touch him. While I was flying, it seemed to take some of the weight of my sadness away from me.

The trip itself did not go to plan, though. We both tried our best to make the most of it, and when we arrived in Australia we attempted to put a positive spin on things. We were to stay in Jim and Moira's house, where they would look after us and try to help us through our difficulties. They couldn't have been more welcoming, but even they could see from the outset that things between Denise and me were not good.

They organized simple trips for us, like a day out to go and see the world's biggest rocking horse, and we would have meals out and go for drinks. Denise went shopping with Moira and some of her friends. They deliberately didn't lay on anything too strenuous in case we didn't feel up to it.

Jim and Moira could see the problems between us, and in the end I felt very sorry for them. Denise and I tried our best to be civil to each other, but every time we had an argument it kept leading back to James, and Jim and Moira were stuck in the middle. They tried to help us work it through, but the damage was so deep-rooted it felt as if the marriage was imploding and nothing was going to stop it.

We spent a total of six weeks in Australia, living a fairly normal life out there, but any hopes that we would be able to mend our marriage seemed to be flying out the window, and we were both wishing we were back home with Michael. It felt as if we were trying to put a small sticky plaster over a huge gaping wound, hoping it would solve the problem, but it was not to be. The rows intensified and the trip became something of a nightmare.

By the time we touched down at Heathrow Airport in the late autumn, I knew in my heart that our marriage was over, although we hadn't talked about splitting up and there was no huge scene or fight. But I had made my mind up that I was not going home with Denise. I didn't leave Denise for Eileen – I left for me. I really thought that I would lose my mind if I stayed.

When we got back to Liverpool, Denise and I went into

the house and I told her I had to leave. I began to pack some things and later the same day I went to stay with Jimmy and Karen. It was a horrible day and I felt very bad that I was hurting Denise, but looking back I wonder if she wasn't partly relieved. The situation had probably become unbearable for her too.

I cannot say hand on heart that it was definitely James's murder that destroyed what we once had. Who knows what would have become of Denise and me had he not been taken from us. But I believed then, and still do, that the horrific events of the previous year had played a major part in driving a wedge between us. We did try to support each other, but it wasn't enough. We had spent weeks on end holed up in our flat or at Denise's mother's, stunned into silence and unable to cope with the enormity of what had happened. Every time we looked at each other, it was like tearing open that wound all over again. Denise was a living reminder of what I had lost. I imagine she felt the same when she saw me. I think if we had stayed together any longer we would have ended up destroying each other.

I couldn't make myself return to being the man I was before our son was killed, and so I knew I had to go. People might judge me for leaving Denise after what had happened and I have been criticized in the past. Perhaps I was taking flight from our grief, just as I had done when I used to drive for miles on end in a bid to get away from the nightmares in my head.

The biggest wrench for me was leaving Michael. I had lost two children and now it felt like I was losing a third. I knew he was safe and well looked-after by Denise, and I knew how much he meant to her, and so I had no choice but to move out and make sure I got to see my son as regularly and as often as possible.

I have questioned myself time and time again about my actions, but I know I never set out to hurt anyone, least of all Denise, who had already suffered so greatly. Neither of us are bad people. But what we endured was beyond what most people suffer in a lifetime, and instead of growing stronger together, the marriage shattered into pieces. Denise bore me three amazing children and I will always be grateful to her for that. Grateful that I had the chance to meet James, even if his stay on this earth was so short. I am sorry that I wasn't able to make the marriage work because the last thing I wanted to do was inflict greater hurt on my wife. Perhaps if my head wasn't so messed up things would have got better with time, but I didn't know how to fix myself. I left Denise because I had to sort my own head out, and I knew I had to do it now, or else I really feared I might have ended up topping myself.

Karen and Jimmy, as ever, gave me the most incredible support at a time when I had nowhere else to go, and I will never forget what they did for me. It was a difficult period of adjustment. It felt like a very lonely place to be. I tried my best to get on with life but I had little motivation. I seemed to go round in circles and it was hard to see the point in anything. I guess it is called depression by the doctors, but all I know is that I was deeply unhappy and struggling to cope. Beer and my family, and Eileen, kept me going through the darkest days when I saw very little hope for the future.

I settled in at Jimmy's and tried to get some structure in

my life. My mum, Helen, was a great help too, and I would spend quite a lot of time back at home with her to give Jimmy and Karen a break from me. Denise and I worked out a system where I looked after Michael at the weekends. Other than that we had very little contact. These were my favourite days of the whole week and the time when I felt most complete. I would either pick him up or Denise would drop him down to my mum's. I was used to caring for the kids and so I was more than capable of feeding Michael, winding him and changing his nappies. It was just a comfort to have him with me, even though as a small baby he still didn't do a lot, but I knew those days would come.

After several months, in early 1995, Eileen and I decided to move in together. It was quite a normal relationship in contrast to the shared traumas that Denise and I had been through. It felt like a new beginning for me, even though I knew I would always have to carry the weight of losing James. I found that I was able to sit still more and take stock. When I was troubled, Eileen always dragged me back from the brink. She had a natural ability to sit and listen when I needed to talk. I warned her many times that I was a lot to take on, but she was determined to try to help me, and she cared deeply for me, as I did for her. Slim and pretty with long dark hair, she seemed like a free spirit and I always felt immediately relaxed in her company.

Our new home was still in Kirkby and so I was still very close to my family and Michael. Unsurprisingly, our life together was very simple, but that suited the pair of us. We liked spending time together and I began to feel a little less tense and wound up. Despite it all, we found the time to laugh together too. This was hard for me at first, because I felt a huge guilt for any small happiness that came my way, but I began to realize that it was OK to let go of some of the misery, some of the time. It was a small step in the right direction.

Eileen was also very supportive of me with Michael. It was far from ideal that I didn't get to see him more, but at least I was able to spend time with him at the weekends. As he began to grow, I would play with him in the back garden at Mum's and he brought me a lot of joy. It wasn't a chore for me to spend time with my son; I cherished every last minute. He was very bubbly and funny, just like James, although I don't think he was quite as boisterous. That would have been a hard act to match for any toddler! He was as spoilt as any of the kids in the family and I loved him with all my heart. His life seemed so precious because of what had happened to James, and not a day went by when I didn't count myself lucky to have my son. There was little I could do about the circumstances. Neither Denise nor I could have predicted the way our lives would turn out, and when I thought back to the carefree days when James was a toddler, it was hard to see how we had managed to come through the nightmare. Michael was a strong driving force for both his mum and dad to keep going.

I can't say that life changed much from day to day, but I just tried to get on the best I could. I was happy with Eileen and we made a happy home together. By February we discovered that she was pregnant, and although it was sudden and unexpected, it was not unwelcome news. She was still only a young woman herself but, as I have already mentioned, she was wise beyond her years and she relished the chance to become a mum. I just felt blessed to have the chance to be a dad again. I think this was a big turning point in my personal life. With another baby on the way, I had to make some changes. It wasn't going to be easy but I was at least going to try.

It was also the time of year to face dreaded anniversaries again. It was two years since James had been murdered, and a month later, in March, it would have been his fifth birthday. That was a massive hurdle to get over. I couldn't help but try to picture him as he would look on this special birthday. In my head I could see him having grown, but I thought he would still be quite short and stocky. I thought his hair might be a little darker but still fair, and some of the chubby baby fat would have gone from his face. But I knew his bright blue eyes would still be shining and that big grin would have remained unchanged. The one thing that escaped me was his voice. I couldn't imagine what he would sound like.

He would be in school by now, and pictures flashed through my mind of a happy little boy in his school uniform, racing out the door as quickly as possible every morning to join his new mates in the playground. James embraced life so fully that I have no doubt he would have been popular at school. I am sure he would have had loads of friends he would have looked out for, and they would have been up to all sorts of fun and games together. I reckon he would have been footie-mad and knocking a ball about with his mates from an early age. They were all such sad reminders of what his killers had robbed us of.

As Eileen's pregnancy progressed, stories began to filter out in the media about Thompson and Venables. I was trying my hardest to move forward, but every time a newspaper wrote about their rehabilitation in detention, it dragged me backwards again. It was as if I was never going to be allowed to escape from the onslaught of information about James's killers. Time doesn't heal; I know that for certain. I'm not even sure you learn how to deal with the pain better, but you have to try to change the way you do things and look at the world. At this point, I still felt James's death like a permanent knife in my back. I was still tortured by the knowledge that my little boy must have wanted me to be there for him on the day he died and I had failed him.

It had already been widely reported that the boys were serving their punishments in two separate juvenile detention homes under the care of the local authorities. Under the terms of the gagging order, it was never revealed where they were being held, although unpoliced reports on the Internet revealed their locations, which made a bit of a mockery of the injunction. There were obviously lulls in the press reporting, but from time to time another new 'exclusive' would rear its head and that would prompt my thoughts to become obsessed with James and his killers once more.

Then some very strange events happened that I have never been able to explain. As a family, we were all very paranoid by now and worried about speaking to anyone we didn't know or trust. I returned home one afternoon to my house. My garage door had always opened very easily and so I had left a bin against the inside of the door to prevent anyone gaining access. The garage and the house were linked by a door, which led into my kitchen. When I went inside, I could see that the bin had been moved and I was sure someone had been in the house. The mop in the kitchen was not where it was always kept and letters had been displaced from the side of a cupboard. Something was not right, but nothing had been stolen.

A neighbour came to see me and said that two strangers had been at the house earlier that day. He said they appeared to have a key to the property, checked the lock for a while and then let themselves in. It was all very odd. I knew of no one who would have had a key, other than family, to gain access. Some time after this incident, another neighbour saw Jimmy and pressed a piece of paper into his hand.

'I didn't give this to you,' he said.

The note read: 'The Men In Black have been watching you. Men in black suits have been seen entering Ralph's house.'

The note also gave the registration numbers of two cars seen at the house and we made a formal complaint to the police, but they told us that the registration numbers we had filed did not exist.

It all seemed very cloak-and-dagger and bizarre. I didn't for a moment suspect that it was over-eager journalists trying to get a scoop, because they wouldn't have had a key or picked a lock in this manner, which really left only one option. Were the security services watching us? Tight security always surrounded Thompson and Venables and I suppose anything was possible, although I didn't see why that would merit my family being watched. Perhaps they were concerned one of us might attempt to take revenge on the two boys or that we were being fed information they didn't want us to have. Jimmy had long suspected his phone was tapped and years later, when he began to use a computer, his Internet service was continually disrupted by some unknown, outside force. Jimmy recalls:

In the space of six months, five different computers were disabled. It was incredible. The computers were bought from PC World and at first I thought it was just a faulty machine, but a pattern began to emerge. Every time I looked up something sensitive on the Internet regarding Thompson and Venables, the images on the screen scrambled and became encrypted. After several trips back to PC World, I became known as the PC Assassin because the hard drives on the computers died completely each time I accessed those sites. One of the managers asked me if I had been logging onto any sites that I shouldn't have access to. I said no. He said that whatever sites I was going on, I should back off because an external force was shutting the hard drives down and killing the computers stone dead. I knew then that this was not a computer error, but a deliberate act to close my Internet access down.

To this day, Jimmy and I have no proof that we have ever been watched by members of the security services, but we have our suspicions that someone was keeping a very close eye on us and our activities. The truth of the matter is, we have never encouraged a mob mentality regarding

Thompson and Venables. On the contrary, we have always asked people to back off and not take the law into their own hands.

If the security services were interested in us, I don't know what they were hoping to achieve. We will never know the truth about who it was, but it certainly felt that we were being watched and treated with suspicion even though we were not the ones who had committed the crime.

Eileen was a brilliant support to me on my down days, because while she was caring, she also remained positive and upbeat, and that had a great influence on my way of thinking. I had a baby on the way and a future to look forward to. Instead of drinking, I tried to put more focus on my training, and that helped too. I was still running but the weight training and gym work also allowed me to let out some aggression. If I went a few rounds on the punchbag, I would think of Thompson and Venables and hit the bag even harder. This tired me out and took away the need for me to constantly drink myself to sleep. The nightmares didn't stop and neither did the thoughts about what had happened to James, but I had to accept things as they were and make a different life to the one I had always imagined. I knew I was never going to be the person I once was. I was changed for ever and not in a good way. I wouldn't allow myself to be happy in front of other people. I would put on a fake smile that was hiding the dark and ugly feelings inside of me because I could never show them to anyone. Indoors with Eileen I felt safe. I could share some simple laughs with her because I knew she wasn't going to judge me. I guess I was scared that if other people saw me laughing they would think I was over James, and that I had moved on and didn't care about him. Nothing could have been further from the truth.

12

Trying to Have
A Family Life

In November 1995, Eileen gave birth to our first daughter, whom I will refer to as Ree. It was a very happy day for both of us even though, as at Michael's birth, I couldn't help but think of James. I tried my hardest to shove any negative feelings away and to concentrate on enjoying the arrival of our little girl, who was beautiful and healthy. Eileen was overjoyed at becoming a mum for the first time, and instinctively I knew she was going to be brilliant at it. I prayed this was going to be a turning point for me and I was determined to be the best dad I could for my new daughter.

The sleepless nights that go along with having a new baby didn't bother me, for not only was I used to them by now, I didn't kip well at the best of times, and so I would regularly help out by getting up in the small hours to bottle-feed and comfort Ree when she woke. She was a dote and I adored her. Life was quite busy at home with a new baby on board and I also continued to see Michael at weekends. I had constructed a swing in the back garden for him to play on, and my time spent with him was fantastic. I loved watching him grow, learning to walk and talk and start playing like any normal kid. He was a gentle and loving boy, just like James, and never caused any bother.

Family life was pretty normal apart from the constant stress of trying to deal with my emotions over James, and keep them at bay. I was better at dealing with things, but I would be lying if I said I had got everything under control by the time Ree was born. I hadn't. Instead, I started to separate the different parts of my life into boxes, and that made it a little easier to cope with. Eileen and Ree were in one box, and when I was at home I tried to act normally and take care of them both. Then there was Michael who was growing up rapidly, and when I was around him I put on a happy face because I didn't want him to see his dad miserable. As for James, well, I would still go out and get drunk sometimes, and that was when a lot of my feelings would spill out uncontrollably. Eileen was patient and under-standing when this happened and she was always there to pick up the pieces.

It was in April of the following year, 1996, that things really started hotting up legally regarding Thompson and Venables and their sentencing. Lawyers acting for the two boys had filed applications on behalf of their clients to the High Court in protest at Michael Howard's raising of their minimum tariff from ten years to fifteen. It was to prove a lengthy legal battle that would stretch over a year before a final decision was made.

In the first hearing of the case Mr Edward Fitzgerald QC, acting for both Thompson and Venables, challenged Mr Howard's ruling, claiming that he had acted in response to public opinion instead of considering the relevant social and psychiatric reports on the boys to make his decision.

He claimed that the coupons from the *Sun* and signatures collected from the family calling for whole life sentences should have been placed in the bin, and further insisted that Mr Howard acted to make an example of the killers in a blaze of publicity. Further, he said that Mr Howard's fixing of the tariff had been unlawful.

The purpose of the hearing was to seek a judicial review of the circumstances and to overturn the fifteen-year tariff. It was a huge body blow, but Mr Howard and the Home Office were prepared to fight the application and defended the decision. It seemed that it was one step forward and two steps back all the time. One of the major arguments that would come out of this long legal process was whether it was the job of the Home Secretary to fix a minimum tariff, or the courts, and a lot rested on the outcome.

Much of this was very confusing for me, but we had recently instructed a great criminal lawyer called Robin Makin to help us pick our way through all the complicated issues that arose in the case. It was Jimmy who had suggested bringing Robin on board because he could see that there would be many obstacles that would need addressing, and we were not capable of doing it by ourselves. This was the kind of thing that Jimmy was brilliant at. He was having a hard time of things himself following James's death, and yet he was determined to continue looking after me. The legal side of things was really up his street because he had a sharper academic mind than me, and with Robin's help he was able to understand the system and explain things to me.

Karen had by now given birth to their youngest child, and so she really had her hands full with three young daughters of varying ages, but she also had to support Jimmy, whose mental state had been shattered much like mine. I don't think he ever got over seeing James's body, and I think most people would have been damaged if they had to go through that. Jimmy's escape was through drinking in the pub and so family life for Karen was extremely hard. Jimmy was in the pub a lot of the time while she remained at home with her family, trying to hold everything together. By his own admission, the drink turned him nasty and aggressive and the atmosphere at home was often tense and difficult. It shows Karen's strength that she cared not only for her children but for her husband too, and she was determined to see things through. I would often sit and chat with her at her kitchen table, and I remember countless times when she confided how hard it was.

'I can't take much more of this, Ralph,' she said to me once. 'Life is a nightmare and the kids are suffering. I sometimes think I'd be better off on my own than living here with him. Most of the time he's in the pub drinking, and when he's here he's miserable and narky to everyone. He's changed so much that I don't even recognize him any more.'

I understood what Karen was saying, but I also found it hard to criticize Jimmy because I knew he was struggling and out of his depth. He was doing exactly as I had done by finding comfort in the drink. I knew he loved his family, but he had shut himself away from everything that had gone on and it was awful to see. He is a good man but he was also a victim of the things he had witnessed when James died.

However hard things got, Karen refused to cave in and leave Jimmy. She felt that if her marriage broke up then she would be giving in to Thompson and Venables and that they would have won. She was not prepared to let them take anything else away from our family at any cost, even though the road ahead was to be very rocky for them.

After the initial hearing at the High Court a judicial review was launched, and all we could do was sit back and wait to learn the findings. Robin was all over the case like a rash and he was outstanding at his job. He was, and still is, like a little terrier dog who refused to let go of something once he had got hold of it. He is only a small, thin man, with tight curly hair and spectacles, but he was like a giant when it came to legal matters. Without him we would have been lost, and while we tried to get on with our family lives and our grief, Robin remained in the background constantly working away for us. He knew the law inside and out, and he fought for us tooth and nail. In July, the Court of Appeal ruled that in setting the fifteen-year tariff Michael Howard had been wrongly influenced by the public petitions. One of the three judges, Lord Woolf, who had recently taken over as Master of the Rolls, said that this was unfair as it would be impossible to 'test or match' the material. The other two judges agreed and in addition criticized the Home Secretary for failing to give his reasons for raising the tariff to Thompson's and Venables' lawyers, as a judge would have done, so they could respond with relevant psychiatric and social reports.

It seems significant to me that Lord Woolf in his judgement referred to two psychiatric reports on Venables, one of which showed he had had an 'excellent' response to the therapeutic work he was receiving. The other report had concluded that there would be major concerns for his wellbeing if he had to progress through young offender institutions to prison, which, Lord Woolf said, was likely if the present tariff was maintained.

The decision of the Court of Appeal was a setback as it meant Michael Howard had to reconsider his tariff, but he immediately said he would appeal to the House of Lords, so I tried to keep my hopes up that we'd get the result we wanted in the end.

Later that year, Eileen and I were blessed to have another daughter, whom I will call Bobbi. She was another very welcome addition to our family and both Eileen and I put all our energies into parenthood. I loved being a dad more than anything else and, while I might have failed in many other areas of my life, I always put one hundred per cent into my children. My family was growing and I couldn't have been happier. It never took away my loss of James and I never tried to see my other children as replacements for him, but I loved all my kids as much as I had loved James. My children made my life worth living and they kept me going through some of the darkest days of my life. They were so innocent and vulnerable, the complete opposite of the darkness I carried around with me over James. That made it all the more important for me to split my life into compartments to protect them.

It was a constant source of happiness for me to see the kids growing. Michael by now was a smashing little boy who was playing football with his dad at weekends, and Ree was toddling and making us all laugh. I would sit her on my lap and she would cock her head from side to side as she looked at me and laughed. I knew she was going to be able to wrap me round her little finger when she got older.

It was in June 1997 that we would learn the decision of

the House of Lords regarding the sentencing of Thompson and Venables. The law lords decided by a 4–1 majority that Mr Howard had acted unfairly and unlawfully by taking into account public opinion while reconsidering the sentences of the boys. They also said that home secretaries may not treat children detained at Her Majesty's pleasure the same way as adult lifers. A new tariff for the killers was not set, but it was still a devastating verdict because Mr Howard's fifteen-year ruling was now quashed. That only meant one thing to me: the boys were likely to be released far earlier than we had hoped.

It was fair to say I was fuming at the outcome. All it did was refuel my anger towards James's killers. I didn't believe that justice was being served for my son. It was a terrible ruling for us and I felt that it was James who was being let down.

I just couldn't help thinking all along that no one wanted to punish these boys for their crime. They couldn't see beyond the small schoolboys in the dock, but then they had never stood before the tiny severed body of my James, as his uncle Jimmy had. Perhaps if the system showed more interest in the crimes being committed and the victims who have to suffer, then things might be very different, but to me it all just felt like the law was one big game of chess, weighted in favour of the criminal. Unlike politicians, judges are not elected by the people of this country and yet they had the final say on something as crucial as allowing James's killers to be freed earlier than they deserved. The whole system sucked as far as I was concerned.

It was a hard job to get on with family life with all this going on in the background. Sometimes the obsession with

James and the legal system got the better of me and I could think of nothing else. I still woke every day with a feeling of dread, anger and fear, and it was so hard to shake, even though I really tried for the sake of my other children. But when you carry such enormous emotions around with you all the time, it is exhausting and eventually it takes you to breaking point. Whenever I got to that level of grief, I would take myself off fishing for a few days for a period of quiet reflection. It never made the suffering go away but it helped to calm me down.

I had to find a balance between fighting for James and being a good dad at home. Michael was easy to please and a very easy-going boy. A knockabout and a laugh between dad and lad was all it took to put a smile on his face. I would make him little wooden toys to play with in the garden, a truck or a duck, and he would sit for hours, quite content with anything that came his way.

I would make sure there were special treats for him on Saturdays too, which Ree also loved. The kids would have their meals but there would always be cakes and sweets and biscuits. Michael loved Ree too, and was very protective and gentle with her. They would play together in the back garden and follow each other around constantly. These were the times when I would shut my feelings for James away and smile and laugh with the family. I wanted them to be care-free in their lives. I wanted them to be everything I wasn't.

At the same time, I was determined to protect them at all costs. I knew that I was paranoid, but I couldn't let go. Michael still lived with Denise and I know she shared my fears, which made her very overprotective of him, keeping him by her side and only letting family look after him. It was the same for Ree. She was only young, but Eileen and I never let her out of our sight and certainly never let her out of her pushchair in public.

Alongside our very ordinary domestic life, the case of James Bulger was rarely out of the papers. It would be impossible to recall all of the many things that have been written about James and his killers – it must run into millions and millions of words around the world – but every time something was printed I would get a phone call from a relative telling me what was being said. They knew I wouldn't go out and read a paper, but often it was to warn me in case reporters came knocking. If a newspaper printed something in the morning, very often it would be followed up in the regional papers, and by lunchtime bulletins would be running on the national and local television stations.

The first reports that began to filter out described the life that Thompson and Venables were leading inside their secure units. I think this caused me the most anger because, far from being punishment, their lives appeared to be cushy and comfortable and far better than when they had lived at home. It seemed to me that the state was bending over backwards to give these boys every luxury they wanted, and all because they had killed a two-year-old baby.

Newspapers reported how they were given their own bedrooms kitted out with not only a bed, but a desk and chairs and table, an en-suite shower and toilet and luxuries like TVs, games consoles and personal photographs on their walls. Other reports in the popular press described how they were also treated to the latest in designer trainers and clothing, were being given a five-star education and took part in leisure activities such as football and pool. I had no way to verify if these reports (and others since) were true or not, and the authorities have never commented one way or the other. So what was I left to think? I assumed the press had access to sources I did not, and so in the absence of any other evidence I have found myself accepting most of the reports that have come out over the years, and they have made my blood boil.

It was also reported at this time that top psychiatrists and psychologists were employed by the Home Office to work with the boys to try to uncover why they had abused, tortured and murdered James. One journalist described these sessions as extremely intense and painful for the boys, and it almost made me want to scream. Compared to how they treated James, this was not pain. My son was the only victim who suffered pain and yet, somehow, I was supposed to feel sympathy for two kids who had put him through so much and were now having to undergo psychoanalysis.

It was as if James's family didn't matter any more. Only once had Jimmy and I been offered medical or psychological help to overcome our trauma and devastation. Ever since Robin had started working for us, he had been trying to set up professional medical assessments, and it was during this period that he organized some appointments for us. It turned out to be a disaster, as Jimmy recalls:

A young man arrived at our house to carry out an assessment on me and I couldn't believe how events unfolded. One of our girls was still only a toddler and Karen was caring for her at home.

The 'shrink' told me that no one could be in the house while he was talking with me and asked Karen to leave. I wasn't happy, but I just wanted to get the whole thing out of the way, and so Karen agreed to go out. For nearly two hours she sat out the front of our house with the baby. It was a disgrace.

The guy asked me loads of questions about my experiences and what I had seen when James was killed. I didn't hold back and told him straight about the terrible sight of James's body. I could see this young man wincing as he tried to digest what I was telling him and I knew he was not finding it easy to listen to. He then asked me a range of different questions about how I responded to what I had seen and I found that a lot harder to answer. It's much easier for people closer to you to see you changing. I knew I was disturbed, but I just covered up my feelings by drinking.

When the session was finished, the young man practically ran down our path and couldn't get away quick enough. Karen came back in and immediately thought I had given him a flea in his ear, but I hadn't.

'What happened?' she asked.

'Not a lot,' I replied matter-of-factly. 'I answered all his questions and told him everything he wanted to know, and then he got up and left. He said he wouldn't be coming back because he couldn't cope with what I had told him.'

'What? You are joking me?'

'No, I'm not. I'm totally fucked, Karen, if even the head doctors can't deal with what I have seen.'

It was a ludicrous situation and I didn't have any faith that there was anyone who could help us. Ralph was supposed to have an assessment, but he pulled out when he heard about *what happened to me. After that our family just closed ranks and tried to muddle through the best we could.*

Some days were better than others, but there were times when I was like a volcano just waiting to erupt. Karen became adept at walking on eggshells, always trying to suss out what my mood was for fear of irking my rage. But it wasn't her fault, ever. She just had to live with my anger and mood swings and, along with the problems I faced, I just felt incredibly guilty for putting her through such nonsense.

I was very lucky that Karen was so strong and such a fighter. By rights I should have lost her years ago, but she stayed by my side and never, ever gave up on me. I am a very lucky man to have a wife who is supportive of her husband who behaved terribly sometimes. She was wise enough to know that I was badly affected by what I had seen of James, but it didn't make life any easier for her.

It was incidents like this that made the treatment of Thompson and Venables all the harder to stomach. I admit, we didn't seek out psychiatric help, but neither did Thompson and Venables ask for it. They were automatically treated by the system because they were being looked after. I couldn't help but feel that victims should have the same attention and that the system should make it their duty to provide care for people who have been affected by violent crimes. I was suffering, Denise was suffering, Jimmy and his whole family were suffering, and there was no safety net for us even though we had not committed any crimes. It all felt so unjust that we were overlooked while Thompson and Venables were being mollycoddled instead of punished. I wasn't saying that they should be taken away and beaten.

We live in a civilized society and I wouldn't want that replaced by some brutal regime, but I believed James's killers should have a sense that they were paying for their crime, and I didn't think that was the case. Surely punishment has to mean that they know they had done wrong and were treated accordingly?

There was one man who clearly disagreed with me. About this time Robin made Jimmy and me aware of an American lawyer who had involved himself in this case from the other side of the world. Tom Loflin, from North Carolina, had taken a great interest in the trial of Thompson and Venables. He was, apparently, outraged that two boys as young as eleven had faced trial in an adult court and by their subsequent sentences. After their conviction he began writing letters to many people connected to the case. He lobbied the trial judge and Michael Howard, and then contacted the lawyers for Thompson and Venables to urge them to fight against their sentence to have them freed. He insisted their human rights had been breached and since 1994 had been travelling to the UK to work with the boys' lawyers to strengthen their case. He also began to visit Jon Venables in detention and befriended him over a period of time. It has never been made clear exactly when he saw Venables, but he did speak with broadcaster Jane Corbin of his involvement in a television programme for *Panorama*. Here is what he told her.

'I decided that it was just a monstrous injustice to these young children which had to be corrected. Something effective had to be done for them. I was shocked that a country that I thought was as advanced as the UK would actually be stooping to such barbarism as putting two very young children on trial as adults in public and engaging really in the fiction of the wishful thinking of saying they are adults when they clearly are not.'

He continued to tell the programme about his visits to see Venables and their growing friendship and how he had received many letters and cards from the boy and, in return, Loflin sent him mementos of his favourite baseball team, the Durham Bulls. When Jon was twelve, he made Loflin a ceramic mascot of the baseball team.

'Jon has a lot of creative artistic talent. He has a wonderful sense of humour, a really great sense of humour. He is a lot of fun to be with when you're with him. Each time I visited I could see he had made progress.'

I think when I found out about Loflin I was more shocked than anything that a lawyer from another country would take it upon himself to fly over to England and start interfering in a case that I felt that had nothing to do with him.

It was during this period that he had been working with Thompson and Venables' lawyers to prepare a case to take to the European Court of Human Rights at Strasbourg.

In March 1999, the first of two European rulings on the case was made. The European Commission of Human Rights concluded that the trial for James's murder had been held in a 'highly charged' atmosphere, which led to an unfair judgement. As a result, the trial had been a breach of the human rights of Jon Venables and Robert Thompson. Then, in December of the same year, the European Court of Human Rights echoed the findings of the Commission, ruling that James's killers had not received a fair trial.

Under the Children and Young Person's Act 1933, the age of criminal responsibility is ten, but a child aged between ten and fourteen can only be found guilty of an offence if it is proved by the prosecution that the offender knew what he or she was doing was seriously wrong. As far as I was aware, this had been done at the trial, but the age of criminal responsibility in this country is lower than in most European countries, and I wonder to what extent this had a bearing on the Strasbourg ruling, which also reinforced the earlier High Court ruling that the now former Home Secretary Michael Howard was wrong to intervene in the sentencing of the two killers.

Their solicitors argued at the Strasbourg hearing that Thompson and Venables were distressed and frightened at their trial. Judges agreed with counsel for the killers that the pair did not receive a fair trial because it was held in public, and subject to intensive press coverage. However, they did say that the killers had not been treated in an inhuman or degrading way. They accepted that special measures were taken in view of their youth, for example, the trial procedure was explained to them, they were taken to see the courtroom in advance and the hearing times were shortened. But they felt that the formality and ritual of events in a court must at times have seemed incomprehensible and intimidating to the eleven-year-old children.

Part of their verdict said that some of the modifications to the courtroom – particularly the raised dock so that the boys could see what was going on – had actually increased their discomfort as it made them feel more exposed to scrutiny. The judges concluded that although their legal representatives were seated within whispering distance, it was highly unlikely that either applicant would have felt sufficiently uninhibited in the tense courtroom and under public scrutiny to have consulted with them during the trial. And that they were too disturbed and immature to cooperate with their defence outside of the courtroom.

It was a damning report on our UK legal system and our Government, and my heart sank when I heard the ruling. My first fear was that the two boys would have to be retried under a different system and that would mean the same agony all over again. Surely they couldn't force English courts to hold another trial? It was one small mercy that it never came to that, as the pair had already served six years in detention centres, but it did have huge implications for the way in which juveniles would be tried in the future.

Not only were we floored by the ruling, but our whole family was livid at the way we felt an American had interfered and influenced the way this case was being handled. Tom Loflin should spend just one day walking in my shoes and he might then learn about the consequences of what they had done. Jack Straw was the Home Secretary at the time of the ruling and he insisted that James's killers would not be released early as a result of the hearing, adding, 'The real agony is felt by James's parents. They have to endure, and will continue to endure, the profound grief of losing their son.'

The whole issue was totally sickening for me. Once again, it seemed those in charge had treated James's killers with kid gloves and sucked up to their so-called human rights when they were the ones who had committed the crime and denied James his whole life. Why did we let a European court start dictating what is right or wrong in British law? It felt like our system had lost its backbone and turned into a whipping boy for anyone who wanted to stick their noses into our business. I couldn't get over the argument that Thompson and Venables were distressed and frightened during their trial. I was at the trial and have not forgotten how I watched the boys shuffle and lark about together as the most terrible evidence was laid before the jury. I didn't see one bit of remorse or fear. This felt like just one more way in which the system benefited the cause of two ruthless and wicked young murderers.

The high regard that I'd once had for our legal system was totally gone. The idea that victims in this country get justice is nothing more than a pathetic joke to me. Over the years, I have met many people through a support group called MAMAA – Mothers Against Murder and Aggression – which was set up as a direct result of James's murder. After he was killed, three members of the public, Lyn Costello, her husband Roger, and Dee Warner, came together in a desperate bid to do something, and the result was the formation of this amazing charity. It helps people who lose a loved one to murder or manslaughter when they feel there is nowhere else to turn, just listening if that is what you need, or offering practical help and advice. Through this group I have heard some horror stories from bereaved relatives who, almost without exception, have said that their treatment at the hands of the legal system has been a disgrace and that, in many cases, the experience of going to court or trying to punish the guilty was almost as traumatic as losing their loved ones in the first place. Victims' families came away humiliated and in despair at their treatment.

The fact is that our legal system is currently heavily weighted in favour of the rights of criminals, and is willfully neglectful and dismissive of the rights of victims. In these

days of political correctness, we have a system that is petrified of its own shadow and heavily influenced by the
European Court of Human Rights. We have become too
scared to stick up for ourselves as a nation and defend what
we think is right for Britain. Instead we allow foreign judges
in a faraway state in Europe to dictate how we should punish
our own citizens.

At the time of James's murder, then Prime Minister John
Major responded to the crime by saying, 'It is time for us
to put the victim before the criminal. We must condemn
a little more and understand a little less.' It was so desperately sad that his words were ignored.

I had no choice but to soldier on even though we had
been hammered by the European rulings. Some days I just
felt like giving up. It didn't seem to matter what we did or
how we felt; the legal system, both at home and abroad,
was against us. I am not a legal expert, although I have
learned much over the years about the way the system really
works, but it was more than apparent to me that common
sense just didn't enter into things. It feels to me like the
system is controlled by a powerful few who privately strike
deals that the public will never know about. I was extremely
bitter at the way the law had continually let James down,
and his murder hardly ever came into the equation any
more. It was always about Thompson and Venables – their
treatment, their recovery, their progress, their education
and their human rights. I think that, morally speaking, they
gave up their human rights the day they battered and
murdered my son. They had been given a fair trial and in
my mind they should have received a far higher tariff than
the fifteen years set by Michael Howard.

Why is punishment in our country seen as such a dirty word? We are not a cruel or barbaric country, and so any punishment of these boys would have been fair and humane, but instead they were treated as victims who had to be fixed in some way.

Liberals argue that it was enough punishment for these boys to lose their liberty, but I believe both Thompson and Venables were happier in detention than they ever were at home. They were safe and warm, cared for and educated, and they weren't even locked up all the time. Many years later, newspaper reports claimed to reveal details of a regime that seemed pretty soft to me. Punishment is supposed to act as a deterrent, to be something that offenders don't wish to go through again, but reportedly James's killers didn't even want to leave their detention centres when the time came.

After this kind of setback I would feel an overwhelming need to talk to James, mainly to say sorry to him once again. I went to visit his grave soon after the ruling and I sat beside him and began chatting with him in my normal way.

I must have stayed for at least a couple of hours that evening. It was dark and still and I felt comforted to be next to him. It was days like this that I felt the fight just go out of me, but I knew that I would bounce back and pick up the challenge once more. It was the very least that I owed to James.

I couldn't get to sleep that night even though I was exhausted. As I lay down and closed my eyes all I could see were the faces of Thompson and Venables smirking and laughing with cold, cruel eyes. Was I the only one who could see this? When I compared their faces to the wide-eyed innocence of James, it was as if they had been born on different planets. These boys were getting away with a cold-blooded murder that was evil beyond belief and there was absolutely nothing I could do to change that.

I thought back to the time of James's murder when we had received such amazing support from the public, from complete strangers who shared our grief and shock with us. Over 1,000 death notices had been placed in the city's local newspaper, the *Liverpool Echo*, and then there were the donations in their thousands, many of which went to Liverpool's Alder Hey Hospital – the largest children's hospital in western Europe. I tried to console myself as I lay in the dark that people did care about James and the horrific ordeal he went through, even if the legal system in this country was proving to be unaware of our suffering.

There has to come a time when the victims of crime and their families get put before the rights of the criminals. Failure to do so makes a laughing stock of justice and a system that should be working for the people who need it the most. I passionately believe that punishment must come first, before rehabilitation and reform. But from what I have seen, we are a very, very long way from achieving that.

13

The Fight Back

The European ruling in December 1999 came at the same time as the birth of my third daughter with Eileen. We nicknamed her Naigs, and she was as gorgeous as all my other kids. How lucky was I, to have this brood of lovely children to look after despite all the bitter blows I had faced elsewhere. They certainly kept me on my toes and there was never a dull moment in our house!

The best way I can describe it is that my kids became like the light against the dark. I only had to look at them and realize that I had many good things in my life. This didn't remove my obsession to fight for justice; it just made the journey a little easier.

Michael had started school and was as happy as could be, while Ree became leader of the pack among her sisters. She and Bobbi were right little tomboys in their early years, and they would rough and tumble with each other all the time. They never meant each other any harm but occasionally I had to step in to break them up when things were getting out of hand. Eileen and I tried to bring them up well, but we did spoil them sometimes too. We loved them so much that we couldn't help it, but we tried to keep a balance by teaching them manners and discipline, just as my mum and dad had done with me and my brothers and sisters.

Ree was as bright as a button and quieter than Bobbi, who was so noisy it was untrue! Bobbi was ear-splittingly loud but very funny. It was hard to get cross with her, even though earplugs would have come in handy on some days. I'd take our girls up to Jimmy and Karen's house, and they'd play for hours on end with their cousins. Jimmy's three girls were all a few years older than mine and so they would look after Ree and Bobbi. They would play dressing up and Karen's make-up bag took a real battering every time they all got together. I'll never forget the time that Bobbi yelled the place down when she got her foot stuck in Jimmy's tiny pond. You would have thought her world was coming to an end, but of course all the other girls couldn't stop laughing at her, which I think made her scream even louder.

What was missing was the parties we once threw for all the kids' birthdays and different events throughout the year, like Easter and the Halloween party James had enjoyed just a few months before he died. As much as the adults tried to keep things jolly for the kids, none of us felt comfortable throwing parties. It's hard to explain why, but it didn't feel right. We had all changed from those rowdy, happy days when we would pile into Jimmy and Karen's and have a blast. What's more, Jimmy and Karen shared my sense of fear for the safety of their kids and shielded and protected them beyond what was normal. I guess it was a natural response to what had happened to James, but it meant that Jimmy's girls were never allowed out. It made them stand out from their mates and they hated it. They didn't know why they couldn't go beyond the garden path or stay out later with their pals. But it was drummed into them that they weren't allowed to do it.

Jimmy's youngest daughter, who was born in September 1993, the same year James died, rebelled against such tight discipline and earned herself the nickname of 'the great escape artist'. The background was certainly no laughing matter, but her antics in trying to beat the rules were hilarious. The youngster caused Karen's heart to miss a beat many times when she went missing. She would hide around the house or try to burrow through the back garden fence to get out. Once Karen thought she had gone out the front door when she couldn't find her, and ran down the road in blind panic even though her daughter was only hiding out in the back garden, probably plotting her next big escape.

Naigs was still a baby at this stage, but I would also take the girls to McDonald's for a Happy Meal and they were always delighted with the little toys they got. They weren't demanding girls at all, but they wore me out nonetheless. Their energy was full-on, but that is just the way it should have been at their age. I could have done with some of that same energy for what I was about to face next.

The new millennium was coming and for many it was seen as a significant time of hope and a brand-new era. But for me, I couldn't see beyond the immediate future, which meant more uphill battles with the legal establishment. The Strasbourg rulings were just the start of a new wave of complicated legal and political decisions that would affect everyone, from my family to Thompson and Venables. It was such a minefield; thank God we had Robin Makin by our side. He believed in fairness, real justice and a transparency that we had so far been denied. I will always be grateful to Robin for what he did for us but also, most importantly, for what he tried to do for James.

The issue of the minimum tariff the killers had to serve had been a political hot potato ever since the boys' original conviction, and the goalposts kept being moved at every juncture. After Mr Howard's tariff was quashed, no new one had been put in place, as politicians and lawyers waited to see the outcome of the European rulings. When the Home Office was defeated, it had fallen to Jack Straw to refer the case back to the newly appointed Lord Chief Justice for England and Wales, Lord Woolf, who had inherited the final decision on how long Thompson and Venables would remain behind bars. The outcome was solely in his hands.

In the summer of 2000, Lord Woolf publicly announced that he would consider the opinions of James's family on how long we thought the murderers should stay in jail. Our views were already firmly recorded in the public domain, but the fact he'd said this meant at least the door had not been totally slammed in our faces, even though we had already had earlier indicators, as I have said, that Lord Woolf had thought Venables was making great progress, which he might take into account when making his next decision.

He said, 'I think it is very important that all those involved should have an opportunity to have an input into the process in this decision.

'I am waiting for representation from the Director of Public Prosecutions, who will be taking the views of the victims and, in the case where someone has been killed, that means their family.

'The family are going to express their views to the Director, and the Director is going to be the method of communication to the courts of their views.'

As ever, Robin was like a Rottweiler in his approach to representing our family's views. We were unequivocal: don't ever release these boys because they will reoffend and another family will have to go through what we have suffered. That had been our message from the beginning and nothing had changed. Those feelings were submitted to the Director of Public Prosecutions and then forwarded to the Lord Chief Justice, and now all we could do was wait until he had made his decision. Denise and her new family felt the same way.

Thompson and Venables were approaching the age of eighteen and this was a crucial factor. If their tariff was to extend beyond their birthdays, then they would have to be transferred to a young offenders' institution and begin serving a real jail sentence, instead of living in the detention centres they had become used to.

In October 2000 my worst fears came true. After all the legal posturing, and despite our hopes that our views would have a decisive impact, the Lord Chief Justice reinstated the original minimum eight-year tariff that had been set by the trial judge. We were back to square one, but even worse, the killers' tariff expired immediately, paving the way for their release back into society.

Home Secretary Jack Straw followed the Lord Chief Justice's decision by immediately referring the cases of Thompson and Venables to the Parole Board, to decide if it was safe to release them on licence in the coming months. The board would have to take on lengthy assessments and it was announced that their decision would be unlikely to be made until February of the following year. According to Lord Woolf, the time the killers had spent in detention by that stage was the equivalent of a court jailing an adult for sixteen years, who could expect parole halfway through the sentence. The long and the short of it was this: when Lord Woolf made his ruling to end their tariff, Thompson and Venables had served just seven years and eight months.

He said, 'The one overriding mitigating feature of the offence is the age of the two boys when the crime was committed.'

He went on to say that he believed if the killers were to be transferred from local authority secure units to young offender institutions, it would 'undo much of the good work' that had been carried out to rehabilitate them. He believed they would not be able to cope with the 'corrosive atmosphere' and exposure to drugs they would inevitably encounter in such places. He also said that while information about the impact of James's death on his parents had been of real value, he had never invited us to give our views on what the appropriate tariff should be. That, he said, had to remain strictly a legal decision.

It was the first time that a judge had set the tariff for a young person's release. Until that point, the Home Secretary had always decided when a child sentenced to detention under Her Majesty's pleasure should be considered for release. The European Court of Human Rights had changed all that by insisting that the setting of a tariff, which was effectively fixing a sentence, had to be done by an independent and impartial tribunal and not by a politician.

So there it was: what felt like the final kick in the balls. We believed that our views amounted to nothing and had been merely lip service to a judicial system that had already decided that it wanted to release Thompson and Venables back into society. It felt like we had been tucked up in our own country by a bunch of interfering lawyers from Europe who had hijacked the laws of Great Britain to defend the 'human rights' of two young psychopaths.

The decision brought outrage across the country and, once again, the case of James Bulger was back on the front pages and in the headlines on television news. The liberal do-gooders were rubbing their hands with glee but politicians from all sides of the fence were furious.

Gerald Howarth, MP for Aldershot, said, 'It is monstrous that a matter of huge national importance like this should be decided by unaccountable judges. These cases, which raise matters of huge national importance, should be decided by politicians who can be held to account on the floor of the House of Commons.'

Lord Tebbit said, 'Whatever the merits or demerits of this particular decision, it emphasizes the extent towards the unelected judiciary overriding the elected Government's decisions. This is a dangerous trend and, if continued, it will bring both Government and the judiciary into disrepute.'

I sat with Jimmy and vented my anger. 'How the fuck can they do this, Jim? How can they say it is OK to let these monsters go free after just eight years after what they have done to James?'

'We'll just keep fighting, Ralph. We will never give up and we all owe that to James.'

'But they don't care about James. They don't care about his grieving relatives and how our lives have been destroyed. We're just numbers to them – it's cruel and it's wrong. How are we going to fight this?'

'We will find a way, Ralph, don't you worry. Robin won't allow this to drop.'

Jimmy was right. Robin was not going to bow down at the first hurdle. We knew it was a tough fight against politicians and legal hierarchies, which seemed to have their doors firmly closed to ordinary people like me. But we had to keep trying. And it was time to ramp up the public's attention.

Robin made an immediate public announcement that our family was to explore all possibilities to appeal Lord Woolf's decision, even though it had not been something that had been tried before.

And that was not the worst of it. As soon as Lord Woolf ended the boys' tariff, lawyers acting for Thompson and Venables launched a lightning-quick High Court action to give James's killers lifelong anonymity. They wanted the boys back in society but for no one to know who they were.

To say I was devastated doesn't even come close. I felt just like I did when James was first murdered: angry and helpless. We had huge support from the general public, and the following month, in November, MAMAA organized a peaceful protest in Liverpool against the planned release of James's killers.

Denise had also been fighting her own justice campaign for our son, by organizing marches and rallies and publicity. We still didn't speak to one another following our divorce, but we both had the same voice when it came to fighting for our boy. The rally, which was held on the steps of Liverpool's historic St George's Hall, was the first time in more than five years that Denise and I came together in a show of solidarity for James. Denise was by now happily remarried and we put our differences to one side with only one common aim between us: to show the world we were fighting for our boy. Hundreds of people turned out to support the rally, including Bill Jenkins, the father of murdered schoolgirl Billie-Jo Jenkins, and Winnie Johnson, the mother of Keith Bennett, who was murdered by Moors killers Myra Hindley and Ian Brady. June Richardson, whose son was killed by child murderer Mary Bell, also spoke at the rally.

Many of them offered both Denise and me words of comfort because they had all suffered terrible losses. There was a bond between all the bereaved relatives. Bill Jenkins stayed in Jimmy's house for the weekend, even though none of us had never met before that day. Bill was a lovely man, just an ordinary bloke who felt that the legal system had let him and his daughter down. He had had some terrible battles with the establishment over the years, but it felt good to have others to talk to who knew what we were going through.

Denise and I didn't talk at the rally but we stood shoulder to shoulder as James's parents, because we had both lost so much. Neither of us addressed the march but we remained composed and dignified in honour of our boy. It was a very emotional day and I was choked listening to some of the speakers.

Dee Warner addressed the rally on behalf of MAMAA with real passion. She said, 'MAMAA first came here to Liverpool when James was killed and I can't believe we are back here again now, just eight years later, trying to keep these boys locked up. The law in this country is for everyone, but it seems that justice is only for those who can afford it. All it takes for evil to prevail is for good people to stand by and do nothing, which is why we are here today to make our feelings known. One day these boys, who are now eighteen, could be living next door to you or me. They could win our confidence and one day be babysitting our children because they have new identities and we will never know who these boys are. If they were capable of doing what they did to James at ten, God help us now they are eighteen. They don't deserve compassion and we don't want them released.'

June Richardson also addressed the rally: 'Something good inside each and every one of us died the day they killed James Bulger. His killers have never been punished. We may just be ordinary people but we demand that they be properly punished.'

It was a heartbreaking sight when Winnie Johnson, who sadly died in 2012 without ever finding where the Moors killers had buried her beloved son Keith, took the stand to speak to the crowds. Visibly shaking and sobbing, Winnie had to be held up by friends but insisted on having her say. She said, 'In 1964, my lad was taken from me by Brady and Hindley. I have never had peace of mind and that is all I have ever wanted. I want my son's killers to stay in prison, as I do the killers of James Bulger.'

Winnie really touched my heart that day. Like all parents of murdered children, she had never got over the loss of her son Keith. I knew how she felt and I also realized I was going to feel just as she did for the rest of my life.

The rally was a very public statement that gave ordinary people the chance to support us in our campaign, but the hard work was going on behind the scenes, and Robin would be the man to lead us forward.

Jimmy and I put in applications for legal aid to bring

action through the courts in protest at Lord Woolf's tariff but they were turned down. I couldn't help but feel it was an attempt to silence us – and so we decided to launch a public appeal to help us with our fight against Lord Woolf's decision. Much of the legal language was beyond me, but Robin always explained it to me in simple layman's terms. In essence, he was preparing on our behalf to challenge Lord Woolf's decision through the High Court in a bid to overturn the ruling to release Thompson and Venables. It was a long and complicated process but I knew that Robin would do an excellent job.

Together with MAMAA, we set up the Human Rights for Victims Fund to pay for the legal process. I made an impassioned appeal at the time, begging the public to get behind us. I gave a rare media interview to the *Mail on Sunday* and, even though I hated the spotlight, I agreed to go on television to get our message across. We had also arranged to release a never-before-seen video of James for the television networks to play. For a few brief moments, it brought James alive again, and the world could see just what a lovely, bubbly little boy he was. The footage showed James on a trampoline at a family birthday party. He was bouncing up and down and laughing his head off. You also heard him calling out my name and attempting to sing 'Happy Birthday'.

I had never appeared in a television interview before, because I was just too shy and ill equipped to deal with the intensity of questions. My only experience of television cameras had been at the press conferences when James was missing. Against my better judgement, I went on GMTV's early-morning breakfast show to highlight our campaign and to speak alongside the release of the video. It was a public relations disaster. I was just not cut out to do public speaking. I had neither the right words nor the confidence to speak in public, and as a result I came across as hostile and difficult. I'm not either of those, but as soon as the interview went live, I froze like a rabbit caught in the headlights. My defences went up and I scowled at the camera. Inside I felt like a terrified child and my jaw clenched tight as my hands began sweating.

It was an uncomfortable interview for the TV hosts as well, and although I tried my best, I found it so hard to find the right words. Then, as the short interview drew to a close, I was asked what I would do if Thompson and Venables were released. My instant response was to say, 'I'll do my best to hunt them down.'

It was the worst possible thing I could have said, but it came from my gut. I have talked already in this book about the difference between what you would like to do and what you would actually do, and they are a world apart, but I had just blurted out on live television that I would like to hunt down James's killers if they were ever freed. I would be lying if I said that it had not been a part of my fantasy thoughts. Can any other parent honestly say that it would not have crossed their minds? Of course I felt the need to avenge the brutal murder of my child, but I would never have done it. As I've already written, unless you have been through something like this, it is impossible to understand the difference between the thoughts in your head and the reality of how you act. It is no different to considering the possibility of suicide; it doesn't mean you are actually going to go through with it.

However, the damage was done in a very public way, and I regret with all my heart what I said. It didn't help my cause either. As the debate raged on about whether Thompson and Venables should receive lifelong anonymity, my comments were seen as another reason for the powers that be to give them secret identities, because they believed there was a very real danger to their lives should their names and whereabouts become public knowledge. It was a hard lesson for me to learn about the media, not that it was the TV show's fault. I was just not media-savvy enough to know the right things to say, and instead I just spoke from the heart in the only straightforward way that I knew.

The general public were quite remarkable in their response to our appeal. Not only did they make donations in their thousands to help pay for the legal challenge, they got behind us with moral support too. Despite the nightmare television interview, total strangers came up to me in the street and patted me on the back and wished me luck for what I was doing. Robin, as ever, led the way, with Jimmy riding shotgun for me the majority of the time. Jimmy is far more articulate than I am, and so he was a natural bridge to interpret the ins and outs of the legal case.

With every passing day, the media spotlight intensified, and in January 2001 our legal challenge began. Robin had prepared our case in meticulous detail and I was so very, very proud of him. The challenge he was mounting was making legal history, and even though we knew there would be a rough ride ahead, we were determined to make as much impact as possible. The game plan was to seek a judicial review of Lord Woolf's decision as a way of reversing the decision to reduce the killers' tariff to eight years, ensuring they remained locked up for as long as possible.

Robin went through the court papers with us in fine detail, explaining what the implications of the case would be. He warned us that it would be a tough fight that we may not win, but, like us, he believed wholeheartedly it was the right thing to do. He had listened to our fury and represented our views immaculately. We pulled no punches and accused the Lord Chief Justice of putting the killers' interests before those of the victim, insisting that they needed to be punished for longer for the terrible crime they had committed.

We also claimed that the Lord Chief Justice had 'erred' in treating the rehabilitation of Thompson and Venables as more important than their punishment and that the eight-year tariff was too low for the enormity and brutality of the murder. Concerns that the boys would have to be transferred to a young offenders' prison if their sentence continued was irrelevant, we concluded. In fact, I believed they deserved to go to a harsher institution than a local authority secure unit.

Robin Makin told reporters, 'This is a unique case which we believe must be addressed publicly and thoroughly. It goes to the very heart of how decisions are made in a democratic society. Every legal challenge is flawed with difficulties, but on its merits, we believe we have a very good case. We hope the justice system is able to deal properly with this very serious issue.'

The papers were served not only on Lord Woolf, but on Home Secretary Jack Straw too as part of our application for a judicial review of the decision. We were trying to hold both politicians and judges accountable for the huge errors we believed they were making.

The legal hurdles kept coming at us like rapid gunfire. As soon as the papers were committed to the courts, we faced another huge drama. As the Parole Board continued its assessments of Thompson and Venables to establish if it was safe to release them, another major court ruling loomed and that was to establish if this pair, who were now young men themselves, should be allowed to have secret identities and lifelong anonymity if they were released from detention.

As much as I tried to believe that our justice system might for once be on our side, I think I knew in my heart what was coming.

On 8 January 2001, Thompson and Venables won an unprecedented court order to allow them to have anonymity for the rest of their lives. They were also to be given brand-new secret identities so that on their release, no one would know who they were.

The ruling was made by England's most senior family judge, the Honourable Dame Elizabeth Butler-Sloss, to protect the killers from possible revenge attacks by James Bulger's relatives and the public. The draconian order banned the media from disclosing information about the new identities, addresses, appearance and even the accents of the pair. Even if information was widely available on the Internet, they could not report it. In addition, the media was banned from publishing any information about the eight years they spent in local authority detention for a full twelve months after their release.

The application for new identities had been lodged by the lawyers acting for Thompson and Venables and had been vehemently opposed by some of the biggest newspaper groups in Britain, including News Group, Associated Newspapers and the Mirror Group, which insisted that secret identities for the boys would damage open justice, press freedom and the public's overriding right to know the identities of those who committed serious and detestable crimes. But because Dame Elizabeth felt that the lives of Thompson and Venables would be at risk if they were identified, in her eyes this outweighed the importance of freedom of expression and the right of the press to publish.

The biggest sting in the tail for me was when Dame Elizabeth quoted me insisting that I would hunt James's killers down. So my disastrous interview had come back to haunt me.

I was beside myself with rage but, of course, totally unsurprised. What really distressed me more than anything was that this new ruling, one of the legacies of my son's murder, meant that other monsters in the future would be able to use it as a tool to live in secrecy too. That was the last thing I wanted to result from what had happened to James. I believe that the treatment of Venables and Thompson always made the Establishment nervous, because if they changed their policy of rehabilitation to punishment they would be admitting they had got it wrong first time round. And they were young men by now, so they should have been treated like any other adult murderers. The pair may have been notorious and they may have faced dangers if their identities were known, but that also applies to many other adult killers who earned infamy through their crimes and were later released into society. Why should these two be treated any differently?

This was the first time that child killers had been granted lifelong anonymity, and I had been right to fear it would set a precedent. In 2003 Dame Elizabeth would be called on again to rule on a second similar case – that of Mary Bell.

In December 1968, Bell was convicted of the manslaughter of two boys, four-year-old Martin Brown and three-year-old Brian Howe. She was ten when she killed Martin and eleven when she took Brian's life. She was released in 1980, aged twenty-three, after serving twelve years' detention, including time in an adult prison. She was granted anonymity but it was not for life. Four years after being released from jail she had a daughter, who was unaware of her mum's past as she grew up. When a reporter discovered Bell had a daughter, the courts granted anonymity to the child until she reached the age of eighteen. Two years after Thompson and Venables were granted secrecy for life, Bell applied to the court to be given the same lifelong anonymity, which was granted. June Richardson, whose son Martin was one of Bell's victims and who had earlier attended the protest for James in Liverpool, called for conditions to be attached to the anonymity so that at the very least Bell could not make money from her crimes by selling her story.

It was hard to take everything in, especially as Robin had worked so hard on our case for us and it had got us nowhere. I remember going round to see Jimmy and sitting at his kitchen table. I was spouting venom until I was blue in the face. I could hardly get my words out I was so mad. I was letting off steam and Jimmy felt the same way as me.

'What kind of bloody message are we sending out when we protect these bastards who have done such evil things?' I vented at my brother. 'What can stop other monsters like Myra Hindley and Peter Sutcliffe from using this ruling if they are freed to live in our midst without anyone being allowed to say who they are? How fucking dare they do this in my son's name.

'Are they gonna protect all killers from now on? Are all the bad people gonna be given new names and secret lives when they do something wrong? It's just sick, really sick. It is totally warped and corrupt that the public will be the ones who are at risk from evil people because they don't know who they are potentially living next door to.

'They have not been punished yet but are gonna be set free anyway to live among normal people who have no idea who they are. They have been given everything to make life easy and privileged for them – everything short of a pat on the back and a gold star for savagely murdering an innocent baby. What next, a sodding knighthood?

'I hate the world we live in, Jim, I hate it! These bastards in their ivory towers are saying that if you brutally kill a two-year-old baby, you'll be looked after in every way. This has to be some kind of sick joke.

'We are the only ones being punished for this terrible crime. These evil cretins have had better lives as a result of killing my baby than they ever would have if they had stayed at home.'

I sat with my head in my hands after letting rip and then I started to cry. I was crying in frustration at the injustice of the way my country was treating us. I felt violated. I felt James's memory had been desecrated and spat on and that his name had been used and abused for the benefit of the boys who had murdered him. How dare they? The treatment we received at the hands of our legal and political system was almost as bad as losing James. I felt like a snarling animal in a cage that was being prodded with sticks by the upper classes. We didn't matter because we were ordinary, working-class folk who just wanted to get on with our lives.

I couldn't even say goodbye to my boy at his funeral because he had been so badly mutilated. The judges may have forgotten that. But I never can.

When my tears dried up, Jimmy, who had remained silent, said gently, 'We are never going away, Ralph. We are going to be a pain in the arse of each and every one in this system that doesn't seem to give a monkey's about James. Don't you worry about that, Ralph.'

As ever, my big brother was right.

14

Justice for James Denied

Without question, we all knew what was coming next. After serving our legal challenge on Lord Woolf and Jack Straw, we were told that a decision would be made within a few weeks. We didn't have to wait long for the inevitable answer.

On Friday, 16 February 2001, three High Court judges sat to deliver their verdicts. I couldn't face going to court myself because I felt sure that our challenge would be thrown out and I didn't want to face any further humiliation. I'd had a bellyful of courts and judges with too much power. Jimmy, as ever, stepped up to the mark for me and travelled to London for the hearing with Robin. Jimmy recalls:

None of us wanted to be there really, because we had been shot down and ridiculed so many times over the years that it had become exhausting. We were all drained by the events of the last few months, and although we retained some hope that our legal fight would continue, we also felt pretty certain that we would be chased out of court unceremoniously.

When we arrived at the High Court in the Strand, we were met by Lyn Costello, her husband Roger and several other supporters from MAMAA, who had turned out to protest at the release of Thompson and Venables. It was a sight for sore eyes. Just like us, they had never given up the fight, and as we stayed chatting on the pavement, along that busy London street, taxi drivers and motorists drove by and honked their horns in support of our campaign. It was like there were two different worlds. One for the millions of normal people like me and Ralph and Lyn and Roger, and the other world that seemed to be inhabited by the few – a lofty elite who appeared to be out of touch with the rest of us.

As I stepped into court, I took a huge, deep breath as once more I steeled myself for rejection. And it wasn't long before I got it. The proceedings were led by Lord Justice Rose, who was sitting with two fellow judges, Mr Justice Sullivan and Mr Justice Penry-Davey. It was not a long hearing as the three senior judges outright rejected our accusations that the Lord Chief Justice had set a minimum sentence for James's killers that was so low in comparison to the enormity of the crime that it threatened to undermine confidence in the criminal justice system. They continued to say that Ralph did not have any legal standing to challenge the tariff, refusing him permission to apply for a judicial review.

Lord Justice Rose said, 'Despite valiant efforts, it seems to me there is no arguable grounds for challenging the decisions of either the Lord Chief Justice or the Secretary of State.'

And there it was. Another door slammed in our faces and the end of the road for us to try to keep James's killers off the streets. I knew Ralph would not be surprised. We had been expecting the knockback, but I was still dreading telling him.

Jimmy phoned as soon as the hearing was over and told me the bad news.

'The bastards have knocked us back, Ralph. They have refused permission to challenge the tariff. I'm sorry, kid,' he told me.

'It's nothing that we didn't expect, Jim. But we had to do it anyway for James. Tell Robin thanks for everything he has tried to do. We will just keep fighting another way.'

I was devastated by the news but, as Jimmy rightly pointed out, not in the least bit surprised. We well and truly knew the score by now.

I really felt for Robin too. He had worked for almost two years to get this back to court, and in just a few short minutes, his attempts had been dashed. There was nothing more he could have done and I will always be grateful to him. When Lord Woolf had reduced the tariff back in October, he said that neither of the boys had shown any aggression or propensity for violence during their detention. We had tried hard to show in our legal challenge that there was evidence that Robert Thompson had been involved in at least two known incidents of violence in his secure unit, which had been reported in the press. The hearing denied that one of the reports, published in the *Sunday People*, was true. The *Sunday People* had gathered evidence of a vicious fight between Robert Thompson and another inmate called John Howells, but the High Court branded official papers that recorded the fight as fakes. These were documents that had originally been leaked to the *Sunday People,* which said the fight took place at 3 p.m. According to officials, Howells was in court at that time and the fight did not appear in any official logs. However, the *Sunday People* said they were confident the documents were written by someone 'with intimate knowledge of the running of that secure unit' and that they had not been asked for money in return for the papers and couldn't understand why anyone would want to carry out such an elaborate forgery.

The paper then reported that two separate taped conversations between Howells and his lawyer confirmed that Howells had told his lawyer of a punch-up with Thompson. There was also an incident with another boy who claimed that Thompson used an electrical flex to try to strangle him. Our QC had a statement from this boy who also complained that Thompson had made himself out to be the victim to the authorities when this was not the case. The barrister acting for the Government didn't deny the attack had taken place but said the event had been thoroughly investigated and the boy had not only exaggerated a minor incident, but in fact he had seriously provoked Thompson.

So despite what we believed was damning evidence to show that Thompson clearly still showed signs of being violent, our case was dismissed. But I couldn't help but believe that the courts didn't want to accept our case because it would show that their grand scheme of rehabilitation and release had failed.

After the court hearing, Dee Warner, speaking on behalf of MAMAA, issued a public statement. She said, 'The law in this country has been taken from the people. The law belongs to one man who is out of touch and that is Lord Woolf. He doesn't live in the same streets as our children do.'

There was one journalist who did grow up on the same streets as Robert Thompson and Jon Venables, and just two days after we lost our High Court challenge she wrote a brilliant article, published in the *Sunday People*, that I think is worth revisiting. So much has been written about the case, but this provided an unbiased, compelling argument to keep the killers locked up. Senior BBC presenter Winifred Robinson grew up on the estate where Venebles lived. From a deeply personal viewpoint, she argued convincingly that it was too early for the murderers to go free. Here is an abridged version of what she had to say:

The myth that has grown up since the trial is that these two boys came from the worst possible homes and that the cruelty and neglect of adults drove them to do what they did. I spent six months investigating their backgrounds for a BBC documentary. I found nothing in their home lives to explain what they did. Thompson had the worst start in life. His father left his mother for another woman and never bothered to see his children again. Afterwards his mother turned to drink and Robert, the fifth of seven boys, was left to fend for himself. The older children bullied the younger ones.

It was a violent household and one brother asked to be put into care when he was threatened with a knife. But friends of Ann Thompson who lived across the road told me she loved her boys. She even took Robert's shoes away to try to stop him roaming off at night. She had stopped drinking in the two years before James was murdered because she had met a new man and had another baby. And in the seven years since the trial, she has not deserted Robert. She is a regular visitor at the secure unit where he is held.

And anyway, it wasn't Robert Thompson who was

known for violence. Jon Venables had made a nuisance of himself at school, hurting other children. His parents, Neil and Susan, were separated but they both looked after the children. They decided to move their son to a school near his dad's flat in Walton to give him a fresh start. It was there he met Thompson and started skipping school.

Venables lived with his mother on the Norris Green estate. I know it well. I grew up there. My sister lives there still and I visit her often. Like most council estates, it has problem tenants. But most people are decent. It is not and never has been a rough estate. When I called, the Venables' house was deserted, but a neighbour told me Susan and Neil were good parents. Susan had suffered from depression; so have thousands of mothers whose children don't hurt anyone. The neighbour didn't like Jon Venables, though, remembering him as a boy who hit and poked other children on the sly. When he was late home his mother reported him missing to the police and both his parents scoured the streets for him, proof that they cared. After he was arrested they were at his side during the police interviews. He only confessed when his mother said she'd always love and care for him no matter what he had done.

At the time of the trial, I was the only journalist to meet Susan and Neil Venables face to face. They struck me as honest and I believe them when they told me that Jon had had more love and care than a lot of other children. They denied reports that he had been brainwashed by a horror movie his father had rented, *Child's Play 3*, saying he had never seen it.

It is a combination of what we are born with and how we are raised that makes us what we are. I concluded that Thompson and Venables were both by nature warped. Together they probably did something far graver than either of them would have done alone. But who can say for sure?

Now they are on the brink of being freed, we're told psychiatrists, merely by speaking to them, have sorted all their problems out. I find this hard to believe when psychiatrists are so plainly powerless to help in so many other cases. In fact, when it comes to the most heartless killers, like the Yorkshire Ripper Peter Sutcliffe or the Moors Murderer Ian Brady, many doctors write them off as personality-disordered people who cannot be treated, let alone cured.

If psychiatrists have all the answers now, they should out of basic decency share their knowledge with James's parents. They have nightmares to this day as they struggle to comprehend what happened on that lonely railway line. Neither Venables nor Thompson told the truth. They blamed each other. Police had to rely on forensic evidence to prove they both took an active part. There were bloodstains on Venables' coat. Thompson had kicked the baby so hard that he left the print of his boots on James's face.

They said nothing about which one of them sexually abused James or what exactly was done. The toddler had been stripped from the waist down, his foreskin had been pulled back and torn, there was clotted blood in his anus from a tear. Sex offenders remain a danger for life. So which of these two killers will go on the sex offenders' register and how can they be tracked or monitored with assumed names?

When he set the tariff at eight years, Lord Woolf said Thompson and Venables must be spared the corrosive influence of young offender institutions. He didn't explain why these places are all right for everyone else except these two. It seems to be an argument for making special arrangements for them, rather than setting them free.

Mary Bell who was eleven when convicted in 1968 of the manslaughter, on the grounds of diminished responsibility, of two boys aged four and three, was detained for twelve years. She served her time in a secure home for boys, a women's prison and finally an open prison. The Bulgers do not want their son's killers to be treated with the cruelty they meted out to James. But they feel strongly that eight years is not long enough to reflect the evil of the crime or to act as a deterrent to others.

In ruling that James's father Ralph has no legal right to question the decision of Lord Woolf, the most senior judge in England and Wales, the system has robbed victims of their voice – a very dangerous precedent.

How can any of us have faith in the courts to deliver justice when the voices of the innocent can be so cruelly ignored?

What Winifred Robinson said in her article summed up so many of my own thoughts, and she had first-hand knowledge of these boys and their families. She believed they bore the traits of psychopaths, that they were warped and that there was clear evidence of sexual abuse. As she rightly pointed out, you cannot cure a sex offender – they remain a danger for life – and so why was I being denied the right to question this tariff when it was clearly not safe for these boys to be back on the streets?

As I've already written, we have never found out why they acted so wickedly, but my belief has always been that it was a sexually motivated crime and that after they had nastily molested James, they had to kill him.

And if the psychiatrists had so successfully sorted out these boys' heads, then why were we being denied the right to know why they killed James? My own real worry was that it was because the doctors didn't know. But surely it is wrong to even consider releasing dangerous criminals if you are not one hundred per cent certain they will not re-offend. Could those in the legal system or on the Parole Board put their hand on their heart, look me in the eye and tell me they were certain Thompson and Venables were no longer a threat? If they couldn't, they would be taking a huge gamble with the life and safety of every child – and not one I would ever have been prepared to take.

As for the judges and politicians who crushed my bid to keep Thompson and Venables locked up, I made my feelings very clear. They all had my son's blood on their hands.

But even though we had lost the ruling, I felt we had gained a moral victory. We had stood up to the might of the law and for what we believed was right. We had overwhelming support from so many people, ordinary decent folk who believed we were doing the right thing.

*

When Jimmy arrived home from London, we were asked to submit a victim impact statement to the Parole Board before they made their final decision on whether to release the boys. Could we persuade the members of the panel to see sense? Or had they already decided to toe the line and do what the judges had wanted all along? It was one last stab at trying to convince someone that these savages should not be roaming our streets again.

Robin helped us to prepare our victim statements in thorough detail. While it wasn't easy, Jimmy and I both knew the importance of these reports because they were being prepared specifically to show the board the continuing effects that James's murder had on us. We knew we were messed up but we had no grand names for it and didn't always know how to describe ourselves. Robin organized for us to see Dr Mike Berry, a clinical psychologist, at his office in Liverpool. His report showed that I had been deeply psychologically damaged by the murder of my son. This was something I already knew, but for the first time it was given a name: post-traumatic stress disorder. It was a big awakening to me to know that the symptoms I suffered came from a very real medical condition when I had always put them down to prolonged grief. But even so, I didn't see how identifying this was going to make it go away.

Dr Berry's analysis formed the basis for Robin's detailed report, which said that I also suffered from chronic depression, powerful intrusive thoughts, nightmares, sleep problems, guilt and anger, and that I was overprotective with my other children. He added that I suffered from social isolation and social avoidance of situations that provoke memories and public attention, resulting in low self-esteem and no confidence to deal with life. This was an official report, but it totally fitted with my more simplistic way of describing my life. I didn't like going out or being around people and that had not changed in all the years since James's death. It made sense when I thought back to the panicky feelings I experienced if people recognized me and why I chose to go and visit James's grave at night when I was alone. Dr Berry also diagnosed Jimmy as having post-traumatic stress disorder and other associated symptoms following his identification of James's body.

In particular, the report stressed that both Jimmy and I remained acutely disturbed by the evidence of sexual abuse on James. If Thompson and Venables were wired to be paedophiles, then surely that was going to manifest itself later in life, especially now that they were young men and no longer children themselves. We genuinely believed that this was not being taken seriously enough by the authorities and that they posed a real danger to the safety of other children. We confided the fears we had for the safety of our own children. We felt that if these two were released, the 'ultimate thrill' for them would be to return to Liverpool and snatch another one of our own children to sexually defile and murder all over again. Right from the beginning it was almost as if the sexual element to James's murder had been brushed under the carpet because no one wanted to consider the concept of two ten-year-olds being capable of committing a blatantly sexual murder.

As the day approached when the Parole Board was due to meet, I went to see Jimmy to talk things through. We had done all we could and now it was out of our hands.

'You know they're gonna let these little fuckers out, don't you, Ralph?' Jimmy stated matter-of-factly.

'Yep, I do. But if there is even just the slimmest hope left, we have to go for it. We have to try it for James.'

'Yes, I agree. I just didn't want you to clutch at straws when we both know what is coming. Before long they are going to be free and wandering the streets again.' Jimmy laid a hand on my shoulder. 'Ralph, we need to prepare ourselves for what is going to happen.'

15

Killers Free Once Again

'I've got bad news, Ralph,' Robin said. As soon as I'd heard his voice on the other end of the phone my heart had started thumping. I knew what he was going to say, but I listened quietly as he told me that the killers were being released on licence. As much as I had tried to prepare myself, it still hurt deep inside my soul and, once again, I felt that I had failed my son. I was floored by the decision, just as if I had been run over and crushed by a juggernaut. It was the final insult to my son's memory.

The next day, Friday, 24 June 2001, Home Secretary David Blunkett, who had by now replaced Jack Straw, made the news public. Ironically, it was also my birthday.

I had met David Blunkett when he was named as Home Secretary and I genuinely liked him. Of all the politicians I have come across, he was one of the few who seemed genuinely to care. I remember him grabbing my hand and saying to me, 'I am so sorry about what happened to your son, Ralph.' And I believed that he really meant it.

Here is how he broke the news to the world.

'The Parole Board has informed me today of their decision, subject to conditions, to direct the release on life licence of Robert Thompson and Jon Venables . . . I would wish to make it clear at the outset that this means that Thompson and Venables will be on licence for the rest of their lives. They will be subject to strict licence conditions and liable to immediate recall if there is any concern at any time about their risk.'

After expressing his sympathy to James's family, he stressed that the Parole Board would have been satisfied there was no 'unacceptable risk' to the public, and that they heard evidence from expert witnesses. And he went on:

'I can say that the call on public funds will be the minimum necessary to ensure their self-reliance, further education and training, and the safety of themselves and the public . . . The life licences include conditions which prohibit Thompson or Venables, whether directly or indirectly, from contacting or attempting to contact the family of James Bulger, or each other.

'They will also be prohibited from entering the Metropolitan County of Merseyside without the prior written consent of their supervising officers. The National Probation Service now has the duty to supervise them and to review routinely the risk of reoffending.

'There are grave doubts about whether this duty could be carried out effectively without some degree of anonymity. I am assured that Thompson and Venables will be kept under very close supervision and scrutiny by the Probation Service, whose principal aim is to ensure the protection of the public.'

And so there it was. The little bastards were set free, with immediate effect. It has always been recognized that both Thompson and Venables were cunning and manipulative, and now they had managed to con the Parole Board that they were safe to be released.

I was told in confidence that David Blunkett had fought tooth and nail against the decision of the Parole Board, but in the end the twisted logic of our legal system got its own way. This was one of my darkest hours since James had died.

These were difficult days, once again. I was by now living back at my mum's house after Eileen and I had agreed to split up several months earlier. It wasn't like we'd had some huge row or bust-up, but I had spent so much time and focus on the legal fight that I felt we had drifted apart. Yet again, I was so consumed with the need to find justice for James there was nothing left to give to a relationship in my own life. Although I still cared for her, I knew it was unfair to stay with Eileen when I was wrapped up in my own troubles and I think she understood.

Thankfully, Eileen was happy for me to call up to the house to visit the girls and so we were able to share the responsibilities for our kids. In her own way, she continued to be there for me by caring for the children when I was battling for James. It was sad, but I count myself lucky that we were able to stay civil and friendly to each other, and we remain so proud of and committed to our daughters. Naigs was only young and so really knew little difference, and as I had only moved around the corner to my mum's, Ree and Bobbi still saw me all the time and they adapted very quickly, as young kids do. And I wasn't constantly rowing with Eileen so they didn't appear to suffer any trauma as a result of the break-up.

The day Mr Blunkett made his announcement, my phone

never stopped ringing. Family and friends kept a close eye on me to make sure that I was OK. My first call of the day was from Jimmy.

'Bastards,' he barked down the phone. That's all he needed to say.

Later that day I took an unexpected phone call that left me reeling. It was from an anonymous man who said, 'Ralph, you don't know who I am, but I have information that I think you should know. I have access to information relating to the release of your son's killers. As part of the preparation for their return to society, care workers took them to visit your son's grave to complete their rehabilitation and to help them deal with the crime they committed. It's despicable and I just thought you should know.'

The line went dead but I stayed rooted to the spot. For the love of God, how much more was I supposed to take? This was the very same as my recurring nightmare – the image of James's killers standing at his graveside. I didn't want to believe it to be true, but the caller had sounded genuine and concerned, not like a crank. Why would he make something like that up? Given all the other attempts to rehabilitate these boys, it made perfect sense they'd be taken to where James was resting.

I phoned Jimmy back and told him. 'They took the bastards to James's grave. That is the one sacred place where I wanted my son to be safe from his killers and they took those evil rats to gloat over him. I hate them so much.'

'What's happened?' Jimmy quizzed.

'I had a call from a well-wisher who says they went there. How could they do that to us, Jim? Are they trying to finish us off?'

'Just try and stay calm, Ralph. This is a shite day and I'm with you every step of the way. We will keep a close eye on everything that happens and we will carry on fighting for James, don't you worry about that.'

We have had no confirmation from the authorities either way, but if they did visit the grave then my chats with Dr Berry also suggest it was likely that, for the same reasons, and in a bid to get them to face up to their crime and avoid curiosity at a later date, Thompson and Venables would have been taken back to the scene of the murder at the railway track.

The decision to release Thompson and Venables sparked real fury across the country. The Internet almost went into meltdown as people threatened to kill the pair and placed bounties on their heads. In a press interview two days later, Jon Venables' mum, Susan, said she feared her son would be tracked down and killed within a month of being freed and that the pair would forever be looking over their shoulders as revenge-seeking vigilantes vowed to hunt them down. They were predictable responses because public feeling had never really faded over James's death, but, while I recognized their notoriety, I didn't feel Thompson and Venables were any more at risk than other violent killers. The decision to grant them anonymity set the precedent to allow any other killer to justify the same treatment, creating a society where violent offenders can move around in freedom and secrecy.

The mood in the country was so ugly that David Blunkett was forced to call for restraint and calm. Several days later the *Mail on Sunday* reported in detail that the killers didn't even want to be freed because they were so terrified of revenge attacks and wanted to remain in the security of their detention homes. Both the teenagers were apparently sobbing with fear when they had to leave the comfort and security of the units that had become their homes for the last eight years.

It was a terrible and bitter irony. The public wanted them to remain locked up, James's family wanted them behind bars, our Home Secretary agreed and if the *Mail on Sunday* report was accurate then even Venables and Thompson wanted to stay incarcerated. And therefore it seemed to me their release was down to the liberal agenda of a few who wanted to prove that young killers could be rehabilitated and that they were not intrinsically evil. If that's right, it was a deeply flawed and dangerous experiment, if you ask me.

Upon their release, Thompson and Venables were given new names, birth certificates and National Insurance numbers, and all traces of their old lives were destroyed. They had disappeared back into society and the rest of us did not know where they were or what they looked like.

Several days after they were freed, tensions were still running high across the UK and I was continually being asked by the press about my response to people threatening to kill Thompson and Venables. I made a statement, which was published on the front page of the *Daily Mirror* under the headline 'Leave Them Alone'. I thanked the public for the support they had given us over the years and for caring so deeply about the terrible crime committed against James, but I also urged people to refrain from seeking revenge on the two boys. My biggest fear was that an innocent teenager might be mistaken for Thompson or Venables and bear the brunt of a nasty attack, or worse. I could never allow that to be a part of James's legacy because no other innocent family should have to suffer the way we had over the years. As I said, 'Thompson and Venables have not paid for their crime, but I cannot live with the thought that the wrong person may ultimately pay the price for their evil. I think the time has come for there to be some restraint and for matters to fade away to allow everyone some time to reflect and allow what has been set up to take effect.'

I hoped this would go some way towards redressing the balance and show that James's family were not looking for vigilantes to track these young men down. My plea to the public was mirrored by David Blunkett. He addressed the nation, saying, 'I understand that people have strong feelings about the release of the boys after eight years. But there is nothing that can bring James back and we have to address ourselves to the future. I think we all need to take a deep breath and to view what is said and done as we would view it if it were taking place in any other country. We're not in the Midwest in the mid-nineteenth century; we're in Britain in the twenty-first century and we'll deal with things effectively and we'll deal with things in a civilized manner.

'If people continue to provide the emotional adrenaline for others who are sick of mind to go and attack the boys then there will be a great danger. The greatest safeguard we can offer to people in the community is to rehabilitate Thompson and Venables effectively.'

I didn't agree with Mr Blunkett that the killers were capable of being rehabilitated; however, I still didn't want vigilante attacks being carried out in my son's name.

I think the power of public opinion had caught the Government and the legal system napping, because now they could see how the people of this country really felt. It looked like they hadn't just let James and his family down; they had let the whole country down.

Details of how the Parole Board had come to their decision to free the boys began to emerge in the days after. On the Monday before they were released, a panel of three people had sat in the visitors' room in a former borstal in an unknown area in the north of England. The team was made up of a judge, a psychiatrist and a lay member. Also present were the lawyers for each boy, probation officers and security men. Jon Venables was the first to be interviewed by the panel and his grilling lasted for two days. Thompson was called to the panel afterwards and also faced two days of questioning.

Press articles reported that Venables fared far better than Thompson during the assessments, dealing confidently with all manner of questions, while Thompson appeared more awkward and quiet. The panel also studied the pair's psychological dossiers, which showed that Thompson was apparently a quiet but caring young man who had come to terms with his awful crime. Robin had put forward a report to the board showing how expert psychiatrists suspected that Thompson could be an undiagnosed psychopath, which was also considered. (I believe that Thompson and Venables knew exactly what they were doing the day they abducted James and enjoyed the pain they inflicted on my son. If that's not psychopathic, then I don't know what is.)

The first key issue the panel had to consider was whether

the boys felt remorse for their crime. Venables, by all accounts, was able to convince the panel easily of his remorse, but it was said to be trickier for Thompson. For several hours he was questioned about the crime and how he had responded to the intense therapy programmes he had undergone while in detention. At the end he was able to convince the panel and answered all their questions unflinchingly. The pair of them had ticked all the boxes and passed the test to be released. They were home and dry.

The parole panel was made up of professional, intelligent people, but in my mind they had simply been tricked. The teenagers were by now adept at therapy, having encountered many counselling and psychology sessions. What's more, they had been taught to lie by the state in order to safeguard their new identities. Fakery and deceit is how they had been prepared to live their new lives, and so it wouldn't have been hard for them to weave past the Parole Board. I believe they would have known how to answer the questions put before them, how to tell the panel what they wanted to hear. I felt pretty sick when I thought about how these two had managed to pull the wool over the eyes of the parole team.

Even though the boys were now eighteen, I think people still didn't want to accept that ten-year-old boys could have been so evil. It was like the authorities were saying, 'Look at us, aren't we noble, we have saved these boys from the depths of hell and put them back on track.'

It was reported that Thompson and Venables were likely to be initially moved to safe houses in a large town or city to ease them back into the outside world and set them on the path to enjoying independent living as young men.

Harry Fletcher of the probation union NAPO said at the time, 'If they feel genuine remorse, then how will they live with what they have done? People working with them will know that there is a high risk they will try and block out the guilt with alcohol and drugs and that there is a real possibility of mental illness further down the line.'

But the boys had been given a thorough grounding to start their new lives. Both reportedly came out of detention with A-levels and a wealth of hobbies and interests. Thompson was said to be a talented young fashion designer, while Venables was a keen Manchester United fan, who idolized David Beckham, loved reading and writing and wanted to go to university. This was all well and good, but it didn't remove the fact that it was James who lost his life, and as a result his killers went on to be given a great start in life instead of a punishment. My son didn't even get a chance to start school, let alone get his A-levels and go to university.

Everyone in my family was furious they had been released. And unfortunately the very real fear we felt for the safety of our children only grew. When Jimmy and I had filled out our victim impact statements, we had expressed our concerns that Thompson and Venables would deliberately target other children in our family. The details of our children's names, ages and schools were all included in our report, which was supposed to be a confidential dossier for the eyes of the Parole Board only. But to our shock, Robin had to tell us that the document was then shared with lawyers for Thompson and Venables, who in turn could have asked to see them. If they had, they would have read our family details. James's killers could now know exactly how many children Jimmy and I had, their ages and the schools they attended. It couldn't have been a more horrifying situation and it was made worse by the fact we couldn't even show our kids photos of the boys so they could be on their guard should anyone try to approach them. Our children could be walking along the street and not realize they were passing these murderers.

If we had been overprotective already, now we all became exceptionally paranoid and terrified for our families. I didn't want to upset the girls, but at the same time my fear got the better of me and their safety was my priority. It wasn't as if they were old enough to go out on their own yet anyhow. They were still only six, five and two, so the biggest impact fell on Ree who had started school but was already having her freedom clipped because of our worries. We didn't like her to go to friends' houses to play. It was fine if they wanted to come to our house, but we didn't like her to be out of our sight when she wasn't in school. Likewise, we felt safe if she was playing in the back garden with her younger sisters, but I wasn't happy to let her play out the front because I was scared she'd be abducted like James. This would be our pattern of behaviour with all the girls as they got older and wanted to go out more. It was tough on them but they began to understand why as the years went by. That is the stress that was put on us all by releasing these two.

Jimmy and Karen felt the same way, as Jimmy recalls:

Ralph and I were in turmoil and we began living our lives like virtual prisoners ourselves. Mine and Karen's children couldn't move to the point that we didn't even want them to go out and play with their friends. They noticed it more than Ralph's kids because they were a few years older and so they were constantly complaining that it wasn't fair that they were being kept in.

I remember one incident clearly when Karen took our youngest to school and there was a camera crew in the playground. It was not long after the killers were released and so the media had been in the neighbourhood in force. This particular cameraman had nothing to do with the news. He was there at the invitation of the school to film everyday life as a way to promote the school. He didn't have a clue who Karen or our daughter were, but when he innocently zoomed his lens around the playground to capture the kids playing and landed on our daughter, Karen freaked out. She started screaming and yelling to get the cameraman away and all the other mums who knew her ran over to the poor guy and almost threw him out of the school. It had been a mistake on her part, but we were all on high alert and so wound up that even the smallest of things would set us off.

It was sad to see how the younger generation of our family was being affected by the release of Venables and Thompson. And the fear I had over my children's safety brought back every bit of self-loathing I had for being unable to protect or save James. It was hard just to get through each day. The whole thing left me feeling hollow and empty because everything we had ever done to seek justice for my son had been for nothing.

16

The Tenth Anniversary

The tenth anniversary of James's murder was on 12 February 2003. By that time his killers had already been free for almost two years. The irony was not lost on me. It was a bleak and miserable day and I can say with my hand on my heart that my pain and sorrow were as huge as on the day my baby boy was stolen from me. My life had been shaped and rearranged by the death of my son and now, after years of hurt, it had become twisted and buckled beyond all recognition.

The anniversary was not forgotten in Liverpool and the atmosphere in the city that day was dark and sombre. Once again the people of Merseyside showed how much they still cared. At the Strand, where Thompson and Venables abducted James, shoppers stood in sorrow for a two-minute silence and flags flew at half-mast across the county as a mark of respect. Churches everywhere dedicated their services specially to James and children in school said prayers for him at morning assemblies. I was so very grateful that my fellow Liverpudlians had not deserted us or forgotten my son. His anniversary also dominated the local TV news channels and papers, and the anger was still there in the hearts and minds of ordinary people. But alongside the fury lay a calmer and more reflective attitude. Things had most certainly settled down a bit from those early lynch mob days.

But while the people of the city were calmer, I had no idea how to get rid of my anger and sorrow, and, despite a ten-year period of mourning, I had not moved on one bit. It's not that I wanted to be like this, all chewed-up and mangled inside, I just didn't know how to feel any other way, and my rage had been stoked by a legal system that trashed my son's right for justice. I would have done anything to wake up for just one day and not be consumed by anger and bitterness.

Several weeks before James's anniversary, I flew to Cork in Ireland to visit Father Mick. He had remained in contact as he had promised, and he was still one of the few people I felt comfortable talking to about James and my feelings. I don't know why really. I think it was because I trusted that he was such a good, kind man and that he didn't expect me to be anything but myself.

I was delighted to see him, and his welcome for me was as warm as ever. He had a very rare gift of connecting with people and making them feel good.

'It's wonderful to see you, Ralph. Come in, come in,' he beckoned when I arrived at his front door.

'It's great to see you too, Mick.'

No sooner was I through the door than he embraced me in a massive bear hug and instantly I felt the tears welling up in my eyes. It was a sudden rush of emotion that I had not been expecting.

The first thing he did was put the kettle on to make us

a cup of tea, and then we both sat down to catch up in the comfort of his cosy living room.

I spent hours chatting to Mick that day, and even though I eventually broke down into tears, it was a very calm and peaceful visit. Sitting with him was like emptying my emotional dustbin. For just a few moments, I was able to shed the feelings that normally lay festering in my heart and soul.

'I just don't know how to do this any more,' I admitted to Mick.

'What don't you know, Ralph?' he gently replied.

'I don't know how to cope with these feelings any more. It's like they are just too big for me to handle.'

'You have to give yourself permission to have compassion for yourself, Ralph. And you have to ask yourself if you really want to let go of those negative feelings. Maybe you are frightened of what you will be left with if you let them go. The healing process has to start with forgiveness, Ralph. And if you can't forgive the boys who murdered your son, then try to begin with forgiving yourself. You are carrying so much guilt and hurt inside, but you are not to blame for James's death. There was nothing you could do to prevent it. You weren't there and you didn't know about it, so you couldn't have saved him.'

'But I should have been there, Father Mick. I should have been there for him and I wasn't. I just can't get the thought out of my head of James begging for mercy and crying out to his dad for help. I am so angry with myself and I don't even know if I can forgive myself. I want to, I really do, but I failed him as his dad. He was my flesh and blood and I failed him, and I don't know if that will ever go away.

How can I get rid of it? Please tell me. I think I'm going mad sometimes.'

'You have to slowly try to let go and have compassion for yourself. James would want you to forgive yourself. He was a loving and kind boy who would have wanted to help his dad feel better.'

We had never really spoken in such detail before. He had always tried to bring me comfort and was forever telling me it was not my fault, but I was so angry during our early chats that I don't think this gentler approach would have helped at the time.

It was an incredibly emotional afternoon as I wept buckets of tears to Father Mick and felt not one ounce of embarrassment. Afterwards, I went for a walk in the quiet countryside and I thought about what Mick had said. Could I ever forgive myself? Could I ever stop blaming myself for James's death? I just didn't know if that was possible. The truth is that my anger was the only thing that kept me going sometimes, but I also knew that it was eroding every fibre of my humanity. I knew I could never forgive Thompson and Venables, and I didn't want to, but I desperately wanted to feel normal again. I couldn't remember what it felt like to start each day with joy and happiness, as I had before James was killed.

My trip to see Father Mick was a delight. Despite the deeply emotional nature of our chats, there were some very short periods of light in the darkness for me as we spent time together and talked. As well as comfort, he gave me a little belief that maybe one day I will be able to move forward, no matter how long it takes. Father Mick taught me that it was OK to feel the way that I did and that, despite the passing of ten years, it was normal to still feel the pain of losing James. He reminded me that you don't get over something so horrific as James's murder and that time doesn't heal. You just find different ways to cope.

I returned to Liverpool feeling better prepared for the anniversary, thanks to Father Mick. I thought a lot about the conversations I had shared with him and it dawned on me that I had a lot of unresolved issues. It wasn't just my guilt; the fact that I would still binge drink at times was another problem, as was my anger. The time had come for me to confront a lot of things and Father Mick had helped me see that. There was one thing in particular that I was finally ready to face. I had never been to the railway track where James was murdered – the last place he was alive. For ten years my subconscious had been nagging away at me to go there. I think I carried some deep, primal need to connect to the place where my son had drawn his last breath. It was almost as if it was one of the missing pieces of the jigsaw. I thought about it for a long time before I committed myself to going. I questioned why I wanted to go there and how I would react. And I spoke to Jimmy and Karen about it.

'Do you think I should go to the railway track where James died?' I asked them.

'Why do you want to go?' Jimmy responded.

'I'm not sure. I just feel that I should go. It's where my son died and I have never been there in the ten years since he has been gone.'

'If you feel it will help, then you should go,' Jimmy replied with certainty.

'What if I can't handle it? What if it makes things worse?'

'I don't think it will,' he said. 'It sounds like you need some closure around this and by going there just the once, you will feel as if you have paid your respects to James at the place where he died.'

'I've never been able to face this before. I didn't think I could ever go down there, but it's a part of James's life I have never confronted and I think I need to. I can't explain it very well but I just feel a strong need to do it.'

'Then you have answered your own question, Ralph,' Jimmy concluded.

He was right. It wasn't something I relished the thought of, but I did need closure on it. I needed to go there and then move on. It was a few weeks before the official anniversary that I decided to be brave and face my fears head on. I ordered a wreath crammed with yellow and white flowers, all bright and sunny just like my James. Across the rim of the circular arrangement was a pure white ribbon, bearing the words 'For James'. It was with a heavy heart that I set off for the railway track that day, and I must have tried to change my mind a hundred times, but I kept returning to the belief that I somehow owed it to James to visit the place where he had been killed. I thought about many of the conversations Father Mick and I had shared, and I knew I had to do right by my son in his death.

Jimmy and Karen had offered to come with me, and I was very grateful to them, but it was a moment I needed to spend with James alone. The railway line where James's body was severed in two by a freight train was still used occasionally so I'd had to get permission to go onto the tracks at a safe time. As I climbed the steep grassy hill to reach the embankment, I thought about how hard that must have been for my son with his little legs. He had already been walking for nearly three miles by the time he reached the railway and he would have been exhausted.

I think the short walk to the spot where his body was found must have been the longest journey of my life. I felt exactly as I had done when I carried James's coffin into his funeral. It was bleak, dark and soul-destroying. It didn't take a lot of imagination to conjure up how frightened my son must have been. Weary, scared and crying for his mummy and daddy, he was dragged onto the embankment of that desolate track and tortured repeatedly. There wasn't a sound on the trackside that day, but in my head were the screams of my son as these boys ripped his clothes from him, battered him with bricks and smashed him with an iron bar. I saw his face screwed up in agony as they dripped the tin of paint in his eyes and mouth, as James begged them, 'Please don't hurt me. I want my daddy.'

Every last detail of my son's murder, already ingrained in my mind, sparked into replay in vivid technicolour, and the rage and shock coursed through my blood once again. How could they have done this to such a loving, helpless child? And how could our legal system have released his killers to enjoy the rest of their lives as if the murder had never happened? I tried to place myself in James's shoes on the day he was murdered. He would have been looking up at the boys with fear and confusion, crying as he begged for mercy. And he would have suffered so much pain. It was almost too unbearable to be there, revisiting his attack in my head.

I knelt slowly down to place the wreath on the track in

the exact same spot where ten years earlier these boys had laid his battered and dying body to be finished off by a train. The beautiful wreath of flowers looked frighteningly out of place against the dirty stones and railway sleepers, just as my bright and vibrant boy would have looked as he was stretched on the track to die.

'I'm so sorry, James,' I whispered.

It was time for me to leave this place. I began to walk away and didn't look back. I don't know if I did find any closure that day, but it was one last job that I had needed to do for my son. And it had been torture. It certainly didn't bring me any peace, but I realized it wasn't for my benefit. It was all about James. He had suffered so much that day, and perhaps I wanted to make a small sacrifice of my own to show him how sorry I was. Perhaps I was even punishing myself, I don't know. But it was over and I knew I would never go back there again.

On the day of the anniversary itself, I just wanted it to be over. When I woke up, my mind drifted back a decade. I could still see James waving goodbye to me from the front step of his grandma's house, as if it were only yesterday. He gave me the widest, most loving grin you could wish for, and that would be the last I ever saw of him. Inevitably, regret flooded over me once again, remorse and self-hatred for not taking him with me that day to go and fix the wardrobes, and that horrible knot in my chest rose up with a passion as if to remind me what a terrible father I had been.

I didn't really want to be around anyone that day and so I spent many hours alone, quietly reflecting and mourning the son I had loved so much. Eileen knew what day it was and offered me her support, but the girls were still too young to realize and I didn't want them to see their dad unhappy. I tried so very hard to think about James and the amazing love he had brought to all our lives. I wanted to banish all thoughts of his killers from my mind but it proved to be impossible. I thought about how much of his life James had missed over the past ten years, and then I compared it to how Thompson and Venables were just twenty years old and free to live their lives.

I decided to visit the James Bulger Memorial Garden and sat for over an hour under a small circle of trees opposite a stone memorial tablet which was inscribed, 'James's Garden – A place of peace and beauty'. When it was time to leave, I laid a small posy of flowers and a card next to the plaque, which read:

'James, I miss you today more than ever, but I know you are at peace now, son. I think about you every day and I love you with all my heart. Stay safe and warm with the angels now and keep laughing, my little "smiler". All my love, your Ralph (Dad) xxxx'.

It was hard to leave the garden that day because it was so quiet and dignified, and it brought a small touch of calm to the madness inside my head. I missed my son so much that my body hurt both inside and out.

Just a few weeks after the tenth anniversary was James's birthday, on 16 March. He would have turned thirteen and become a teenager. I spent hours and hours fantasizing about what he would have been like and I had a clear vision in my mind of how he would have looked and sounded. I'd had so many dreams for the son who never even got to three.

I imagined the pair of us still playing football together, laughing, and sharing private jokes. In my head I could hear us chatting about what he wanted to be when he grew up – a rally driver maybe, or an airline pilot? He could have chosen to do anything he wanted because he was smart and bright and clever. It didn't really matter what he wanted to do. If he had told me he wanted to be a dustman or a brickie, I would have been delighted for him, just so long as he was happy and healthy. My greatest sorrow is that I never had the chance to do the ordinary things with him that fathers do with their sons.

I know if James were alive today, I would take him fishing and we would talk about anything and everything. I would have bought him his own rod and tackle and we could have set off together on days out, wasting hours away side by side on the banks of a river. I know he would have loved that. What's more, he would have been the older brother to Michael and his three little step-sisters. I know in my heart he would have been a brilliant big brother and that he would have looked after each and every one of them. So many people lost so much when they took James away. He lost the chance to grow up and welcome his new family, and his brothers and sisters never had the opportunity to get to know him.

I think my son would have grown into a tall, strong and handsome young man with a winning smile, sparkling eyes and a kind heart. As each year passed, I imagined James that little bit taller and wiser, just getting on with his life. I would love to have heard his voice as he grew from a boy into a man. But all I am left with is the sound of him as a baby. I still carry his picture in my wallet and talk to him all the time. That will never change, but I wish with all my might that I could once again just be that ordinary man with my extraordinary son by my side.

Even after the boys were released the newspapers continued to report on Thompson and Venables and their new lives, and each time they did, it reignited public fury. At the time of James's tenth anniversary, it was reported that the two young men were to be spared reminders of their crime by being whisked away to adventure holiday parks at the taxpayers' expense. They were said to have been taken to separate outdoor pursuit centres for a ten-day break with twenty-four-hour protection to guard against the threats from gangsters who had placed a £100,000 bounty on their heads. These were the types of stories that repeatedly surfaced over the years and did nothing to appease public fury. As I've said, I have no idea which of the stories were true, but they kept coming thick and fast. Some of them sound highly unlikely, but to some extent that almost made me believe they must be true.

The Internet also played a very dangerous role in the reporting about the killers. On several occasions innocent young men were accused of being Thompson or Venables and had to go into hiding as a result. Up-to-date photographs said to be of the pair were also posted online and often they would be emailed to Jimmy. We both saw them, but so often there was no proof that they really were images of Thompson or Venables. While the authorities acted swiftly to shut the sites down when they appeared, it wasn't before thousands of people had had the chance to view them or copy them. It made a mockery of the injunction in place, because from the day they were released, it was always going to prove an uphill task to keep their identities secret in an age in which technology can spread information so quickly.

The public was furious to read reports that both killers independently went on unsupervised foreign holidays in Europe, even though both were meant to be strictly monitored under the terms of their parole. Venables, it was reported, was given permission to go clubbing in Norway. One of the most shocking allegations was that Venables had also had sex with a female guard at the secure unit where he was held while still a teenager. That just about summed up our system to me. Not only did it appear that those boys had enjoyed every privilege they could have wanted – clothes, computer games and a sterling education – but now it was claimed one of them had had sex with a grown woman who was supposed to be guarding him.

The newspapers widely reported that in 2000 Venables had sex with the woman shortly before he was granted parole and while he was still in detention at Red Bank secure unit in Merseyside. He was seventeen at the time.

According to the reports, instead of punishing the guard, it was alleged that Red Bank hushed it up, although she was later suspended and never returned to work after staff at the unit filed reports on the incident. The local council that runs Red Bank denied any cover up and said the matter had been properly investigated. It was never confirmed whether Venables had or hadn't been involved. But if he had then I can't help thinking this woman must have been as twisted as Venables to want to have sex with him in the first place, and it would have been a grave breach of trust by someone who was supposed to part of a so-called re-habilitation process. It would also have begged the question of whether the Parole Board knew about the incident when they made their decision to free him.

17

Life Goes On

James's tenth anniversary was definitely a major turning point in my life. Perhaps it helped that our legal battle seemed to be over – there was no more we could achieve. Thompson and Venables had been freed. I knew the very best thing I could do was look after my family, so I finally stopped the binge drinking and, when I wasn't looking after the kids, I would go training for hours on end or take myself off for a spot of fishing. I didn't go on some mad teetotal campaign, but my attitude had changed and I became healthier and more positive, and occasionally I would enjoy a social drink without going over the top. I was trying to focus on the future of my children.

The girls were growing up fast and they kept me busy. I loved every minute of it. One of their favourite games was when I would deliberately scare them with a pair of coyote slippers that I would wear. When you pressed the ears the slippers began howling and the kids would squeal in mock terror and run off to hide behind the sofa. I would deliberately chase them and they loved it. These were the silly, simple games with the children that kept me grounded and sane.

I took my daughters shopping one day and stupidly said they could have money each to buy whatever clothes they wanted. I had no idea the sort of mayhem that could break out in a shop from making that kind of offer to fashion-mad young girls. In seconds there were clothes everywhere and their arms were filled with items they liked, until I got so embarrassed I dragged them all out of the store insisting their mum could bring them back another day! I took them all to a café for egg and chips afterwards and we laughed our heads off. The girls said the look of horror on my face was hilarious. They were cheeky and funny, happy young girls, just the way they should be, and I couldn't have asked any more of them.

It was in the same year as James's tenth anniversary that Ree turned eight, and she dropped a bombshell on me that I hadn't been expecting. She came home from school one day and began to ask me about her brother James. All the other kids at school had been talking about him and she wanted to know what had happened to him. Ree was far too young for me to fill her head with horrible things. I told her that James was her lovely older brother and that when she was a bit older I would tell her more about him. A couple of years later the issue came up again, only this time she really began to dig deeper.

'How did James die?' she asked out of the blue one day.

'I'll tell you one day, but not right now.'

'Kids at school say he was killed.'

'Bad things did happen to James, but he's in heaven now. He was a lot like Bobbi. Noisy and lively,' I joked, desperate to lighten the moment.

Jimmy and Karen had faced similar issues with their girls.

By this stage, two of them had looked up a lot of the details on the Internet at school and knew far more than their parents were aware. Their eldest daughter became extremely protective of her mum and dad, and if any of her siblings attempted to ask them about James, she would give them a tug.

'Don't you be asking Mum and Dad about that stuff. If you wanna know anything about James, you come and ask me,' she demanded. It was as if the girls had created their own little secret service to protect their parents and it was very touching.

And so it went on. We had the ordinary days without drama and then there was a burst of activity, which was nearly always prompted by something in the papers about Thompson or Venables. One particular story really shocked us. In 2006, the *Sunday Mirror* reported that Robert Thompson had become a dad himself. By now he had turned twenty-three and the report said that the mother of his baby had no idea of his criminal past.

We didn't respond to a lot of press reports, but if this was true it was terrifying. Jimmy and I decided to ask Robin if he could find out for us but we were always met with a wall of silence. It was a story that was repeated many times over the years and never denied by the authorities. The follow-up to this was another report that Robert Thompson had left the mother of his child and was now gay and living with his male lover, who knew all about his conviction for murdering James. Again, we had no way of proving whether this was true or false, and we learned not to get too wound up by every single story that came out. It's fair to say that my emotions always went up and down, but I knew I couldn't let the press stories get to me, or my health would begin to suffer and my head would get filled up with anger again.

Unfortunately, while my life did improve during this period, the same couldn't be said for Jimmy, who seemed to be stuck in the same rut of self-destruction. As Jimmy himself says:

Without question, I was never the same man again after seeing James's body in the mortuary. It has been years of mental torture. I can only begin to guess what it must have been like for Ralph and Denise to lose their child in such a brutal and savage way.

Just like Ralph, I began to be consumed with anger. It was impossible not to, after seeing the sheer brutalization of little James's body. It was utterly beyond comprehension how a human being could inflict such suffering onto a tiny young boy. From that day to this, life has been a struggle for everyone. Of course, it affected Ralph and Denise the most, but my family life would never be the same again. I was furious all the time and that spilled over into my own behaviour at home. I didn't know how to deal with what I had seen and all my feelings remained locked up inside, as they still do now. My health has suffered greatly over the years as I struggled to look after myself. I drank too much and smoked too much as I tried to block out the raw and horrific images I had seen, and this caused massive health problems. In some strange way, it was almost as if I felt I didn't deserve to be well. I felt that my own life and wellbeing just didn't matter any more, because nothing could ever compare to the pain that little boy went through. When something like this happens, there is a part of your soul that dies too. Your faith in human nature is destroyed when you have seen humanity at its worst. Along this journey, there have been plenty of people who have helped to restore that belief in goodness – the kind of people who have unselfishly tried to help Ralph and Denise and our entire family. But it can never erase the awful truth that there is so much evil in the world too. James was the one who suffered the most, but his parents and loved ones were left with a lifetime of misery too. The flashbacks I have experienced for many years now will never go away and I can still imagine James's pleading voice as he was being tortured. I wake up covered in sweat and I can hear James crying in the dark.

Where once I was an outgoing, happy man, today I am a very different character. Over the years I have become a loner, with horrendous thoughts locked in my head. I have never been able to talk to anyone about it and that, in turn, has affected my own family, including my children, some of whom were not even born when James was murdered. I could never have got through these years without my devoted wife. She has been there for me solidly even though she, too, has been to hell and back trying to keep everything together and bring up our children. Ultimately, feeling terrible becomes the 'norm', but on that awful day in 1993, I vowed I would do everything in my power to help Ralph seek justice for his son. At times, it became like an obsession and completely took over our lives. But we all knew we could never give up fighting for baby James.

Karen has had to watch me fall apart over the years and there was nothing she could do to stop it. She was there that night with me when I identified James and says she will never forget seeing how ashen and stunned I was when I came out of that room. She said that I looked like a ghost, a living spectre who had just glanced into Hell. She was right. The terrible image of James's body stays with me all the time, but I have never learned how to talk about it properly. It has always felt easier to cover it up and deal with it alone. And for my wife, that almost felt like losing her husband. The feelings remained trapped in my body and I had nowhere to put them. When my anger boiled over, I would erupt with fury and frustration and this affected our family life. My outbursts at home were both terrifying and tragic. The kids didn't know why their daddy was so angry all the time or why their mummy was crying or upset. My girls bore the damage of losing their cousin too. I often felt so sorry for them because our paranoid fear for their safety meant their lives were so different to the way they should have been. We almost tried to keep them under lock and key, which meant they never got to enjoy normal things like going to youth clubs or having sleepovers at their mates'.

The enormity of the case really hit home for me when my daughters began studying for their exams. Two of my girls studied psychology at school and part of their curriculum was to learn about the murder of James Bulger. I remember clearly the day one of the girls got back from class with homework about her own murdered cousin. It was quite flabbergasting and it upset the girls greatly. There was very little that a textbook or coursework could tell them about the grisly death of young James.

I have never been able to share my feelings with Karen. I don't know if that is because I tried to protect her or whether I just wasn't capable of getting them out. Ralph was better at expressing himself than me, and he was able to cry, which was very healthy and part of a healing process. I think it has been a lonely journey for all of us in our own ways, but when things got tough we just dug our heels in and waited for the storm to pass.

I did settle down over the years but sleep never came easy to me. I would sit up most nights researching the case on the Internet until the early hours of the morning. My disillusionment with the legal and political system turned to loathing as they shafted us time after time.

Karen and I both saw at close quarters what this all did to Ralph. When his marriage broke down, he came to live with me and Karen for three months. If you look at photographs of Ralph in the newspapers, he always looks so hostile. He scowls and tenses his whole face, but that is very much part of his protective armour. When he is not in the spotlight, he looks less harsh and at ease. He has always been a thoughtful and kind man and he is gentle, a trait which his son James inherited from him. But Thompson and Venables instilled anger in him, too.

Peace is a luxury that has been stripped from our family because of two evil young boys who killed for kicks and ripped so many hearts wide open, but we will never give up the fight for James.

18

Recalled to Prison

It was late afternoon on 2 March 2010, around 4 p.m., when the doorbell rang. I wasn't expecting any visitors and so when I opened the door to see two official-looking callers, a man and a woman, I knew it had to be something serious. They introduced themselves to me and said they were from Merseyside CID and the Ministry of Justice. My heart quickened as I knew it could only be related to one thing.

'Mr Bulger, we have some news for you. Do you mind if we come in for a while?' the middle-aged man, a plain-clothes detective, asked. I opened the door to him and the woman from the ministry. I showed them into the living room and invited them to sit down.

'I am afraid we have to tell you that one of your son's killers, Jon Venables, has been recalled to prison for breaking the terms of his release and we wanted to inform you before the news became public.

'Unfortunately, we can't tell you the extent of what he has done, only to say it is an extremely serious matter that is being treated with the gravest of concern.'

The man in the suit continued talking but his voice seemed to get fainter as my mind began to work overtime.

'Please, God, don't let him have harmed another baby,' I prayed in silence.

I realized that he was still talking to me as I tried to gather my thoughts.

'Ralph, can I ask you how you feel about him going back to prison?' he urged.

I shrugged my shoulders and told him, 'To be perfectly blunt, I am not surprised at all, and as much as I appreciate you coming here, your visit is a bit of a waste of time because I said a long time ago that I knew this was going to happen.

'No one listened to me then and I doubt they will listen to me now.

'Has he killed another baby? Has he done it again? No one else should have to go through what James suffered.'

The man looked at me apologetically but, as expected, his reply told me nothing.

'As I said, I'm afraid I don't have any details at the moment, but I am sure more will become clear.'

That was the extent of my 'briefing', and in less than ten minutes they were gone. As a parting shot, the woman who had stayed quiet until now added, 'Oh, you might see news of this on the television and in the media. Just to let you know.'

There was the punchline. The recall of Jon Venables to prison was about to become headline news and I strongly suspected that this was the only reason I was getting a personal visit. If their hand had not been forced by the media getting wind of events, I believe I probably would never have learned that Venables had reoffended and been taken back to jail.

I had a million and one questions that the ministry was unable to answer and, once again, I was in the dark about the real truth of what had happened.

I got on the phone to Jimmy immediately. 'Venables is back in prison, Jim.'

'What?' he stuttered.

'Yeah, he's back in jail for breaching his licence but they won't tell me what he has done. I hope he hasn't hurt another baby, Jim.'

'Jesus, Ralph, are you OK?'

'Yeah, I guess. One down and one to go, eh?'

'Yep. It was only a matter of time and we both knew that. Let's try and find out what he has done.'

'It will be all over the news later. The media have already got hold of it.'

'OK, well, maybe they will shed some light on it for us.'

By 6 p.m. that evening, just two hours after my visit, the national news had broken the story and the media went crazy. It was the lead story and headline news around the world.

The Ministry of Justice released very few details that day, just a short, terse statement. It read: 'We can confirm that Jon Venables has been recalled to custody following a breach of licence conditions.'

I was wracked with torment because I didn't know what this man had done. I thought about James and the torture the ten-year-old Venables had inflicted on him; I shuddered to think what he was now capable of as a twenty-seven-year-old man. I was also furious with the Government for trying to keep the reason for his return to prison secret.

How dare they? The public had a right to know. We don't live in a police state where information is concealed from ordinary people.

As the hours ticked by, public indignation began to gather pace. This was one of the few occasions when I felt compelled to speak out publicly and I blasted the Government for throwing a veil of secrecy around Venables once again. Politicians were not even prepared to say whether he had committed another crime or had been recalled for breaching one of the conditions of his licence, such as the ban on him returning to Merseyside. The only hint that he had carried out a crime was when the Home Secretary, Alan Johnson, said that he expected criminal justice proceedings to follow.

For days we continued to receive mixed messages from the Government. While Mr Johnson came out and said he believed the public had a right to know, Jack Straw, who by now was the Justice Secretary, kept insisting that the reason for Venables' return would not be divulged because he believed it was not in the public interest. It was a shocking turn of events.

In a press release to the media, I let rip at the Government: 'I always said that the judges and politicians who let these two boys out had James's blood on their hands because they just didn't care enough about the precious life of my little boy.

'Venables might be back inside but his other killer is still roaming free and no one knows who he is because of the anonymity they were both granted. Knowing that one of them is behind bars again is little comfort when they won't even tell us what he has done. And why did it take a week to let me know what had happened? Is James's family really so unimportant? Jack Straw protected these boys years ago and now he is doing it again. He is saying it is not in the public interest to reveal why Venables has been jailed, but once again he is wrong. What have the Government got to hide over this? We all have a right to know the truth, and how dare the Government try to cover it up?

'What these boys did was so horrific it is beyond belief they were ever let out. When we fought to keep them in prison we were told they would never reoffend because of their so-called rehabilitation. The Government got it wrong then and now they should hang their heads in shame. If we are to be told that Venables is back in prison, then we should also be told the reasons why. Our legal system danced on the grave of my innocent son without a hint of shame or compassion by letting his killers go free. Now their actions have come back to haunt them. Venables is back where he belongs but he should never have been let out in the first place. If he has reoffended then he should now be stripped of his anonymity. As far as I am concerned, once evil, always evil.

'Now is the time for our Government to stand up and give us the justice we have never had for our baby James. No more hand-wringing and looking the other way. God knows our family has waited long enough for justice. We have had seventeen years of hell because of these bastards and we must be told what Venables has now done. He should not only be punished for his recent crimes but he must now pay as an adult for what he did to James and any other poor souls who have had the misery to cross paths with him. He was offered the chance of rehabilitation and freedom, but he has blown it. It is only a matter of time before Thompson is caught reoffending too.'

Such was the secrecy surrounding Venables that we were not even allowed to know which jail he had been sent to because of the injunction that still remained in place. There was just one seed of hope: Venables was now serving time in an adult prison, and I prayed he would remain there for a very long time.

My head was full of all sorts of anxiety about what Venables had done. I was certain it would have to be something serious and, as the days dragged on, Mr Straw continued to drip-feed the public information, finally confirming that Venables had committed a very serious offence and would be appearing before a Parole Board panel before the end of the month.

Almost a week after we learned that Venables was in jail, another bombshell was dropped on us. The newspapers began to report that James's killer had been recalled to prison for child sex offences. The *Sun* newspaper revealed that Venables had hoarded a stash of vile child pornography on his laptop.

I admit that I was stunned. I shouldn't have been shocked, but it was such a revolting revelation that I felt sick. How many children had been preyed on by perverts so this evil man could satisfy his sick urges? I took no pleasure in being proved right that Venables was, and always would be, a predatory paedophile and a danger to children. My heart sank when I heard the news and all I could think about were the children like James who had been harmed by Venables and other warped men like him.

The laptop had been seized by police from Venables' home and when they examined the computer they discovered child porn images rated at category four on an official scale of one to five, with five being the worst. Mike Hames, former head of Scotland Yard's paedophile unit, said at the time, 'All child pornography is serious, but category four images are particularly vile. They are among the most serious and depraved images of child pornography it is possible to possess and involve an element of sexual violence against children. Given this individual's background, that must clearly be a huge concern to the authorities.'

Venables had not changed one bit.

Jack Straw and the rest of the Government were facing embarrassment over the recall. In an about-turn, he invited Denise and me to meet with him to discuss what had happened, but I was so incensed that I refused. Denise did go, but I don't know the outcome of that meeting. For me it was all too little, too late, and once again we had only found out the truth from the newspapers. Mr Straw had been forced into a corner, and I viewed his invitation as a damage-limitation exercise and a cheap publicity stunt to save face. I had been in this position before, back in 2001, when we met with Mr Blunkett as we tried to prevent James's killers being released. He said all the right things and sympathized – but then let them out anyway. I wasn't about to face a second humiliation by going all the way to London to be told absolutely nothing.

It also began to be claimed in newspaper reports that Venables had been dangerously out of control during his years of freedom, and on several occasions had almost been recalled to jail even before the child pornography offences.

His probation officers had been concerned about his daily abuse of drugs and alcohol and he had become involved in a string of violations, including two brawls, during one of which he was stabbed.

Despite being banned from ever visiting Merseyside as one of the conditions of his release, Venables flouted the rules and regularly snorted cocaine on nights out at Liverpool nightclubs, receiving a police caution in 2008 for possessing the drug. Reports claimed he had downed cider and cocktails and taken cocaine and ecstasy in a number of bars across the city. He also visited The Cavern Club, where the Beatles started their careers, and watched Everton Football Club play at their ground at Goodison Park in Liverpool.

He repeatedly ignored his licence conditions, despite the fact that he was supposed to be under constant state supervision. In short, his so-called rehabilitation had been a disaster. The whole thing was laughable and our politicians had some serious questions to answer.

It had been nine years since he was released from detention and only now were we beginning to uncover what Venables was really like. He was reported to have a raging temper, just as he had when he unleashed his fury on my son's body. Sources close to Venables insisted he was snorting up to a gram of cocaine a week and was a regular visitor to the V Festival and Glastonbury, where he was said to get 'wasted' for several days on end. He also worked as a nightclub bouncer and had a reputation for being aggressive and confrontational.

In another incident outside a nightclub, he got into a fight with the boyfriend of a young woman. He was punched in the face by the girl's angry lover and Venables spent the night in police custody. All these shocking revelations had been known to his probation officers, but still he was not recalled to jail until the child pornography images were uncovered.

How could our Government have got things so wrong? The warning signs had been there. Once again, they had chosen to ignore them.

But it wasn't just Venables who was in the spotlight again. A week after Venables' arrest, a social worker who had supervised Thompson for eight years in detention came forward and gave a startling account of what the killer was really like in an interview with the *Mail on Sunday*. Reporters Ian Gallagher and Andrew Chapman described how Thompson had been treated with kid gloves while in detention, was cunning, knew how to 'work the system' and showed no remorse for the killing of James.

The social worker was quoted as saying, 'He was monosyllabic and sullen when we were first introduced, like all the children when they first arrive. But then it became apparent that he was a typical "care kid" – even though he had never been in care. These children are cocky and streetwise, know the system and know their rights and what they can get away with.

'He'd say things like, "I want a drink. Get me one now. You've got to get me one."

'From the outset he was a star prisoner – and played up to it. There were frequent visits from Home Office officials who were always fussing over him, checking with him and the staff that he was all right. He was treated with kid gloves and underpinning it all was this fear that something might happen to him, that something might go wrong.'

The newspaper article confirmed everything that my family had always suspected, and in some respects it was worse than we had thought. He was not only pampered inside, but treated almost like a celebrity prisoner. The article was really important to us and it must have made uncomfortable reading for the politicians and lawmakers. The social worker went on to describe how he took Thompson on many days out to shopping centres, parks, swimming pools and restaurants, and that his room was decorated with Lowry paintings and others by a Russian abstract artist. It didn't add up to much punishment to me, but then this was what we had always insisted. I think what the article really highlighted was how much power Thompson had over his carers and guards, and that was frightening.

The social worker gave a good example of this when he described a bust-up in Thompson's unit. He said, 'Once, he was involved in a confrontation with another youth, and he was really angry, but in a controlled sulky way. He stood rooted to the spot in the lounge area. It was bedtime, but he wouldn't go to his room. I said to the other staff that we should take him back to his room and take away his TV or some other privilege, which was the procedure. But they were against it.

'It was a good forty minutes before he eventually went to his room. It was ridiculous. I made a representation to my superiors that he was being treated differently from the others but it was shrugged off. He was extremely persuasive, and used this to extract what he wanted from senior staff. In fact, after this incident, he even secured himself a later bedtime. When the others went to bed, he'd stay up for a further twenty minutes watching television. He was also close to the manager at the unit and they'd sit talking and laughing together. The manager would even send someone to get them a cup of tea while they chatted . . . no one wanted to upset him because they were afraid of what the consequences might be.'

A lot of information about the treatment of Thompson and Venables in detention came out a good many years after they had been released, and this report was no exception, but it did show up very specific privileges the boys were treated to. Their routines and luxuries were more than I could ever have afforded to give my son and my other children. For example, they were given around £60 a month spending money and clothing allowance and received £25 on their birthdays. At Christmas time they gave present lists to their social workers who would go out and buy the gifts. Details also emerged that when he was sixteen, guards allowed Thompson to form a relationship with a red-headed girl who had a troubled past and had been placed in secure detention for persistent thieving.

Amazingly, the social worker finished his graphic account by recalling how he saw Thompson after he had been released working as a steward showing people into a major stadium.

To me, this was one of the most factual articles that we had seen on James's killers, and it was from a source who had actually been there. It really hammered home how privileged he had been. Venables received very similar treatment, but it had not stopped him from reoffending.

*

On 21 June 2010, Venables was finally charged with down-loading child pornography and was facing up to ten years in prison. He was accused of downloading fifty-seven in-decent images of children from the Internet and distributing seven images to other paedophiles. The first court hearing was held in private at the Old Bailey in London, but the judge, Mr Justice Bean, lifted reporting restrictions and allowed the charges to be printed in the interests of open justice. It was alleged that Venables amassed the indecent pictures between February 2009 and 2010.

Mr Gavin Millar QC, prosecuting, said, 'The first count, the making of indecent photographs, covers downloading onto his own computer. Count two covers the distribution through the Internet of indecent images. The Crown's case is that fifty-seven images were downloaded by Venables between the 1st and 27th February 2010, but he used and had available peer-to-peer software on his computer. This made it possible for other Internet users who searched for photos to download them.'

I was so relieved that Venables had been charged, but my biggest concern was that he would somehow get away with this too and wriggle out of trouble again. In the run-up to his trial, Venables was kept in complete isolation in prison, where his true identity was thought to have become known to other inmates. Prison governors confirmed that his status was 'high-risk'. It was some of the most unset-tling and disturbing times we had ever endured, because the outcome of his pending trial was on all of our minds the whole time. I couldn't bring myself even to think that Venables might one day be back on our streets, and I prayed that finally this might be the one thing that kept him locked up for good.

He came to trial on 23 July 2010. The hearing was held at the Old Bailey again, but Venables would only appear before the judge via video link from prison. The judge was the only person to see the defendant on a TV monitor placed directly in front of him.

This was to be Venables' first court appearance since he appeared in the dock back in 1993, when he and Robert Thompson were on trial for James's murder. He pleaded guilty to all the charges laid against him but the details that emerged of his seedy life were truly sickening. The court was told that some of the pictures he had stored on his computer involved children as young as two – the same age as James when he was abducted and killed. Videos he had watched showed eight-year-old girls being raped and forced to perform sex acts.

Prosecutors outlined how Venables had an extensive history of searching for and downloading child porn, but the details of how he posed as a young mum who was prepared to allow her own daughter to be abused by another paedophile in return for cash left everyone reeling. In 2008 he wooed fellow perverts in Internet chat rooms by pretending to be a thirty-five-year-old mother called Dawn from Liverpool with an eight-year-old daughter. He begged for photos of parents abusing their own children. 'Dawn' told one man that she and her husband abused their daughter and the paedophile responded by saying he would like to meet the daughter and abuse her himself. He then gave 'Dawn' a telephone number on which he could be contacted. Venables kept the conversation going so he could keep receiving indecent images and he struck up negotiations to agree a price for abusing the young girl. Venables admitted that he was sexually aroused by the indecent images, but broke off contact with the paedophile when he asked to meet with the girl.

Venables was only caught for his sickening crimes after he panicked that his true identity had been uncovered in February 2010. Terrified for his own safety, he rang his probation officer who told him to pack his things and get ready to flee to a new home. When the officer arrived to pick him up, Venables was found trying to destroy the images on his computer by hacking into the hard drive with a tin opener. A detective inspector arrived at the premises and Venables and his laptop were taken away to the police station, where the pornographic images were discovered. After his arrest he had bragged that he considered his behaviour to be 'breaking the last taboo'.

Venables' lawyer, Mr Edward Fitzgerald QC, told the hearing that his actions could be partly blamed on his 'abnormal' situation of living under an assumed name and with the very real and prolonged fear of reprisals. His isolation, he said, had led him into a downward spiral of drink and drugs and he had become addicted to cocaine and mephedrone. His lawyer said that Venables had tried to live as normal a life as possible, but was forced to lie to friends about his true identity and was unable to form any close relationships with women.

Judge Mr Justice Bean jailed Venables for two years for his offences and banned him from owning a computer with Internet access for five years. He was also banned from ever working with children and was told he would have to register with police as a sex offender for ten years. The Ministry of Justice announced they had launched a probe into his re-offending and whether he should have been recalled to prison earlier. No public inquiry was ever launched and I've certainly never been told of the outcome of any investigations by the ministry, and probably never will.

The final sting in the tail was a statement that Venables released after his trial through his solicitor, John Gibson. He claimed that he thought about the killing of my son every day and said he was sorry for his crimes. I didn't believe a word he said; this was just his pathetic attempt to excuse his unforgivable depravity. His statement went on to try to explain why he had become a paeodophile.

'His release involved a challenge, and one that has impacted upon him daily ever since. In the words of the pre-sentence report, he had "a legacy life" – a complete change of identity – "he was trained by the police in counter-surveillance and has had to live and hold a lie for the rest of his life. There was little doubt that if his identity became compromised his life would be at risk." A casual search of Facebook and the internet shows the very real risk to his life . . .

'But, throughout this time, as the pre-sentence report observes, "One of the major impacts in his life has been the inability to share his huge secret . . . he feared he would always be alone" . . .

'The 2008 offences took the form of a hoax online conversation exchanging images obtained from file-sharing sites, which were then deleted. Jon Venables acknowledges that conduct, which came at a time when he was drinking to excess because of the pressures he was under, was crass and unthinking. It was not repeated: the very careful analysis of the computer he owned during 2009 and 2010 shows that, whilst he continued to obtain and view indecent images of children, he took no steps to show them to anyone else.

'He puts forward no excuse for his conduct. He is genuinely ashamed, but he has and continues to express his remorse, and has come to an understanding of how children are harmed by those who have even a passing interest in such material, let alone by those who pass it on . . .

'By pleading guilty to the charges today, Jon Venables has accepted and acknowledged the wrong he has done and the harm he has caused. He is extremely remorseful and knows that he has badly let down those who have tried to help him since his release from custody.'

I'm not sure what was the most shocking part of the whole fiasco. Jon Venables had managed to escape with just two years in jail for serious child sex offences when he could have been handed down up to ten years! It simply wasn't a long enough sentence for the crime he had committed, but it was another example of our lenient legal system letting dangerous and cunning criminals off the hook.

As for his statement of so-called remorse, the only thing Jon Venables regretted was being caught. How could he possibly say that the stress of living a lie led him to enjoy child pornography? He had admitted being aroused by these appalling images and that could only mean one thing – that he was a paedophile through and through. If he is ever freed again, he will without question reoffend because he will never be cured from the sickness in his head. This man is never going to change and I don't know what it will take for the authorities to accept this.

It made me want to retch when I thought back to how he and Thompson had sexually defiled James. That had been their intention all along, to abuse a baby in that way. As he was still on life licence, the Parole Board had the right to keep him inside indefinitely for the murder of my son if they believed he was a danger to the public, but I held out little hope of that happening. What's more, the secret identity he had been given when he was first released from jail had been well and truly blown apart. And so if he were to be freed again, he would have to be given another identity, costing the taxpayers hundreds of thousands of pounds.

As if it were needed, further evidence of Venables' disturbed mind at the time he killed James was now released through the newspapers in the form of a drawing that had never been seen publicly before. It was sketched shortly before he and Thompson murdered James and had been found at his father Neil's house. It was part of a bundle of unused evidence from his trial and appeared to give some insight into the deeply troubled mind of a boy who routinely watched sick horror movies. I don't know why it never came before the court because it was a terrifying image. It showed an attacker with enormous knives, slashing two individuals who are on the ground with blood gushing from their bodies. Venables had titled the drawing, 'My Dad's house'.

The words on the drawing were full of spelling mistakes and grammatical errors but clearly established that he was illustrating a scene from the 1970s slasher film *Halloween*.

Venables wrote, 'In my dads I saw howowen is when you a girl and this man and he kiled people especial girls and he has got a mask on that he robed knifes out the shop and the police that it was pice but it was not it was the man.'

Whatever Neil and Susan Venables believed, Jon clearly had watched horror movies at his father's house and they had made a deep and lasting impression on him. Venables drew his ghastly picture just a few weeks before savaging James.

The whole episode sent shivers down my spine and the only relief was that Venables was back in jail where everyone agreed he deserved to be. On the night he began his new prison term, I hugged my girls extra close to me and thanked God they were all safe.

19

Parole Denied

As Venables began his two-year jail term, Jimmy and I met with Robin to discuss what we could expect in the coming months. We knew we had to be prepared well in advance because Venables would be eligible for parole within a year. We decided that we should seek the chance to put forward new victim impact statements to the Parole Board, with particular reference to what we believed to be the sexual motive for James's murder. We had to do everything we could to prevent the board from releasing Venables halfway through his jail sentence. As ever, Robin worked like a trooper on the groundwork for any future hearings.

At the beginning of May 2011, just a few weeks before the Parole Board was due to meet in June, a photograph showing Venables just before his arrest for child porn was posted onto a website set up to campaign against child abuse offenders. Within just a few hours it had been viewed by 1.7 million people as well as being posted onto social network sites such as Facebook, ensuring people as far away as Australia and Canada viewed it. The founder of the site defended his decision to publish the photo, insisting that it was to protect the public and children from convicted paedophile Jon Venables.

We cannot name the founder of the site because of the draconian injunction that prevents the British media from revealing Venables' and Thompson's identities, but he said at the time, 'I have not singled out Jon Venables on my site, as I name and shame all convicted paedophiles so that the general public know who they are and can therefore protect themselves. The picture has been seen by millions across the world and I know prisoners are using their mobile phones to pass the picture on. The public deserve protection from a man who is a killer and a proven sex offender. My campaign is all about education and information and I don't believe Jon Venables or any other sex pervert has the right to anonymity or a protected identity. It is the public that deserve protection – not the perpetrators of such crimes.'

I agreed with every word this man had said. I only hoped the Parole Board would see that the public needed to be protected.

Venables' parole hearing was set for Friday, 24 June 2011 and I was frightened and nervous about the outcome. I was prepared to do anything I could to convince the panel that Venables had to be kept locked up. Robin had helped both Jimmy and me to prepare our victim impact statements, which contained an explosive and damning indictment of James's killer in a bid to stop him from being freed.

More than ever, I feared that my children would no longer be safe if Venables was let out. As I've said, I genuinely believed that the ultimate sexual thrill for him would be to abuse and kill another one of my children. Now I was convinced that when Venables was caught with child pornography, he was spiralling out of control and on a mission to abduct and torture another toddler for his own sexual gratification. It was only sheer luck that his perverted lust for children was uncovered by police before he had the chance to sexually attack another child.

My own view was that the legal system of this country should have been in the dock alongside Venables, for failing to protect innocent children. I needed the Parole Board to know how I felt because if they decided to release him, I didn't even have the right to appeal their decision.

I was begging the board not just to consider his latest crimes but to look at the whole picture stretching back to James's murder. I was convinced that there was an unmistakable and clear connection between his latest child offences and his killing of James. If the board agreed with me then his life licence should be revoked for all time, or else there was a danger he would be released and would kill again. I just wanted the board to see sense for the sake of all our children. I had to get my message to them before the panel sealed Venables' fate

The Parole Board was sitting for their hearing in an unknown location in Leeds, and so Jimmy and I went to Liverpool Crown Court, where Robin read out our victim impact statements to the panel via video link. They could see us but we could not see them. It was a terrible and deeply distressing experience to have to relive all our suffering again for the hearing, but if it meant that Venables was kept inside, it would have been worth it.

Outside the court, Robin let rip to the waiting reporters and television crews, articulating my family's fear, anger and pain.

He said, 'Ten years ago this month, in June 2001, a decision was made by the Parole Board to release Jon Venables. At that time we very much wanted to make all possible representations to the Parole Board. They refused to allow us to do so. We submitted a lot of material to them. Quite astonishingly, the Parole Board have no records of what happened ten years ago. And the Ministry of Justice don't seem to have been able to locate any of those papers. So we have had to start again.

'It has been an extremely distressful time for Ralph. He has suffered depression, intrusive thoughts, nightmares, sleep problems and post-traumatic stress disorder. The authorities have not yet provided any support or help to deal with those issues over the years.

'Ralph faces a daily nightmare and things have not really got any better. We explained to the Parole Board how Ralph was affected when James was abducted.

'The whole process has transformed him into someone he doesn't really want to be. Whereas Jon Venables . . . in a sense what they have been trying to do is transform him into somebody he really isn't.'

Robin was on a roll and when he had finished speaking at length to the media, it was time to go. It had been an exhausting day and I was glad to get home that evening. We were told to expect a decision within ten days, and all we could do now was wait.

Just three days later, on the Monday, I was stunned to hear from Robin.

'Ralph, I have good news for you. The Parole Board has

turned down Venables' parole,' he said, coming straight to the point.

'That's brilliant, Robin, I'm made up. How long will he stay in for now?'

'Well, no one knows yet, but he will be eligible to apply for parole again in two years, so this could be an ongoing battle. At least it's the right result for now.'

'Yeah, thank God they haven't let him out. Thanks a lot, Robin. We couldn't have done any of this without you.'

The three members of the parole team – headed by a judge – had had to decide whether Venables still posed a risk to the public and they looked at the offence that led to his recall to prison, his offending history and his progress in jail. Reports from psychologists, probation officers and prison officers were also considered, as well as my own address to the panel.

It was a great result, and the only time in almost twenty years that a decision had gone our way. We had fought tooth and nail and had no idea if our pleas had been in any way influential, but we were all just so relieved to hear the news. Finally, one of James's killers was being kept behind bars where he belonged. It was the only legal victory we had ever tasted since they were first found guilty, and it felt amazing.

I slept easy that night for the first time in many years. Everything we had battled for had been worth every bit of sweat and tears. I have no idea what convinced the Parole Board to make that decision, because they never discuss individual cases, but at that moment it was enough. Perhaps they denied parole because they didn't think they could keep his identity a secret if he was released. Perhaps they too believed he still posed a risk to children. Or maybe they finally realized that Venables is a calculating liar who had repeatedly conned the authorities into believing he was rehabilitated. He is not a young man who can be trusted, and anything that comes out of his mouth should always be treated with extreme caution.

It is clear to me that he has a personality disorder, and until the true extent of his mental state is established, he should not be considered for release. The whole episode was a huge embarrassment for the Government and the legal system. They had tried to 'cure' a savage child killer and they had failed. I only hoped that lessons had been learned to safeguard the protection of all children for the future.

What also proved to be a mistake was that his probation officers had allowed Venables to live within a few miles of Liverpool after he was freed, even though one of the conditions of his licence was that he wasn't allowed to go to Merseyside. It was foolish to think that he wouldn't automatically drift back to the place that had once been his home. His presence in Liverpool meant that the people of this city would have been walking past him without knowing who he was, and that could have included me or my family. It was naive and highly risky to place him so close to the place where he had killed James and where we all still lived.

Even with Venables put away, it was still not over. As Robin pointed out to me on the phone, much as I would love for him to remain in jail for ever, he would be eligible for parole hearings every two years, which meant we would have to begin the fight all over again in 2013.

*

Towards the end of May 2013, Jon Venables appeared before his second parole board in secret in a bid to be freed from jail after serving his sentence for child pornography. Just as we did on his first parole hearing, Jimmy and I made an impassioned plea, via a video link, to the parole board. We begged them not to let Venables out, giving the same reasons we gave two years earlier when his parole was denied, including our belief that James's murder was sexually motivated. It was distressing to have to keep reliving the same nightmare over and over again, but if it was the only way to keep this man in jail, then I would do whatever it took.

This time the board told us they would recall all the evidence from the original trial when Thompson and Venables were convicted for James's murder. They assured us they would investigate this aspect of the case very thoroughly, and it gave us some reassurance that they might agree with our fears and refuse to let Venables out.

After Venables' first parole hearing, a decision was made very quickly. This time around things were different. Days and then weeks ticked by and we heard nothing. As more time elapsed, we all had the sinking feeling that he would be getting out and that his new identity and release were being planned by the authorities in secret.

After nearly six weeks, Robin placed a call to the probation and parole board. The response he received was astounding. He was told that they could not say when the decision would be released but that James's family would be tipped off just sixty minutes before a decision on Venables' future was publicly confirmed. The reason for this was because the authorities wanted to avoid a 'media furore'. That was the killer punch. As soon I heard that, I knew he was getting out, if he hadn't already been released. On previous occasions when decisions were made about James's killers, our family always received at least a few days' notice before the public announcements. I got straight on the phone to Jimmy.

'He's getting out, Jim, I just know it. If there's going to be a media furore, it's got to be because he's being freed. Everything is being hushed up and even though it was my son who was killed, we are all being kept in the dark. If they were keeping him in, there would be no furore.'

'I know, Ralph,' Jimmy replied. 'We knew this was gonna come one day. The little bastard is probably out already, shipped out and in a secret new home somewhere. He could be next door to some poor bloody family with kids.'

Later I went round to see Jimmy and Karen to talk and we were all fuming. It wasn't just the fact that Venables was going to get out. That was bad enough, but I thought the way we were treated by the authorities was a disgrace. Why weren't we being told what was going on six weeks after Venables had appeared before his parole board? We felt there had been a cover up from day one because they refused to let us in on what was going on. As James's father I felt I had a right to know what was happening.

'Why don't we go public and make a fuss about it?' I asked Jimmy. 'Humiliate the bastards in authority who treat us like dirt.'

'Yep, I'm right behind you,' he responded without hesitation.

The same went for Karen. We all agreed that we were not going to be silenced any longer, and contacted a trusted freelance journalist to ask for help in getting the story out into the public domain. We passed on the information and left the reporter to sort the rest out. Two days later on Thursday, 4 July, national newspapers ran front page stories under headlines such as 'Bulger Killer's Secret Release.' The story was followed far and wide and it kicked up a real hornet's nest in the media. Sara Payne, whose daughter Sarah was murdered by paedophile Roy Whiting, campaigned and spoke publicly about how furious she was at the way we had been treated.

'This angers me so much,' she said. 'After all the heartache, keeping James's family in the dark about what is happening to one of their son's killers is simply wrong. Why are the family not being told? Why has it taken the parole board six weeks to deliver its decision? It sounds like another part of a secret-keeping culture. Legals chiefs want to avoid a "media furore" by keeping the decision secret but are causing further heartache for the victim's family when these processes should be open and honest.

'After all, it is the families of murder victims who matter most.'

The story also dominated on national television, with Philip Schofield and Holly Willoughby leading the debate with news commentators on ITV's *This Morning*. People seemed appalled at the way we were being treated. It felt like such disrespect and I am sure it made for some very uncomfortable moments among the authorities. But we were not expecting what happened next.

By 5 p.m. that same day, just hours after the media blew the whistle, I received a phone call from Robin.

'Ralph, Venables is being released,' he said quietly. 'I'm sorry it is bad news but it has been confirmed.'

'I knew that was the case, Robin. I'm not shocked in the slightest. We were right all along that they were trying to keep this quiet.'

By 6 p.m. the decision broke on all the news channels and across the Internet on news websites. My response was simple. It was wrong and it should never have happened. I was sickened to the core, obviously. And I was furious because once again I felt that James and his family had been ignored and let down.

I believe Venables is a violent and dangerous sexual predator of children and releasing him just puts kids in danger of being attacked. It was also reported that this would be the fourth time that Venables would be given a new identity, at a total cost now of £1 million to the public. To me it is an utter disgrace and I am disgusted that Venables is now free once again to live a charmed life in secret.

It was a particularly proud moment for the media, who had forced the parole board and the Ministry of Justice into coming clean a few hours after publicly humiliating them for their behaviour. I don't think it was an accident that their decision came the same day they had faced widespread criticism for keeping Venables' release secret, and as far as I am concerned, journalists who shine a light in dark places and get a government department to be open with the public are reporters doing their job very well.

The Ministry of Justice trotted out the usual lines that Venables will remain on life licence and will face strict controls and restrictions. But those same conditions didn't prevent him from reoffending before, and I can't see things being any different this time around.

In the days that followed the decision, Robin tried hard

on our behalf to establish the exact terms of his licence. In particular, we were frantic to know if he would still be banned from entering Merseyside. That had been part of his previous conditions but it was reported that he regularly flouted the rules and frequently visited Liverpool to go clubbing and partying with his friends. At the time of going to press with this paperback edition, we have still not been told the conditions of Venables' release.

In the summer of 2012 a story was printed in the newspapers about a young man in Scotland who killed himself. His mother said that he had been bullied by people in their neighbourhood, who accused him of being the child killer Robert Thompson. She claimed that when the taunts became too much for him, he took his own life. I cannot verify the story, but if this is true, it is precisely the reason why we campaigned for the identities of James's killers to be known. If the public knew who they were, innocent people would not be mistakenly targeted and accused in the way we have seen on several occasions over the years.

I accept that the issue of Venables and Thompson will never go away. I am still subconsciously on guard all the time, steeling myself for the next battle I have to face. And I am still waiting for a knock on my door to tell me that one or other of them has committed another crime, the thought of which fills me with dread.

20

A Ray of Hope

It has been twenty years since that terrible day in Walton when James was murdered. He would be twenty-three by now. My imagination has a field day trying to picture what he would be doing. I like to think he might have had all the opportunities that I didn't. I fantasize that he's finished a university degree course, studying something really grand or fancy. He was such a clever little boy and bright well beyond his years.

I'm certain he would have been a handsome but caring young man, someone who didn't toy with people's emotions, and there is no question that he would have had a cracking sense of humour. James's laughter really defined him. He was always smiling, grinning or cackling away at something, because he genuinely embraced life from the moment he was born.

I would give my whole world to have him here with me now, to hear his voice as a young adult and to hold him close to me one more time. I'd like to playfully ruffle his hair and draw him in tight and hug him for dear life.

I was only a young man myself when James was murdered, just two years older than James would be now. That's a whole lifetime of grieving. I honestly don't know how I am still standing, but I do know it was my enduring love for James that kept me going. He dominates my waking hours and visits me in my sleep. Part of my purpose for living is to continue the quest for justice for my son. But I will not let it take over my life completely. I have to save a part of me for my other children who are still living, and that is an important lesson I have learned along the way. My love for them, their love for me, helped me survive. My three girls with Eileen have grown up fast, and my eldest, Ree, is now eighteen, a young adult herself. She is so protective, not just of her dad, but of her younger sisters too.

Like Karen and Jimmy's girls, my kids also learned a lot about James from the Internet and from their mates at school. I have talked about our family's suffering, but I don't think people grasp just how much it affected not just me or Jimmy or Karen, but the children as well. But we have survived, and today I think I am in a much stronger place than I have ever been before. Writing this book has really helped me to get some of my feelings out into the open, to lay down the truth about how I feel. I hope in the future I won't have to keep hiding behind a fake smile.

James's murder still shocks people all these years on, and it will forever be a stain on our nation's conscience. It still shocks me, and I live with it every single day. But in many ways the strength of feeling, the love and emotion that people from all over the world have expressed, has meant that James has never been forgotten. His angelic face, his dazzling smile, his big sparkling blue eyes and, of course, that giggle encapsulated the very vision of innocence.

I have always been reluctant to be in the public eye because

I find it so difficult and uncomfortable, but there were times when I had no choice but to speak out for James and our family. The relentless media attention that this case attracted certainly intensified the pressure on all of us, but, for all those difficulties, I have to say that I am grateful for our press that battled every step of the way with me for justice for James. They expressed the moral outrage of our country, and on many occasions it was only through the newspapers that I learned about what was going on. The media was gagged to protect these child killers and that was wrong. A free press is vital in a world where politicians seek to hide the truth from society to protect their own backsides. The media has also always treated my family with great compassion and sensitivity, and I will for ever be so thankful for that. As much as I often wished the attention would go away, I remain glad that the newspapers and television channels never forgot James.

My life has changed hugely since *My James* was first published in hardback in February 2013. It was a terrifying moment because while I was 100 per cent sure I wanted to share my boy's story with the world, I had no idea what kind of reaction I would receive from people, not just in Liverpool or the UK, but from around the world.

Writing James's story and revealing how his family have suffered for so long has been like stepping out of the shadows. I lived with so much shame and guilt and hurt that it was beginning to rot me away inside. For the first time I felt as if I was given a chance to tell the story as it was for me and my little boy. I won't say that it has taken away the daily pain. Nothing will do that. But it has changed me as a man and that is in part down to the most amazing response I have been given by the many thousands who read James's story. The feedback from the public was quite overwhelming – kind and loving, just as it was twenty years ago when James was murdered. It has helped me to shake off some of the guilt and the burden that I have carried with me for so long because I have been able to share my deepest and most secret feelings. It taught me that I am not a bad person – just an ordinary man whose son was the victim of a terrible crime. I cannot thank the public enough for their kindness and generosity of heart in responding to James's story. I have received hundreds and hundreds of messages from well-wishers and fantastic people who read the book. Every single one of those meant so much to me and I would like to thank everyone who bothered to contact me.

At the time of writing, more than 300 people have reviewed the book on Amazon and almost all have given it a five star rating. But far more crucial and poignant to me are the comments that people have left that show just how much ordinary strangers care about James. That alone has confirmed my belief that it was the right thing to do, to publish his story in the first place.

In the run-up to publication, I carried out a number of interviews for newspapers, magazines, radio and television. There were a couple of standout moments for me when I met two particularly fine journalists. The first was Winifred Robinson from the BBC who has long supported our family. She is a Liverpool girl who really understood the dynamics of this case and the background of not just my family, but the families of James's killers, and so I felt very comfortable with her when she came to our home to speak with me.

She probed with care and compassion into the dark corners of my soul, getting me to open up in a way I'd rarely done before, in particular when I talked about how I was overwhelmed with guilt at not being able to save James from his killers. I had no shame when I broke down and cried, and it felt almost like relief to finally confess how I had felt inside for so long. Her interview was broadcast on the BBC's *Today* radio programme on the morning of James's twenty year anniversary. It was very moving and I would like to thank Winifred for approaching this job with great sensitivity and professionalism. I know she really cares and it wasn't just a job to her. That made a lot of difference.

I also met with TV broadcaster and writer Gloria Hunniford to film an interview with her for *This Morning*. ITV had deliberately chosen Gloria to talk to me because she has also lost a child, even though the circumstances were very different. Gloria's beautiful daughter Caron, also a TV presenter, died from cancer and so, as a parent, she already understood the heartbreak of burying your own child before their time.

Gloria was wonderful. I felt for her because I know I am not the easiest subject to interview as I don't open up very easily, but she really made me so comfortable that I did manage to speak to her on camera. Again, I felt no shame when my tears welled up because I knew she had walked in my shoes. After filming the interview, I went to James's grave with Gloria where we laid some flowers for him. It was an important moment for me because I was able to show the world how much James meant to me. I really connected with Gloria because I knew I didn't have to explain what this level of grief feels like, and she was a very classy and kind lady who I am glad to have met.

The book was so well received by the public that by the end of February it had hit the number one slot in the *Sunday Times* Best Seller List. For me, this kind of award means little, but it demonstrated just how much support my family had received from ordinary people and that was a huge deal. I felt that I had been able to do James proud by sharing his short life with people who really cared and they all got to know my amazing son that little bit more. I wanted the book to be my tribute to James and I am happy I was able to do that for him.

Today I am seeking to move forward with my life. For the last three years I have shared my life with a new partner after my relationship with Eileen ended. Natalie is on every part of this journey with me and she keeps me grounded. She encourages me and helps me to rebuild my shattered confidence. She is kind and loving and I feel very lucky to have her. It's not easy for any woman to take on a partner who is so damaged and consumed by the murder of his son, but she has compassion and kindness in heaps. While I was working on this book, Natalie fell pregnant and we were both overjoyed, but sadly a few months into the pregnancy she miscarried and we lost our baby. We were both devastated, and on a very minute scale, it showed her a window into my world of grief.

In 2013 Natalie and I moved into our own home. It was a house that needed quite a lot of work and so I have spent months doing it up myself. I plastered the walls throughout, painted the place and am generally putting it together so we can make a comfortable and happy home. It's a lovely little place in Kirkby, close to family and friends as ever.

Dealing with Venables' release in 2013 was tough, although not unexpected, but there has also been some good news along the way, too. Natalie and I are expecting our first baby together. She is due to give birth in October and so by the time this new edition of *My James* is out we are hoping a very healthy and happy new arrival will have joined our family. We are both overjoyed and this has now signposted a new chapter in my life.

It is hard to put into words how much this means to me. My children have always been my driving force but Natalie has completely changed my world. The fact that we are now going to have a child together is nothing short of a miracle. I will never get over the loss of baby James and I accept that, but Natalie has taught me that I can also enjoy some happiness in my life too. It is as if Natalie has helped me to loosen the tight knot in the pit of my stomach that was the never-ending pain of losing James. I thank God every day for sending her to me. For the first time since James was murdered, I can finally smile and laugh without feeling guilty. And I know James would be very happy about that.

Our baby is a true gift and I can't wait to welcome him or her into the world. This is the best thing that has happened to us as a couple and we are both so excited about the baby's arrival. It has brought us even closer together. We are very much in love and it helps me move to a much stronger place. Finally, I am learning not to allow my son's evil murderers to completely destroy my life.

There's no doubt Venables' release has brought added fear to my life. I am going to enjoy and love our new baby with all my heart, but it will always be like sleeping with one eye open to protect my child. I have had to live with guilt for twenty years because I have always blamed myself for failing to protect James that terrible day. I don't know if anything will ever take that guilt away but I know I will never let it happen again so long as I have a breath left in my body. Natalie and I just have to try and count our blessings and not dwell on the miseries and fears of the past. James will remain a part of everyone's lives for ever and with that goes the sorrow and anger, but at last I do believe that I also deserve some joy too. Natalie has brought about some dramatic changes to my life and my whole family has seen this, as Jimmy describes:

Ralph has dealt with everything in his life with great dignity and courage and I am so proud of him. He has been so troubled and grief-stricken for so long that it is a relief to finally see him smile again without guilt or regret. There have been many tears shed these last few years, especially when Ralph relived so many horrors while working on the book. But it has definitely been worth it. Ralph wanted to talk about James. He wanted to tell the world how he felt about his son and what had happened to him. The way total strangers have responded to him has given him a little trust back in human nature again. Before James's murder, Ralph was just a normal lad who wanted to get on with his life in peace. He was comfortable with those who knew him and he always enjoyed a laugh. But after his son was killed, Ralph was forced to deal with the media spotlight and he had no idea how to cope with that. He knew it was important to deal with the media in order to put his message across about James's murder and his continuing fight for justice. But he found it impossibly difficult. To the wider world he put up an impenetrable defence because inside he was terrified of being vulnerable or hurt. Recently, everyone who knows Ralph has seen a massive change in him. The photographs of him with Natalie are proof of that. Smiling and relaxed, his love for Natalie is clear for everyone to see. The protective armour has fallen away and his face is softer and gentler than ever before. A sparkle has returned to his eyes where once he had a stony glare for the world. We are all amazed at how Ralph has changed and Natalie and the new baby are, without question, part of the reason for this fantastic transformation. The book and the public's amazing response have also played a huge role in helping him cope better with this tragedy. The young man who once only ever dreamed of living a normal life and being a good dad to his children has been to hell and back. I can't think of anyone who deserves this happiness more.

It is definitely the start of a new journey for Natalie and me. She is like my missing piece of jigsaw. We just fit together. This is her first baby and I am going to be a very proud dad once again. I will make sure I look after them both the best I can. The biggest sadness is that James will never get to meet this lovely new baby or any of his other siblings. But I can't help believe he is still with us in many ways. He lives on in my heart and I can still hear his little voice calling to me as we played football in the park. I am determined to celebrate my new baby as well as celebrate the precious days I was allowed to enjoy with James before he was stolen from us.

As for my family, I would never have got through this without them. I am so grateful that Jimmy and Karen contributed to this book because they have both played vital roles on this journey. Jimmy has suffered so much because he chose to support me when he could have walked away. His own family has borne the brunt of his torture, but he couldn't have been a better or more loving brother to me if he had tried. He pledged to be with me all the way and he has never let me down. Karen has also struggled as she tried to hold her family together and care for her husband's tormented mind. She too has been a shoulder for me to cry on, and they both know how much I love them.

Above all, this book keeps me closely connected to James. I wanted people to know exactly what he was like and how adorable and loveable he was. But what that amazing little boy brought to all our lives in those three years was nothing less than miraculous. Talking about him and sharing his love and joy in this book has given me one of the first opportunities since his murder to celebrate all that he was. It has been painful to revisit because it is a very sharp reminder that he has gone, but it has taught me to hold on to those memories tightly and let them bring me comfort.

I loved and cherished James with all my heart and soul while he was still alive and I am grateful that I spent every day of his life with him. I still have a little chat with James in my head and think about him every day when I wake up in the morning. But I am certain that he is still with us in spirit and looking down on us from afar. I think he would be very proud and happy to see me smiling again. I have saved my last words for him.

'My sweet and beautiful baby James. Thank you for being the best son I could ever have wished for. You brought me so much happiness and joy before you left us and I will never forget you. I am always with you in your heart and I am only ever a thought away when you need me. Daddy still loves and misses you so much every day and I think about you all the time. I hope you are safe and warm up there with your new friends and still laughing away. Heaven is very lucky to have you. Please stay happy, my special little boy. Until we meet again, son.

All my love, as always, your Ralph xxxx'

Appendix:
The Story of MAMAA

A very special charity called MAMAA – Mothers Against Murder and Aggression – was set up as a direct result of James's murder. From small and humble beginnings, it now helps thousands of people who have had the terrible misfortune to lose a loved one to murder, or anyone who is the victim of serious violent crime. It is a registered charity that does incredible work and it deserves to be celebrated as a positive move forward from a terrible crime.

As Denise and I would find out, there are few places that relatives can go to for help and support when their lives are turned upside down. MAMAA has been on this long journey with us from the very beginning and it is an important part of James's legacy. I would like to say a huge thank you to Lyn Costello and her small team who have shown so much passion and commitment to helping others. They have not had an easy ride and at times they struggled to keep going because of the appalling lack of financial support. I am so proud of what they have achieved and of the vital role that they play in our world that has become increasingly brutal. I have asked Lyn, the founder of

MAMAA, to share her experiences in this book. Here she tells her story:

I was thirty-nine when James was murdered and I had just become a grandparent, after my daughter Shelley gave birth to a baby boy. I was working full-time selling advertising in Kentish Town and lived nearby with my husband, Roger, and our four kids. Roger worked for Whitbread, the brewery, and we did a lot of charity work through them in inner-city London, especially raising money for ChildLine.

I was pretty switched on to the media because of the nature of my job and so I was used to reading about gruesome murders, but, like so many of us, I would read articles, turn the page and go about my business. It wasn't that I didn't care, but because it hadn't affected me directly, I would move on. I remember seeing the reports on the TV news when James was taken. My first thought was, 'Oh no, not another child.' And then the images of the CCTV footage were released as the hunt for James continued and, like a lot of people, I felt relief. If this little boy had gone off with a pair of kids, I felt certain that it was some kind of prank and that he would turn up safe and well. When the news took a turn for the worse and James was found murdered, I was shocked. I assumed it must be some awful accident or that something had gone terribly wrong by mistake. It didn't cross my mind that two children had killed this little boy.

My son Jay was eleven years old at the time, just a year older than the boys who had taken James, and I couldn't imagine that a boy so young could be capable of deliberately causing hurt to an innocent baby like James. You don't want to believe it. With children and grandchildren of my own, living in a tough inner-city area, I know how much trouble kids can get into, but nothing like this. I won't deny that my own kids could be little sods when they were growing up, getting into all sorts of mischief. I had to keep my eye on them all the time, as I know how easy it is for children to go down the wrong path in life; I wasn't the first parent to wring my hands when they got into trouble. But I also remember looking at Jay and thinking, 'Is it possible that he could do that sort of thing to a child so small and vulnerable?'

It was so extreme and so in your face that even tough kids were shocked and devastated by James's murder. People up and down the country were really feeling the impact of this wicked crime. Everything you ever believed in was turned upside down. My kids had been taught never to talk to strangers, or get into their cars, but never before were we faced with a situation in which you didn't want your children to talk to other kids they didn't know. Who was safe any more? Like many people in the country, I asked myself, 'What have we done as a society to breed two boys capable of such evil acts?'

James's murder was a huge wake-up call to everyone in Britain. It really held a mirror up to the kind of society we were living in. The country was morally lost, with crime rates running out of control. Youth crime went to the top of the political agenda.

I knew I wanted to do something in response to a crime so shocking and appalling, but I had no idea what I could do or what I should be doing. It began to nag away at me, and Roger and I talked about it constantly. We wanted to find even the simplest way to show that we cared and that the future of all our children meant something.

At the time a lot of youth clubs were being closed, and so outside of the home and school there was nothing for kids to do and nowhere for them to go. I am not knocking people with money, but it was a very different kettle of fish for middle-class, affluent families who could afford to take their children to private activities and groups. That wasn't the case for the families with little or no spare money, having to go to work all hours and struggling to make ends meet. My initial thought was to set up a youth club and so Roger and I established a kids' group in Kentish Town under the MAMAA umbrella. We hoped it would be the first of many contributions we could make to help change things for kids on the streets.

My family set-up was what you might call dysfunctional. Both Roger and I had been married before, we both had kids with previous partners and we were bringing them up together in the tough inner-city communities. It was far from perfect, but we were not breeding killer kids. I was also struck by the general misconception held by a lot of people, who judged all kids the same if they were from a rough council estate. If you're from an estate, then you obviously must be rotten through and through, but that just isn't the case. If you came from an impoverished back-ground and didn't have pots of money, there was a stigma attached to you, and that made me furious. I didn't want my kids to be judged like that. If you have lived on a tough estate – generally full of normal, decent people – you can very easily pick out and identify the kids who are likely to go off the rails, but it still doesn't mean they will end up as child killers. I knew some of the biggest rogues in our area, but even the most hardened scallywags and tearaways were shocked by the murder of James. When I set up MAMAA, it was from some unlikely quarters that I ended up getting my greatest support.

Some of the toughest youngsters would stop me in the street and say, 'Well done, girl, well done. We're behind you all the way.'

When we held a community street party, a couple of well-known drug dealers couldn't wait to get involved to help. Here were two hardened criminals who were horrified at the murder of James, and so it seemed that this terrible crime had united people on all fronts.

We wanted the parents of the local neighbourhood to run the youth group and, in turn, we would become more involved with the community's kids and their lives. Roger and I ended up running it most of the time, and while a lot of families were very supportive of the idea, the reality was that it turned out to be nothing more than a free babysitting facility.

It was never going to last. Roger and I were both working full time, we had several children of our own, and here we were optimistically trying to run a full-time youth project with little backing from other parents in the community. In the end we were forced to close it down. Of course it was a body blow, a huge disappointment, but I think it clearly showed our own naivety back then.

That is how our involvement in MAMAA started, and the group just began to evolve in its own way. The next step we took was to organize a vigil on the streets of Liverpool, again to show support and raise public awareness

— not that there were many people in the country who didn't know what had happened to James Bulger. We certainly got the measure of the strength of feeling in Merseyside, with huge support and empathy. They were very slow beginnings but, even then, I knew I wouldn't give up trying to do something to bring about changes, to make a difference.

I was an ordinary mum, having the odd holiday to a caravan park once a year and that was it. I have always been someone who has great ideas, but by my own admission, I have never stuck to anything in my life. I have started courses and ditched them, set up organizations and closed them down, but MAMAA would change all that. For the first time, this was something I couldn't get out of my head and I refused to let it drop.

A lot of people came forward to help us with MAMAA, but inevitably, as time wore on, folk slackened off and few remained with the cause. To make MAMAA work, we needed to raise funds. It is impossible to do anything properly with no money, as any charity or voluntary group will tell you. And so we needed to keep our commitment but also start finding practical ways to make our cause work. One of my first projects for MAMAA was a petition. I had been doing some research on how many kids had killed kids, and it was not many. I didn't have the luxuries of Google and the Internet back then, and so I had to go to the library to do things the old-fashioned way. I learned that there had been child killers before, but nothing was as brutal as James's murder. The petition aimed to make it the law that anyone who murders a child, no matter what age, must go to prison for life, as there could never be an excuse for the premeditated slaughter of an innocent child. The petition garnered loads of support and it really encouraged me.

We had been campaigning for a while when I received a phone call at home one night. I had always been aware that when we set up MAMAA, we had never sought the permission of James's family. We had acted on instinct and from the heart, but even so, I was extremely nervous of talking to the family. They had their own grief to deal with and I would never have dreamt of bothering them with what we were trying to do. So when I answered that call, it was a complete shock to me. There was a quiet voice on the other end of the receiver, speaking in a Liverpudlian accent.

'Hello, can I speak to Lyn Costello please?'

'Lyn speaking.'

'This is Ralph Bulger.'

'Pardon?' I spluttered.

Then again: 'It's Ralph Bulger.'

I froze on the spot. Not only did I find his accent quite difficult to understand, I also went to pieces. I knew exactly who he was but, for all my bravado, I couldn't find the right words to say.

'Hello, Ralph, thanks for ringing. Can you leave me your number and I will call you straight back?'

I was deeply ashamed and embarrassed, but I kept thinking, 'What do I say to a man who has lost his son in such appalling circumstances?'

It was my lovely husband Roger who called Ralph back, and they spoke for many hours into the night. Ralph totally backed MAMAA and asked if there was any way he could help us. It was the most amazing generosity of spirit from a man who had lost so much. This was the beginning of a special and long-lasting friendship with Ralph, his brother Jimmy and sister-in-law Karen. But it still didn't stop me being terrified the first time I went to Liverpool to meet them all. I found the family so open, warm and honest about everything they had been through. I will never forget Jimmy describing how he had identified James's tortured body. I was simply lost for words. It hit me really hard, and I thought I was going to faint hearing the terrible reality of what this child had suffered. I also grasped the enormity of what we had taken on and I knew that we had done the right thing in setting up MAMAA to continue supporting the victims of violent crime.

Ralph also made me realize one very important thing: that a man, a father, could feel just as desperate and devastated as a mother. It made us consider changing the name of our charity, but we were established and starting to be recognized, and it was felt we would lose our momentum. But meeting Ralph for the first time brought everything home to me so acutely. From that point on, we made a point of stressing that we didn't just support mums who had lost a child, but any relative. I had seen for myself just how devastated this father was to lose his son.

Times are changing. Traditionally and historically, in times of mourning our society has always focused on a mother's grief and her loss. Mum was always at the forefront while dad stayed in the background, but that is no longer the case. I have learned that a father's love is just as deep and binding as a mother's is for their child. I also viewed at close quarters what Jimmy went through for his brother, not just in identifying that poor, innocent child in the mortuary that day, but in supporting Ralph for so many years, and it takes its toll.

It was a very humbling experience to meet Ralph and his family. They taught me so much about dignity and what it really means to lose a loved one in such terrible circumstances. Before MAMAA, I wrongly assumed that families like Ralph's would be properly cared for and looked after by the Government, the state and the National Health Service. I really believed that all their needs, down to the simplest things like getting financial help and counselling, would be automatically provided for. But it was only when I got really involved and started to help other bereaved families that I realized how little assistance there is for people in this position. We wanted to provide that help, and so MAMAA evolved to become the missing link for families as they started the journey after murder. We began to put victims in touch with other organizations that could help them, and the work quickly snowballed, giving MAMAA a real sense of direction and purpose.

Other times, victims may just want to talk, and so many hours were spent on the telephone, just listening and providing a shoulder to cry on. It becomes a constant part of your life, because you don't just turn off when you have spent hours talking to family members in their darkest moments. It took a lot of years to learn not to talk about MAMAA constantly. It does take over your life and you become drained.

It sounds absurd, but the murder of James took away my innocence as well. I was never again able to open a newspaper, read about some terrible violent act and then just able turn the page and move on. My life had taken a new direction, and if people needed help in such terrible times, I couldn't refuse them. I was angry and impassioned, and I had an awful lot to learn about how to channel my feelings effectively. It got to the stage where people who knew me in Kentish Town would cross the road, rather than speak to me, because I was always getting on my soap box, getting angry about something, which was totally the wrong way to deal with things. I had been campaigning for one of our petitions on the television on one occasion when a woman stopped me near my home.

'I saw you on the telly the other day,' she said.

Instead of speaking to her properly, I snapped, 'Did you actually listen to what I was talking about? Do you actually know what the issues are?'

In that moment, I just stopped myself. I realized I was becoming a preacher, and an angry one at that. I had set out with a genuine desire to help, but now I was trying to force my views onto others, which was wrong. Instead of encouraging people to get on board, I was driving them away with my attitude.

I was never going to get people to back us by wagging my finger at them, telling them they were wrong and we were right. We might have been pricking the nation's conscience, but we were wrong to do it in such an aggressive and dogmatic way. We did learn eventually, but it took a while for the penny to drop.

The whole thing was taking over and I realized I had forgotten how to laugh. If I am truthful, ironically, it was the families we were supporting who had lost a loved one to murder who taught us to start living again and to start laughing again.

The first time we visited Ralph and Jimmy, we sat around the kitchen table for hours and talked into the night. There was much sadness and anger, but there was also real laughter at the right moments. These two men taught me for the first time that life does go on, however hard it is. I learned from them that it was OK to give myself permission to laugh and smile. Until that point, special occasions, especially Christmas, had been really hard. I would feel overwhelmed that I had my family around me when so many had lost loved ones. I would feel guilty for that when I thought of all the families across the country in sadness. So I also had to learn about gratitude and be thankful for what I had been blessed with, and not feel guilty because another family had suffered such misery.

With the greatest of respect for James's family, and in no way meaning to make comparisons with what they have been through, James really did become the nation's child in a symbolic way. He stood for every parent's son or daughter, who could so easily have been the victim of that terrible crime that day. I don't think there was a parent alive who didn't shudder at the sight of that CCTV footage. We all knew it could so easily have been our own child.

MAMAA marks its twentieth anniversary in February 2013, as it was set up at the time of James's murder. It's difficult to quantify my feelings about this because it is a massive milestone in my life, and I am very proud of MAMAA and what we have achieved over the years. But equally, how do you begin even to talk about celebrating when it was set up in response to something so horrific.

Twenty years after James was killed, violent crime offenders in Britain are getting younger and younger still.

In juvenile offender homes, there are boys of twelve and thirteen who have stabbed and killed other youngsters. We set up MAMAA to try to stop this type of thing occurring, but we are living in a society where it happens on a weekly basis. The circumstances are different, I admit. These crimes are not the premeditated murder of a toddler, but are the result of a gang culture out of control. We also now go into young offender homes and talk to them about their crimes and try to educate them. I passionately wanted to live in a country where kids were not killing kids. I just wanted to know what I could do to make a difference.

For many years, we have been on what we call a 'Government round table' that was set up by David Blunkett when he was Home Secretary under Prime Minister Tony Blair. It started because kids were killing and maiming each other on the streets. What we were telling the Government then is what we are still telling them now, and yet successive Prime Ministers are not acting on it.

We have pressed the need for education about crime, about getting tougher on juvenile crime, on early intervention, and yet nothing has changed. If anything, the situation is getting worse. These are not platitudes. The politicians are not taking the lessons on board. The warning signs are always there, and if the right organizations intervened before crimes were committed, more young people would be spared death or injury, and fewer young people would be going to prison or young offender homes for violent stabbings or shootings.

These things do cost money, but they are worth it to provide a better future for all our children. Something is wrong with a society in which you have this level of cruelty being inflicted on children by children. It is unfathomable. And yet we are becoming more and more desensitized to violent crime like this as society changes for the worse. We appear to have become immune to stories of stabbings and killings among young people. Two decades on, we are supporting families of murder victims who have been killed in terrible circumstances, and yet the events barely even make the local newspapers sometimes, let alone the national news. Life appears to have become so much cheaper to us as a society.

With everything I have seen over the years, I often wonder if I can be shocked any more, and then I get a phone call with details of yet another family needing help and it is overwhelming. We receive referrals from all directions and will always help where we can. We were put in touch with one woman by a local gravedigger. He kept seeing this lady arriving at the cemetery in a dreadful state. Her mother had been murdered, so he gave her MAMAA's number and she called us. We started out as tea and sympathy, but it is so much more now. We are a professional and structured organization that can give essential help to those who need it. We provide confidential, practical advice as well as emotional support. I could retire now and be very proud of what we have achieved.

We won funding for two wages a few years back, but that has since stopped. The organization relies on donations and sponsorship, without which we would be in trouble. I don't believe in the church, but someone up there must have been looking out for us whenever we hit a financial crisis, because something always turned up when we needed it most. Roger even cashed in his pension at one point to keep us going. We have worked tirelessly to make things easier on those who lose a relative to violent crime. We have run gun amnesties and been involved in the Victims' Code and Charter. We have helped change stalking laws. And all of this came from James's murder.

Ralph and Jimmy are very proud of MAMAA and also see it as part of James's legacy. That means so very much to us all. Gone is the preaching attitude I used to have. In its place, I try to use everything I have learned from bereaved families to help others in the same boat. I'm still an interfering old cow, but hopefully that will never change. I am proud to do our work in James's name.

MAMAA is a national registered charity that provides an all-inclusive practical and emotional support and advocacy service to those affected by serious violence or bereaved by homicide.

MAMAA is committed to ensuring that our beneficiaries receive a useful and effective service, delivered in a professional and ethical manner.

Our vision is that every individual affected by serious violence and/or homicide receives a nationally agreed, standard level of support and advocacy across the UK.

To contact us for help, advice or information call: 020 8207 0702

For information on how you can donate please go to www.mamaa.org

Charity Reg Number: 1074817

Acknowledgements

We would like to thank Robin Makin of Rex Makin & Co in Liverpool for all his fabulous and tireless work in seeking justice for James. Thanks also go to all our friends and family, including our close friends at MAMAA, Les and Kathy Walker and family, and Yanna and Mary O'Brian and family.

We would like to acknowledge all those people who have offered us their love and best wishes over the last twenty years, including the many kind strangers who have helped to restore our faith in human nature. Thanks especially to the people of Kirkby, our home town, and in the wider Merseyside area, who never deserted us. Their loyalty and respect to the memory of James and support for his family has been outstanding and it has been a very humbling experience over the years.

We would like to also thank author Mark Thomas for his help in researching this book and for allowing us to use his archive material, without which we would never have been able to accurately portray the events of the past. We would also like to thank anyone else who has kindly contributed to this project, enabling us to give it credibility and honesty.

Thanks go to our agent Robert Smith who has been behind us all the way doing a sterling job and to all at Pan Macmillan for choosing to publish such an important book for us, in particular Editorial Director Ingrid Connell whose patience and commitment to this book in some difficult times will never be forgotten. We couldn't have been in better hands.

Picture Acknowledgements

Every effort has been made to contact the copyright holders of the photographs in this book, but where omissions have been made the publishers will be glad to rectify them in future editions.

Pages 1 and 2: © Ralph Bulger
Page 3: *top* © Malcolm Croft/PA Archives/Press Association Images; *middle* © Mercury Press/Sygma/Corbis; *bottom*: Matthew Polak/Sygma/Corbis
Page 4: *top* © Associated Newspapers/Rex Features; *bottom two photos* © Getty Images
Page 5: *top* © Nick Skinner/Associated Newspapers/Rex Features; *bottom* © Billy Griffiths
Page 6: *top* © Malcolm Croft/PA Archive/Press Association Images; *bottom* © Stefan Rousseau/PA Archives/Press Association Images
Page 7: *top* Ralph Bulger; *middle and bottom* © Billy Griffiths
Page 8: *top right and bottom left* © Billy Griffiths; *bottom right* © Ralph Bulger

extracts reading groups
books new
competitions books extracts
discounts extracts extracts discounts
competitions
books new events reading groups
events books extracts
extracts books discounts
events extracts new titles reading groups
new
interviews
events extracts extracts events
discounts events books new
new books events interviews new books
events
discounts extracts discounts books

www.panmacmillan.com

extracts events reading groups
competitions books extracts new